Twayne's Filmmakers Series

Frank Beaver, Editor

SIDNEY LUMET

Sidney Lumet, 1981. The Museum of Modern Art/Film Stills
Archive.

SIDNEY LUMET

Jay Boyer

TWAYNE PUBLISHERS • NEW YORK
MAXWELL MACMILLAN CANADA • TORONTO
MAXWELL MACMILLAN INTERNATIONAL •
NEW YORK • OXFORD • SINGAPORE • SYDNEY

Twayne's Filmmakers Series
Sidney Lumet

Copyright © 1993 by Twayne Publishers

Twayne Publishers
Macmillan Publishing Company
866 Third Avenue
New York, New York 10022

Maxwell Macmillan Canada, Inc.
1200 Eglinton Avenue East
Suite 200
Don Mills, Ontario M3C 3N1

Library of Congress Cataloging-in-Publication Data

Boyer, Jay.
　　Sidney Lumet / Jay Boyer.
　　　　p.　　cm.—(Twayne's filmmakers series)
　　Includes bibliographical references, filmography, and index.
　　ISBN 0-8057-9329-1 (cloth).—ISBN 0-8057-9330-5 (pbk.)
　　　1. Lumet, Sidney, 1924–　　—Criticism and interpretation.
　　I. Title.　II. Series.
　　PN1998.3.L86B69　1993
　　791.43′0233′092—dc20

93-28388
CIP

10 9 8 7 6 5 4 3 2 1

Printed in the United States of America

FOR SOPHIE

CONTENTS

FOREWORD

Of all the contemporary arts, the motion picture is particularly timely and diverse as a popular culture enterprise. This lively art form cleverly combines storytelling with photography to achieve what has been a quintessential twentieth-century phenomenon. Individuals as well as national and cultural interests have made the medium an unusually varied one for artistic expression and analysis. Films have been exploited for commercial gain, for political purposes, for experimentation, and for self-exploration. The various responses to the motion picture have given rise to different labels for both the fun and the seriousness with which this art form has been received, ranging from "the movies" to "cinema." These labels hint at both the theoretical and sociological parameters of the film medium.

A collective art, the motion picture has nevertheless allowed individual genius to flourish in all its artistic and technical areas: directing, screenwriting, cinematography, acting, editing. The medium also encompasses many genres beyond the narrative film, including documentary, animated, and avant-garde expression. The range and diversity of motion pictures suggest rich opportunities for appreciation and for study.

The Twayne Filmmakers Series examines the full panorama of motion picture history and art. Many studies are auteur-oriented and elucidate the work of individual directors whose ideas and cinematic styles make them authors of their films. Other studies examine film movements and genres or analyze cinema from a national perspective. The series seeks to illuminate all the many aspects of film for the film student, the scholar, and the general reader.

Frank Beaver

PREFACE

I have tried to write a book I would want to read, particularly if I were coming to Sidney Lumet's films for the first time, or looking to refresh my memory of them, or beginning a study of my own. I've tried to write an introductory study, to be read from first page to last; but also I've meant this book to be of use when referred to only by section, the way I will sometimes refer to introductory studies in order to verify a point or check my judgment against the judgment of another.

This book deals with a third of Lumet's feature films, *Twelve Angry Men, Long Day's Journey into Night,* and *The Pawnbroker* in chapter 1; *Murder on the Orient Express, Serpico, Dog Day Afternoon, Network,* and *Prince of the City* in chapter 2; and *Daniel, Running on Empty, Q & A* and *A Stranger among Us* in chapter 3. In effect, the three chapters divide Lumet's career into early, middle, and late periods, and organize Lumet's films by decade; the 1960s, the 1970s, the 1980s, and a bit beyond them. Such divisions are not offered as absolutes; they will only prove to be as valuable in the study of Lumet as the uses to which they are put. Neither is my selection of films definitive. I chose to discuss these particular films both because I thought they were likely to be of interest to readers, and because a discussion of their form and content might yield an understanding that could be extended more broadly, should the reader choose to try. In most cases, I've chosen what I believe to be Lumet's strongest and most interesting work of the period. However, I have also chosen with an eye toward what I believe to be Lumet's best-known films and those most readily available for viewing and study. Again, the reader should assume that my selection of films is but a sampling, and my treatment of those films is more an attempt to encourage dialogue rather than determine which films are finally worthy of study.

I have tried to point the reader beyond the films dealt with in chapters 1 through 3, and I have tried to suggest one possible line of thought that follows in consideration: namely, that the underlying critical assumptions generally applied to Lumet's films may be standing in the way of a full appreciation of the director's worth. Critically, there has been an attempt to understand his films by setting up polar opposites, and then reasoning from those divisions. In the final chapter I discuss how Lumet's films have often been divided into his socially conscious, serious work and his entertainment films, opposing his New York (read "realist") work to his stylized work, art to craft, and so on. I suggest in the final chapter that this sort of polarized logic might be best put aside, that Lumet's craft is also his art, that his realist films are often highly stylized, and his stylized films have their groundings in realism.

I make my living studying films, reading and thinking about them, and writing and talking about films to others. I have done my best to make this book readable and accessible to a broad audience. No reader should have to share my profession in order to make use of it. I've done my best to keep the book free of jargon; when I think I've introduced a film term unfamiliar to someone only beginning to learn about cinema, I've done my best to define it simply, and then move on to my point. I've brought this same spirit to my plot summaries and to the dialogue I quote. I've drawn the quotations from the films themselves, rather than the official screenplays and I've tried to bring them to the page in a form that reflects the way the lines were spoken by Lumet's actors. When I want to emphasize something in the speech that the actor did not, I've claimed the emphasis as my own. Since I've found over the years that the official version of the screenplay can vary from the finished film, I've chosen to look to the films rather than their screenplays for my quotations.

I've had help in the preparation of this manuscript from any number of sources, to whom acknowledgments are due. I'm particularly grateful to Arizona State University for the time I was granted away from my teaching and administrative duties; to the SFG Fund for financial support of travel and research; to my editors at Boise State University Press who allowed me to drag my heels on delivering a manuscript I owed them in order to finish this one; to Frank Beaver, General Editor of Twayne's Filmmakers Series, Melissa Solomon, Associate Editor, and Leslie Camhi, Copyeditor, for their cold, critical readings and warm, constructive suggestions; to my wife, whose editorial skills are keener than my own; to Mary O'Hallaran for her diligence and energy when my own were at an ebb; to Al Hart and others at the Fox Chase Agency, from whom I'm afraid I've profited more during the past 10 years than they have profited from me; to

Tim Schell and other graduate students who aided me in various ways and at various times as this manuscript neared publication; to my colleague in Arizona State University's Interdisciplinary Film Studies Program, Nick Salerno who encouraged me to undertake this project rather than write another novel; to novelist Mark Harris who periodically encouraged me to complete it; to colleagues and students too numerous to name, with whom I've had an on-going dialogue as this manuscript evolved. I'm sure I've learned at least as much from them as they have learned from me, if not more.

Most of all, though, I mean to acknowledge my prospective readers. No one writes without the hope of being read. No one performs the labor of research and critical analysis without the prospect of his or her work interesting others. More than anything else, in writing this book I have meant to encourage an exchange of ideas about Sidney Lumet's work. This is meant to be an introduction in the most fundamental sense, one that might set in motion more thought and dialogue in the years to come. A definitive study of Lumet's work has yet to be written. My hope is that one of my readers may write it.

CHRONOLOGY

1924	Sidney Lumet born in Philadelphia, Pennsylvania on 25 June to (actor) Baruch and (dancer) Eugenia Wermus Lumet.
1928	Acting debut alongside his father in Yiddish Art Theater production, New York City.
1935	Makes his Broadway debut in Sidney Kingsley's *Dead End*.
1939	Following some five years of juvenile roles on Broadway, Lumet makes his one and only screen appearance in *One Third of a Nation*.
1942	Enters the Army, serves as a radar repairman in the China-Burma theater of operations; Lumet has credited this experience with teaching him everything he needed to know about sound.
1946	Returns from military service and succeeds young Marlon Brando on Broadway as David in Ben Hecht's *A Flag Is Born*.
1950	Encouraged by his friend Yul Brynner, Lumet accepts position as assistant director at CBS.
1951–53	Directs some 150 episodes of *Danger,* as well as 26 shows for *You Are There*.
1955	Lumet interrupts his television career to make his debut as a stage director, the off-Broadway revival of George Bernard Shaw's *The Doctor's Dilemma*.
1957	Directs first film, *Twelve Angry Men*.
1960	Directs teleplays, *The Sacco and Vanzetti Story*, which earns an Emmy nomination, and *The Iceman Cometh,* which earns an Emmy.
1958	*Stage Struck*.
1959	*That Kind of Woman*.

1960   *The Fugitive Kind.*

1962   *A View from the Bridge; Long Day's Journey into Night.*

1965   *The Pawnbroker; The Hill.*

1966   *The Group.*

1967   *The Deadly Affair.*

1968   *Bye, Bye Braverman; The Sea Gull.*

1969   *The Appointment; King: A Filmed Record . . . Montgomery to Memphis* (with Joseph Mankiewicz).

1970   *Last of the Mobile Hotshots.*

1971   *The Anderson Tapes.*

1972   *Child's Play.*

1973   *The Offense.*

1974   *Serpico; Lovin' Molly; Murder on the Orient Express.*

1975   *Dog Day Afternoon.*

1976   *Network.*

1977   *Equus.*

1978   *The Wiz.*

1980   *Just Tell Me What You Want.*

1981   *Prince of the City.*

1982   *Deathtrap; The Verdict.*

1983   *Daniel.*

1984   *Garbo Talks.*

1986   *Power; The Morning After.*

1988   *Running on Empty.*

1989   *Family Business.*

1990   *Q & A.*

1992   *A Stranger among Us.*

CHAPTER ONE

Lumet's Early Work: *Twelve Angry Men, Long Day's Journey into Night,* and *The Pawnbroker*

TWELVE ANGRY MEN (1957)

Twelve jurors have just sat through a murder trial that has reached its completion as the film begins. All but two of these jurors will remain nameless to us, and those two—Davis and Arnold, portrayed by Henry Fonda and Joseph Sweeney, respectively—are introduced by name only at the film's denouement. Nor do we learn much about the other jurors, at least in terms of biographical detail. Young Jack Klugman has worked his way out of the ghetto; Fonda, we learn, is an architect; Jack Warden sells marmalade; Ed Begley owns several parking garages; Robert Webber plays an advertising executive; George Voskovek plays an immigrant watchmaker; E. G. Marshall plays a buttoned-down stockbroker; Joseph Sweeney, a retiree; Lee J. Cobb, a self-made businessman; Edward Binns, a house painter. Yet, by the film's end, we know these men. Through witnessing them for about an hour and a half, and being made privy to what Lumet has called "the fullness" of their behavior, we come to know how their hearts and minds work. In a number of cases, we find out more than we might want to know about them as individuals.

The action of the film begins with the judge instructing the jury. As they settle into the jury room, we see that they are a cross section of American working men—blue collar and white, labor and management. No one is special or remarkable. For the most part, what they have in common is their having been chosen at random to decide the fate of a ghetto youth accused of murdering his father, and their apparent desire to cast a vote of guilty and get back to their everyday lives.

Lumet initially ponders their commonness, the comfort of being one among many. This point is underscored by their first communal act, when Martin Balsam is selected as foreman. There is no indication that he is perceived as a leader by the others. On the contrary we understand that he gets the job by default. Yet, as a group, they have been given a remarkable responsibility, that of deciding the fate of the defendant. Only the juror played by Fonda seems to be aware of this. He wants to discuss the evidence with which they have been presented. Before sending someone off to die, he argues, a discussion of some sort is necessary. The remainder of the film is this discussion; and, in a sense, it yields little that is conclusive. We leave the jury room unsure of whether the defendant is guilty or innocent of the crime with which he has been charged. That the defendant's guilt or innocence is never really determined, though, is not the point; for Lumet and Reginald Rose are concerned with the dynamics of ordinary people put in an extraordinary situation.

Bringing Reginald Rose's *Twelve Angry Men* to "the big screen" offered Lumet an opportunity to take advantage of the vertical plane of the motion picture camera, a plane much more elastic than that of videography in the 1950s. In addition, it offered the extended, rectangular dimensions of a motion picture screen, and the moving (craning, tracking, panning) motion picture camera, capable of achieving effects that both early television and the legitimate stage had denied him. The opening moments of the film alert us to the fact that this is neither TV nor stage work, as Lumet gives the viewer an omniscience and freedom of movement that the characters we are about to meet will be denied. Very little is seen at eye level. Dimensions are slightly skewed. Often we are a little too high to see things naturally, or too low to see them at eye level. The film begins with a montage that lasts nearly five minutes. We have no sense of editing. The montage feels seamless. It is composed of a series of long, fluid takes. The camera gives us a sense of effortless motion, for we can climb the massive, classic columns of the exterior of a courthouse, then descend from an interior rotunda with equal ease. As the camera descends inside the courthouse, we see that the daily business of justice is under way. Carved in stone on the outside of the building is the motto, "Administration of Justice is the Firmest Pillar of Good Government," and from all appearances, justice is being administered here. We become aware of individuals, of activity under way on the courthouse floors. Gradually, individuals rather than the physical edifice become the center of our attention. The camera seems to follow one, then another, moving from character to character. A pattern seems to begin. The camera follows one character, another character crosses his path, then the camera follows the second character until someone crosses his path. It is the first sense of disorder we are given, almost as if the camera cannot quite find the character it seeks. Finally there is a cut, and a sense of order is restored. We pass effortlessly through the doors of a courtroom just in time to hear a judge instructing a jury in a murder trial. His voice is tired, perhaps disinterested. He might be speaking by rote. Then the jury retires and we cut to a close-up of the boy defendant. The jury room is then composed in the frame. The camera has stopped moving. The room is functional, nondescript; it is any room in any civil office building. The only thing at all unusual is our perspective. We look down on the room from a high angle. The film's title appears, then screen credits are superimposed over pictures of the jury members entering the room.

As the drama gets under way, Lumet continues to use long takes, a moving camera. Rather than splicing footage together, Lumet often makes use of what the camera can do with a minimum of interruptions: the camera tracks, cranes, pans; the focal length of the lenses changes. This has the effect of recomposing what we see as the action unfolds. In effect, the camera becomes the thirteenth juror, constantly revising its position as new information becomes available, sitting in judgment not upon the defendant but rather upon the jury itself.

Lumet would say about Boris Kaufman's cinematography in *Long Day's Journey into Night* that the camera was employed so that it seemed to have "revelations, definitions, and meanings of its own,"[1] and the same might be said here. As the drama begins, the camera seems to act in the jury room as it has in the halls. It follows one jury member, and picks up another when a second character crosses his path. A group is being formed before our eyes, and within that group, relationships are being established. Gradually, the camera seems to come to rest in two-shots as various jury members are paired off, each apparently seeking a kindred spirit. But there is now a hint of claustrophobia. Repeatedly, a wall appears in the background or a window looking out onto a city to which we no longer have access. The door to the jury room is shut tight, then locked. There is also the sense that something is slightly askew. This has to do with the angle at which

Lumet photographs the table and the jurors sitting around it until very late in the film, though the technique is so subtle that it is apt to be missed on first viewing. There is nothing particularly startling about the camera work; on first viewing, Lumet seems to be using "establishing shots," functional shots that are necessary to establish the dimensions of the space in which the drama will occur. And yet, we know that something is not quite right.

Lumet achieves this effect by his placement of the table in our field of vision, for he rarely lets the rectangular table occupy the center of the frame as one might expect. What we might logically assume to be establishing shots of the table and jurors done at long shot range become something else, for Lumet tends to compose his establishing shots so that the table cuts a diagonal across the frame, either from top right to bottom left ("/"), or, less often, from top left to bottom right ("\"). This is doubly disconcerting. The dimensions of the table appear slightly elongated. This has the effect of skewing the faces and torsos of the jurors nearest to us, while putting those farthest away slightly beyond our normal focus. Henry Fonda, too, catches our eye. Fonda's Davis is the only juror wearing a light–colored suit. He seems out of place, and the significance of his clothes is underscored by his place within the visual image. Within the frame, he is kept at a distance from the others. Otherwise, though, there is a general sense of order. The camera tends to be at eye level by this point in the film, or just slightly above it; the lighting of the room is "natural," that is, ostensibly by sunlight entering the jury room through windows. Still, the camera keeps reminding us that Davis has yet to find a comfortable position in terms of the others. His presence is singular, somehow out of balance with the others.

An exploration of the dynamics of the group begins when a preliminary poll reveals that every jury member except Davis believes in the defendant's guilt. When Davis seems reluctant to rush to a verdict, the other members are given the chance to persuade him of their position. Lumet continues to employ primarily a moving camera, complementing it with one-shots as Lumet switches between Davis and the juror who is speaking; then punctuates this pattern with groupings of other jurors in the frame, a reminder that the juror who is speaking to Davis is actually speaking for others as well as himself. The net effect is to emphasize Davis's singularity. Visually separated from the group in the first part of the film, he is now alone in a more pressing sense. The most potent, decisive argument for conviction is made by E. G. Marshall, and while Marshall's skillful acting raises the dramatic pitch of the film considerably, so does Lumet's camera work. The core of Marshall's argument has to do with the murder weapon, a knife owned by the defendant that has a particular, carved handle. Davis produces an identical knife to prove that possession of so common a knife is not in itself proof of anything.

Lumet capitalizes on this moment through his compositional technique. As Marshall makes his case, we see him from Davis's point of view. We are looking over Davis's shoulder in effect and seeing Marshall across from him, along with Jack Klugman to Marshall's left (that is, screen-right). As the sequence begins, Klugman is actually nearer to the center of the frame than is the speaker, Marshall; then, as Marshall's case becomes more precise and well-considered than any we have heard before, the focal length of the lens is extended. Almost imperceptibly, we move over Davis's shoulder until Davis is completely out of the frame. As Marshall continues to speak, detailing the evidence against the defendant in an increasingly logical fashion, the focal length continues to change until Klugman becomes little more than an afterthought in our field of vision. He turns to Marshall, apparently in awe of Marshall's precision of thought. Apparently like all the other jurors who have given Marshall their undivided attention, Davis is ready to vote with Marshall. Now Marshall dominates the scene, visually and otherwise. More articulate, intelligent, and polished than the others, he has become their champion, their spokesman. But his dominance is soon disrupted. The murder weapon is demanded. The court bailiff retrieves it at the foreman's request, who in turn gives it to Marshall. Marshall opens its blade and lodges it in the table. The camera captures the knife lodged in the table in a full-screen close-up, perhaps the most dominating single image up to this point in the movie. Then Davis takes a duplicate knife from the pocket of his suit coat and puts it next to the first. His point is that the murder weapon is a common style of knife, readily available in the boy's neighborhood, and that duplicates could be had from any number of sources. But the point is more far-reaching: facts are not quite the same as the truth. For every bit of persuasive evidence, evidence for a counterargument can be produced. On this note, Lumet employs a series of reaction shots. He photographs the jurors at extreme close-up range, lighting their faces frontally to make the images appear particularly harsh. The faces before us register not only surprise, but frustration. The second knife has put an end to the momentum of Marshall's exposition, though it has not resolved the jury's dilemma. If anything, it has made matters worse. It has given Davis a leg to stand on, and that has made him their antagonist. Complications be damned: their minds are already made up and they are ready to go home.

After listening to the rest of the jury, Davis proceeds to set out his reservations concerning the case against the defendant. Lumet will repeatedly rely on several compositional patterns during this part of the film, three of which are interrelated.

The first concerns the number of people Lumet includes in the frame. Unlike Marshall, who is gradually given the entire frame, Davis is photographed in three-shot and four-shot as he speaks. This surrounds him visually with skeptics and reminds us of what he is up against, of what it means to be a lone individual confronting a solidified group; it reminds us of how many the individual must overcome if he is to be effective.

The second cinematic pattern has to do with the knife. The evidence has been returned to the bailiff, but Davis's knife remains lodged in the tabletop for the second third of the film. During this time, Lumet photographs Davis from the front so that the knife often occupies some small part of the frame. Davis does not claim to be able to establish the defendant's innocence; he claims only that the evidence does not necessarily lead to a verdict of guilty, and the knife visually emphasizes what Davis has said in his presentation. It reminds us of the "reasonable doubt" upon which our trial system depends.

The third compositional pattern reminds us of how subject our system is to human error. This has to do with what Davis sees as he speaks. Across from him sits Marshall, and to Marshall's side, Lee J. Cobb, the two men who will hold out longest against Davis. Cobb has come to a guilty verdict through a combination of emotion and instinct as a result of his psychic scores. Marshall is willing to cast a vote of guilty because he believes the preponderance of the facts argues for such a vote. By keeping them in the frame together, Lumet reminds us that they represent the two extremes, reason and emotion, that are leading the others to rush to judgment. But he reminds us, too, that Davis is speaking to a group of individuals, each of whom brings his own prejudices, passions and value system to bear on the situation at hand. Davis is not simply outnumbered. He is confronting the foibles and failings of the human condition.

Davis stands his ground, gradually enlisting supporters. He argues that some of the evidence against the defendant is circumstantial at best, while other evidence is open to different interpretation, and virtually all of the testimony they have heard is subject to human failing.

Henry Fonda stars in *Twelve Angry Men*. The Museum of Modern Art/Film Stills Archive.

Lumet uses compositional patterns by this time familiar to us to drive home Davis's points. When the jurors reason, for instance, that the one eyewitness to the stabbing, a neighbor, could not have been wearing her glasses when she saw the murder, Lumet uses a series of extreme close-ups of individual juror's faces—all frontally lit—much as he did after Davis plunged the second knife into the jury table. The images are harsh, even stark. But there is a difference in timbre and tone to these shots. While previously the faces registered resistance, now they reveal a moment of recognition. The one bit of testimony they have been relying upon as irrefutable is, apparently, refutable.

As the jurors work toward their final decision, each man is given the chance to explore his own character and motives; but perhaps the key dramatic moments belong to Ed Begley and Lee J. Cobb rather than to Henry Fonda. These dramatic moments deal with self-revelation and forecast some of Lumet's later work, since the director handles them in ways which underscore how self-revelation isolates the

characters from the group. In one scene, for instance, Ed Begley reveals himself to be a bigot who lives in fear and dread of "them," of
"these people"; and as he argues to convict the defendant on the basis
of the boy's ethnic background, Lumet has most of the jury rise from
the table man by man and move away from the speaker. Another such
moment comes three-quarters of the way through the film as Davis is
convincing more jurors with each point he makes. Early in the film
Cobb has revealed that his relationship with his son has been strained
to the breaking point, a situation that has clearly left him wounded
and embittered. It seems to be an unimportant biographical tidbit until
this point in the film. Listening to Davis in effect argue the defendant's
case raises Cobb's ire until finally Cobb is unable to contain himself
any longer. He accuses the others of letting the defendant slip through
their fingers, of relinquishing the chance to sentence the boy to death.
Lumet narrows Cobb's rage cinematically by having him turn on
Davis. Davis, after all, is the immediate embodiment of what disturbs
him, and Cobb must be physically restrained to keep him from at-
tacking Davis. This begins as a group shot. Eight people are in the
frame, with Cobb in center-frame. Lumet then crosscuts between
Cobb and Davis as they exchange angry words. But while Lumet
keeps Davis at medium shot range, Cobb tends to be photographed
in full-screen close-up, isolating him, and—thanks to the anger that
registers on his face—emphasizing the mania which isolates him from
the group as a whole. Lumet's technique is to let us hear Davis's voice
but keep the camera on Cobb, allowing us to see his growing hostility
and malice. Finally, Davis charges, "I feel sorry for you—what it must
feel like to want to pull the switch. Ever since you walked into this
room you've been acting like a self-appointed public avenger. You
want to see this boy die because you personally want it, not because
of the facts. You're a sadist."

"I'll kill him! I'll kill him!" Cobb screams, as the others restrain
him. But it is too late. Cobb, and the others as well, realize that the
charge is accurate, that Cobb's vengeful relationship with his own estranged son is really at the heart of his ardor, that it is his own son he
wants to punish and not the defendant in the trial. The sequence ends
in a way that mirrors its beginning. Cobb is isolated from the group.
The camera shows us the eleven other jury members, then Cobb, all
alone, at the other end of the room.

Lumet's directorial strategy in the first half of the film is mirrored
by what he does in the second half. This is true not only of his work

with Lee J. Cobb, but elsewhere as well. Consider the film's opening moments. The most fundamental premise of Rose's script is that American justice has less to do with marble-columned courts of law, lawyers and judges, than it has to do with us. Our jury system is only as good as we are, only as just as the jurors themselves. By the climax of the film, once Davis has withstood the momentum of the group and led the jurors to an enlightened decision, we recognize this; but we see, too, that Lumet has forecast that point in the movie's initial montage. It all comes down to the individuals in a nondescript room in a civil office building and their interaction. There is no system of justice apart from us. In the end, we are the system, and we are only as good as the best and worst among us. In the film's final moments, Davis walks among the pillars outside the courthouse. It is a most fitting image, a reminder of the scrollwork we saw etched in marble. For the "pillars" our justice system really relies upon are not stone, but the human pillars of a civilized society.

The film's climax and ending mirror the beginning in a number of other ways, most pointedly through the lighting and camera work. By the end of the film it is Lee J. Cobb's character rather than the character played by Fonda who is isolated, who stands apart in the frame. Near the climax of the film the light is artificial. Time has passed. It is now the middle of the night and the light in the jury room comes from incandescent bulbs, not the sun. When Lee J. Cobb is the only juror still ready to cast a guilty vote, there are group shots inter-cut with one-shots of Lee J. Cobb, now all alone in our field of vision. Lumet keeps the camera low on its vertical plane, and as a result the shots distort Cobb's face and torso, accentuating his mania and rage. Lumet also uses the artificial lighting to put Cobb's face in shadow. Lumet is often criticized for using purely dramatic effects. But here, and elsewhere, such criticism is apt to miss the mark. This not only achieves a rather dramatic "low-key" lighting effect. It reminds us of the figurative shadows in Cobb's own past, his unenlightened rela-tionship with his own son, which has caused him to rush to condemn a potentially innocent defendant. "Rotten kids, you work your life out," says Cobb, as he frantically tears up the snapshot of his son that has dropped out of his wallet. But he cannot go further. In full-screen close-up, he collapses on the table, moving toward us, averting his eyes from ours, from the eyes of his fellow jurors. In effect, he is naked before them. More painfully, he is naked before himself. "Not guilty," he says at last. "Not guilty," he repeats to himself.

LONG DAY'S JOURNEY INTO NIGHT (1962)

Long Day's Journey into Night was shot in six weeks and edited in eight. Lumet worked from the playbook rather than a screen adaptation. He put his trust in the original text and cut only about 20 pages from the original 165, then shot the play in sequence out of respect for its dramatic integrity. This was not a stipulation made by the executors of O'Neill's estate, but it was certainly in keeping with the spirit of the agreement they made with producer Ely Landau and Lumet. Lumet must have seemed to O'Neill's executors to be a rather likely choice for director. Although this would be only his sixth film, Lumet had done *The Iceman Cometh* with Landau on television for "Play of the Week," one of the most highly touted productions of the era. Indeed, in *Sidney Lumet: Film and Literary Vision,* Frank R. Cunningham argues persuasively that some of Lumet's cinematic work with *Long Day's Journey* has immediate precedent in *Iceman,* particularly the ways in which Lumet's camera work actualizes the themes of the material.

Cunningham makes a learned and persuasive case for Lumet's literary sensibility in his study, as well as for Lumet's ability to make print literature visual. Cunningham concentrates on 14 of Lumet's films, giving special care to his skills as an adaptor and interpreter. With admirable precision, Cunningham outlines how few liberties Lumet took with Reginald Rose's 1954 teleplay of *Twelve Angry Men,* and this is even more true with regard to the text of O'Neill's play. Perhaps Lumet parted most drastically from conventional theatrical presentations of the material by emphasizing the mother, Mary Tyrone (Katharine Hepburn), over the male relationships, and making her the film's dramatic fulcrum. He paid special interest to her cinematically as well. He used increasingly longer lenses as the film progressed, thereby de-emphasizing the background and isolating her from her world. In a conversation with Cunningham, Lumet remarked, "If you look carefully at *Long Day's Journey*—which is used in film schools for its skill in use of lenses—you'll see that as the film went on, I used longer and longer lenses on Hepburn, and wider and wider lenses on the other three, so that she became more and more isolated, whereas the reality of the room kept imposing itself more and more on the other three, the reality of the place, the reality of the time."[2]

Here and elsewhere, such comments by Lumet demonstrate his awareness of how the text may best be served by the cinematic medium. A choice of lenses that will isolate a character visually is likely to be of interest to Lumet only if isolation is of concern in the text. The film opens with exteriors. We start in the morning light of a seaside summer community. Lumet gradually moves to interior spaces and artificially lit scenes. We have a sense of growing darkness as the film continues, and O'Neill and Lumet remind us of this with discussions of the patriarch's miserliness, his reluctance to waste electricity, and his cloying obsession with light bulbs. The spareness of light, and Lumet's tendency to put characters in isolated spots of light surrounded by darkness, remind us of the theatrical tendencies of the family members, the degree to which they perform for themselves rather than communicate with one another, and the extent to which each enjoys the "limelight." The lighting of the later scenes often suggests that characters are delivering soliloquies rather than carrying on conversations—which, following Lumet's direction, is precisely what they are doing. All of this culminates at the end of the play, as we realize just how fully these are characters who (both literally and metaphorically) long to stay in the dark.

The ending of the play is one of the most famous in twentieth-century American drama, and Lumet does well by it in the film. It is late at night. The patriarch of the family, renowned stage actor James Tyrone (Ralph Richardson) and his sons, Jamie (Jason Robards) and Edmond (Dean Stockwell), are in the sitting room of their summer home. Mary Tyrone comes downstairs in her wedding dress. In the distance, a foghorn periodically blows; the beam from a distant lighthouse occasionally penetrates the room. Mary recalls the winter of her senior year in high school, when she fell in love with James. Although she is physically present, she is mentally removed from the others thanks to a drug-induced reverie that has returned her to a moment in her past that she identifies with innocence. As Cunningham describes Lumet's presentation,

> The camera continues its backward movement, then pulls upward, over them all, as Mary speaks only to herself. Finally the pinpoint of lighted area is a minute part of the frame, surrounded by total blackness, as if to symbolize Mary's total regression from this world into another. And as she grows smaller, so do the men who love her. The only faint reality is an occasional light beam from the lighthouse, crossing the windows in deep background. . . . Then the camera returns to its long-view vantage point, and Lumet's meditative eye ends the film staring at the spot of light that contains them all, now, until even that light is dimmed.[3]

Mary's inability to come to terms with her past, either to break free of it, or apply it meaningfully to the present, has been a central concern of the play since the first act. There we learn of her drug addiction, of her recent hospital stay, and the recovery she apparently has under way here at the summer house. Her drug addiction is only a symptom of still larger problems, we are to understand, just as her inability to cope with her life during the period when we meet her must be understood in terms of long-standing psychological patterns of denial, repression, and avoidance. It is consistent with these insights that in the play's final moments she should be consumed by drugs and her past, that she should be physically present in the family unit but also apart from it, for this is at the dramatic core of the play itself. All of the Tyrones are similarly consumed and estranged from one another, fettered by their personal histories. The poverty James Tyrone knew as a child has turned him into a miser as an adult. Mary's addiction came at the hands of a cut-rate doctor James employed during the birth of Edmond. Life on the road with James has left Mary with a perpetual sense of homelessness so profound that no physical edifice will ever satisfy her, though James tries to provide one. Jamie's displacement within the family after Edmond's birth haunts him still. Edmond's failure to find himself as an adult is traceable to his childhood.

As the play begins, James has turned to another cut-rate physician, this time to diagnose Edmond's ailments—not that anyone doubts their cause. James, Jamie, and Edmond himself all see that he is suffering from tuberculosis, and not the seasonal cold that everyone keeps mentioning. Ostensibly, they are trying to keep this from Mary, whose own father died of consumption, thinking that a blow of such proportion will make her turn to drugs again. The truth is that they are more comfortable denying the problem than confronting it. Here and throughout, Mary's plight is theirs. She prefers living in a fog to seeing life by the clarity of daylight. For the men, alcohol, rather than Mary's morphine, serves to aid this goal. They are all heavy drinkers, perhaps alcoholics. Being lost in a fog is one of the central tropes of the play. Mary Tyrone says, "That fog horn, isn't it awful? . . . . It wasn't the fog I minded, I really love fog. . . . It hides you from the world. You feel everything has changed. Nothing's what it appeared to be. No one can find or touch you anymore. . . . It's the foghorn I hate. It won't leave you alone. It keeps reminding you, warning you. Calling you back." Each family member longs for insulation against reality, for a vision of the world that, no matter how twisted, is more comforting than reality itself. Upon returning from a walk on the beach, for instance, Edmond is confronted by his father who chides him for worsening his physical condition by walking in the damp sea air at night. Says Edmond,

> "I love the fog. It was what I needed. . . . The hell with sense. It was where I wanted to be. Halfway down the path you can't see this house. You'd never even know it was here. Everything looked and sounded unreal. It was like walking on the bottom of the sea, as if I'd drowned long ago, as if I was a ghost belonging to the fog and the fog was the ghost of the sea. It felt damn peaceful to be nothing more than a ghost within a ghost. . . . Don't look at me as though I've gone nutty. Who wants to see life as it is if they can help it?"

The peace that Edmond associates with the fog is identified as well with ghosts and the living dead. For O'Neill, the problem with such an insular sensibility is that it cuts us off from those around us. We find that we are alone, even when surrounded by people; and often we are most aware of this profound human loneliness, when we are among those nearest to us. At one point in the play, Mary laments her mere presence in the house. In a text filled with wonderful, extended, dramatic speeches, O'Neill's simple line, rendered simply by Katharine Hepburn, remains one of the play's most profound moments. Speaking to her husband, she says, "It's very dreary and sad to be here in the fog alone with night falling."

In effect, Mary is speaking to herself, and with the exception of a few rare moments, that is what all of the Tyrones do. They have kept each other at arm's length for so long that they are now too distant from one another to communicate. One would expect a theatrical family to be comfortable using language to build bridges between speaker and listener, but they build piers instead. A failure to communicate is indigenous to "fog people" such as the Tyrones, Edmond reminds us. And it signals still larger problems. The insulation against reality that the Tyrones crave effectively isolates them from one another, which, as Mary reminds us, leads to a life that is dreary indeed. It is a half-life. At its best, it is only playacting at being alive, a point underscored by the theatrical careers of both James and Jamie; and at worst, it is a life broaching self-destruction. Edmond's walk in the fog may well suggest a suicidal impulse. He admits elsewhere in the play to being "a little in love with death" and he refers to an earlier period when, "stone cold sober" he tried to kill himself. The father of James

14

Katharine Hepburn stars in *Long Day's Journey into Night*. The Museum of Modern Art/Film Stills Archive.

Tyrone, we learn, may have taken rat poison upon his return to Ireland. Jamie says that he hates life, that part of him is dead, that he wants to destroy whatever is living around him—including his brother Edmond. Late in the play, Mary elaborates on an event that has been mentioned previously, a night when she fled the house in her nightclothes. Until this point in the drama, the story has not made sense. Now we see that the issue under discussion has been Mary's attempted suicide. As Mary recalls the event, she was heading toward the sea, intent on drowning herself. She admits that she hopes at some point to take an overdose of drugs.

The ending of the film, then, recounted above, is both true and faithful to O'Neill's text. Within the frame and beyond it (both literally and metaphorically) the Tyrones are together and apart by the end of O'Neill's final act, living in the present but tied to the past. Insofar as any light from outside can be shed on their plight, it is apt to be only intermittent, and finally extinguished entirely. Mary here seems to hear only the sound of her own voice; if Hepburn seems lost to her own performance, that is true for Mary as well, and has been throughout much of the film. It has been true in the sequence in which Mary confides to her housemaid Kathleen (Jeanne Barr) about her loathing of the foghorn; it has been true in a more recent sequence in which, after learning that Edmond has been diagnosed with consumption, she holds him but talks about the pains and failures of her own life, rather than what awaits him in his.

Lumet has spoken about the directorial tension between language and "silent pictorial concepts," about the difference between the stage and the screen, and the tension between the spoken word and what the camera sees. In interviews, he often uses this tension to distinguish "Long Day's Journey" from other stage plays that have been made into films. He points us toward how the visual elements of the film attempt to realize the text cinematically, not simply photograph a stageplay. There are several compositional patterns that suggest Lumet's approach, which may be gleaned from even a casual viewing. Lumet films the text primarily in one-shots, two-shots, over-the-shoulder-shots, and reverse-angle shots; and while that in itself is not unusual, the way he combines these shots is interesting. For one thing, he tends to bring characters closest together in the frame when they are farthest apart emotionally. The reverse is true as well: he tends to put them farthest away from one another in the frame when their mutual plight is most clearly shared. The camera composition makes us immediately aware of the others in their world—and that, of course, makes their isolation all the more painful to witness.

Lumet also uses reaction shots, frequently with stunning effectiveness. He reminds us that the drama of this family situation must be understood not only in terms of what a given speech tells us about a character, but also in terms of what it tells another character about the speaker. Lumet uses reaction shots, as in the scene when the father is recounting his youth on the stage, and the waste of his great talent in favor of staying with a popular play that he knew would make him rich and famous, or the sequence in which Edmond recounts at length his life at sea, or at the film's end. As Mary comes down the stairs, it is as if an amateur has assumed control of the camera, and not a very talented one at that, for Jamie's head is kept at the bottom of the frame, even as the moving camera follows Mary around the table and into the room. It ruins the balance, and is clumsy, distracting. But it is also a visual reminder of how Mary's isolation affects all those around her.

These are sequences in which the acting is superb, but then so are the reactions to it, which we might miss were it not for our proximity to them. Were we watching this on stage, at a distance, they might be lost to us entirely. Lumet also had this in mind when he selected camera angles and focal lengths, which he uses to allow us information that would be lost in a stage production. He uses relatively long takes, with the longest generally devoted to Mary. Similar to his use of the long take in *Twelve Angry Men,* here Lumet's camera tends to recompose as we watch, changing our perspective on Mary as she speaks and moves about her carefully circumscribed world. Often Lumet will begin a sequence in which Mary is featured, only to move us gradually into a position where we see that she is looking off into space as she speaks to herself, when we thought she was conversing with others in the room. At a distance, she is a convincing, sympathetic speaker, perhaps the only level head in the house; but as we get nearer, we see that her dilemma is the most desperate of the lot.

Visually, there is not much in the film that offers us a sense of balance, and when the family is together in the same room, Lumet tends to recompose within the frame to particular advantage. Sometimes the camera keeps moving, even when we would expect it to stop to allow a speech its proper weight. For the first two acts of the playbook, and well into the third—that is, from the moment we meet the Tyrones outside their house early in the morning to the point when Mary confides in her maid Kathleen that she has suicide on her mind—it is as if the camera cannot quite find the proper balance. It pairs various characters in ways which suggest an immediate intimacy, only to undercut that intimacy—visually and with dialogue—as the scene develops. Moments of high dramatic intensity, when central familial issues seem to be about to be resolved, are often shot employing angles so high, low, or obtuse to the action, that visually we sense things are not in balance before we realize how out of kilter they are psychologically. This is particularly true when the characters seem on the point of getting their footing with one another. Then the images seem to lack a center of gravity.

Lumet has often been criticized for being cinematically heavy-handed, for having an obvious sensibility more in tune with television than with film. Such critics might do well to look at the editing in *Long Day's Journey,* and particularly at Lumet's sometimes subtle editing of extended sequences of dialogue. By the end of World War II, the standard Hollywood formula for editing passages of dialogue had become largely dependent on the "flat" cut and a crosscutting technique sometimes called "cutting on dialogue." Essentially, this means cutting from one-shot to one-shot, with an occasional two-shot to remind the audience of the physical proximity of speaker to listener. There are two versions of this, both of them simple and familiar to movie audiences. The first shows us the speaker. The person delivering the lines will be in the frame for the duration of the speech, then a cut will be made to the second person as he or she responds. The second version puts the listener in the frame, allowing the audience to see the reaction to what we hear being said off-camera.

Collaborating with editor Ralph Rosenblum (who would work with Lumet again on *The Pawnbroker, Fail Safe, The Group,* and who is best known today for his work with Woody Allen), Lumet employed an alternative to these patterns at key moments in the film, which has since been called "mathematical cutting." To subtly increase the tension during an exchange of dialogue, Lumet and Rosenblum virtually disregard speakers and listeners. They cross-cut from one actor to another, using progressively shorter takes. A shot of one actor that lasts eight seconds, is followed by a shot of the other actor, also lasting eight seconds. Then back to the first, this time employing a six-second take; then back to the other for an equal period, and so it continues. This mathematical cutting increases the tension we feel when witnessing even the most innocuous exchange between family members. It provides a kind of subtext. Like the camera work mentioned above, it gives us the sense of something amiss, a situation out of balance, even when there is nothing precisely to that effect in the dialogue itself. The mathematical cutting used in *Long Day's Journey into Night* marked Lumet's first real experimentation with editing in a feature film, work which would serve him later in *The Pawnbroker.*

THE PAWNBROKER (1965)

Perhaps less has been written about Lumet's editing than any other aspect of his directorial method. That is unfortunate, for it is well worth our attention. The editing patterns of American film had become rather standardized by the time Lumet began his career as a motion picture director. The degree to which he, and others of his generation, broke with them is apt to be overlooked by moviegoers today, because so much of what they did has become so fully integrated into the movies and television we see today. One has to wonder what a 1930s audience would have made of MTV, for instance. Would they have been able to follow the editing at all?

In his wonderful study of editing, *When the Shooting Stops . . . the Cutting Begins,* Ralph Rosenblum reminds us of "the editorial geography" that informed American movies until the 1960s. He reminds us of the vocabulary of fades, dissolves, wipes, and the like, which was so much a part of what we had come to expect from the movies. He also recalls the amount of information and its sequencing that we were apt to demand from the movie director. Much of this "geography of cutting" was challenged after World War II first by the French and Italians, and subsequently by American directors. Nineteen fifty-nine is often cited as the watershed year. Jean-Luc Godard's *Breathless* appeared in 1959, as did Alain Resnais's *Hiroshima, Mon Amour*—both films that flew in the face of Hollywood's conventional reification of time and space through the editing process. Working with editor Cecile Decugis, Godard employed "jump cuts" to whisk his characters from one location to another, and from one time period to the next, daring the viewer to follow the action and sequence of the drama. Resnais's story of two lovers meeting after the Second World War whose lives are haunted by memories that are as real to them as the present moment, dared moviegoers to redefine the familiar "flashback." It takes 24 frames of film stock to produce an image which lasts for one second on screen. Resnais employed images that were six, eight, or eleven frames long. Occasionally there is a four-frame image. "Flash" cuts (or "flash frames") these are sometimes called, for they are less like filmic images than they are flashes of light. Strobelike in their intensity, they demand that we grasp them visually without giving us time to make sense of them.

American and European critics heralded these innovations as the beginning of a new era of world cinema. Public reaction, though, particularly in this country, was mixed at best. While the work of Resnais, Godard, Truffaut, Chabrol, and others played in art houses to appreciative viewers, these were too few in number to promise significant profits. During this same period, producer Ely Landau was trying to put two projects into production: another stage property, Carson McCullers's theatrical adaptation of her novel, *The Heart Is A Lonely Hunter,* a project he had given to Sidney Lumet; and a literary work, *The Pawnbroker,* Edward Lewis Wallant's character study of a Holocaust survivor, to be directed by Arthur Hiller. When the former production fell through, Landau gave *The Pawnbroker* to Lumet. Landau was taking a risk. Of the six films he had directed, Lumet had only two major successes to his credit, one of them a movie made from a teleplay *(Twelve Angry Men)*, the other a movie made from a stageplay *(Long Day's Journey)*. *The Pawnbroker* was neither. It was a novel, and a particularly problematic novel to bring to the screen. It offered a distasteful protagonist with very few dimensions, apparently a cold, Shylock of a man, the formation of whose character was explored through dramatic flashbacks to his experience during the Holocaust. The novel demands that a reader accept that these past experiences (which protagonist Sol Nazerman has repressed for some quarter of a century) take hold of him in a period of a few days, and become so real and vivid that they bring about a thaw of glacial proportions. Wallant had made them an integral part of the story line, setting them off neatly on the page in italics. In some sense, the present action of Wallant's novel is only there to trigger these italicized sections. Screenwriters David Friedkin and Morton Fine voiced some doubt to both director and producer that this could be done on the screen, at least, not through conventional flashbacks. Ralph Rosenblum, in describing the standard flashback, suggests why.

> "In the thirties and forties flashbacks had been very popular and always happened in the same way. A sequence quieted down, Joan Crawford or Bette Davis said, 'I remember . . .' or began reminiscing in a dreamy way about her first marriage, then the camera moved in on her entranced face, an eerie 'time' music saturated the soundtrack, a shimmering optical effect crept over the screen as if oil were dripping across it. . . . And sure enough, during a long, slow 'ripple' dissolve, the star's face gradually disappeared, to be replaced by a scene from the past or perhaps the same face looking 20 years younger."[4]

Lumet agreed with Friedkin and Fine. The conventional flashback was simply not up to the task. It was too formulaic, too familiar. In this film, memory had to intrude itself; immediacy was required. The past, in all of its fragmented power, had to take hold of the present. Memory had to sieze the viewer just as it was taking hold of Sol Nazerman. But how? Lumet was faced with a challenge that was without precedent in his stage or television experience. He could imitate Resnais and Godard, perhaps, but to do so might dismay much of his potential audience. He could give the audience more familiar fare, such as the conventional ripple dissolve signaling a flashback, but to do that would risk turning Wallant's novel into a soap opera. It was a curious situation for Lumet. Thematically, the book put him on familiar ground; but stylistically, he was going to have to become more of a "movie" director than in his previous projects.

The film begins on a Friday, 26 September. The title character, Sol Nazerman (Rod Steiger), is approaching his twenty-fifth wedding anniversary, Monday, 29 September. On his way home from Harlem for the weekend, long-repressed memories begin to surface, of his dead wife and children, and the atrocities he experienced at the hands of the Nazis. These memories surface as miscellaneous flashbacks at first, but as the next week starts, they take on more form, order, and sequence. Memories begin to come back to Nazerman with a force and narrative order that he cannot deny, until by film's end, he can confront life with a better understanding of himself, and a renewed desire to live.

Events in Nazerman's present life—some consequential, others not—begin to trigger these memories. His relationship with Rodriguez (Brock Peters), a Harlem crime boss, grows strained. An old acquaintance, Mendel (Lumet's father, Baruch), dies. His assistant in the pawnshop, Jesus Ortiz (Jaime Sanchez) has begun to look to Nazerman as a mentor, perhaps even a father figure. Ortiz is doing his best to earn a legitimate living, but he is being pressured by a neighborhood gang to turn on Nazerman, to break into the pawnshop safe where large sums of Rodriguez's cash are kept. These two story lines come together through Ortiz's girlfriend, Mabel Wheatly (Thelma Oliver). Rodriguez launders syndicate money through Nazerman and the pawnshop. Nazerman has made a point of never learning the source of syndicate money. He knows the money comes from illegal activities, of course, but that is all. Some of the money comes from Mabel and others like her, for she is one of Rodriguez's prostitutes. She inadvertently forces Nazerman to acknowledge this when she comes to his shop, as she tries to enlist his help in keeping Ortiz employed, rather than letting him return to the street as a gang member. Her visit triggers long-repressed memories of being forced to watch as his wife was sexually abused in the death camp. In memory, Nazerman is forced to confront the degradation of life in the camp, while in his present life, he is moved to confront such things through Rodriguez. He goes to Rodriguez and refuses to deal in money "that comes from filth and from horror." But he is as helpless before Rodriguez as he was before the Nazi guards. Nazerman is mocked, manhandled, then sent on his way.

The more Nazerman confronts the corruption of his present life, the more vivid are his memories of helplessness during the war. The memories build to a crescendo when Nazerman relives his son's death in a boxcar on their way to the death camp, which will have its parallel in the subsequent death of Jesus Ortiz. Ortiz has agreed to the robbery of Nazerman's safe only if the rest of the gang will do the job unarmed. When one of the gang members unexpectedly draws a pistol on Nazerman, Ortiz takes the bullet that was meant for the pawnbroker. Outside the shop, Nazerman kneels over Ortiz's body. His long-repressed pain starts to form itself into one, primeval scream; but when he opens his mouth, nothing comes out. The sound we hear—three tones, run together—is a trumpet, part of Quincy Jones's score. Returning inside, Nazerman goes to the metal receipt spindle where he keeps the pawn tickets. No longer content to be numb to life, Nazerman takes the first step toward reengagement. He wants to feel. He must feel! If for now, horror and pain are all he can feel, so be it. He realizes how much he wants to live; and in order to do that, he realizes, he must try to engage life, if only on a primitive level. He opens his palm and runs the sharp spike through his hand. The camera watches his face.

The Pawnbroker was the first of Lumet's films in which the self-revelation of a single individual was of paramount concern, but it follows in many ways from his previous work. Like the Tyrones, and many of Lumet's "fog people," Nazerman is leading half a life. Blaming himself for his inability to save those he loved, Nazerman has done his best to repress the atrocities he has suffered and those he witnessed against his wife and children at the hands of the Nazis. And in so doing he has cut himself off from the rest of human commerce—not literally, for he is a busy merchant, but spiritually. At one point in the film, Nazerman talks to Mendel. Mendel, a Holocaust survivor, is the aged father of a woman Nazerman has sex with periodically. Mendel says to Nazerman,

"I came out alive, you came out dead. . . . Guilt, there it is, guilt. To find yourself alive. So you wrap yourself in a kind of shroud and feel you share the dignity of death with those who already died. Tell me, does blood ever flow through you, Sol Nazerman? Can you feel pain?"

"No," answers Nazerman.

Says Mendel, "You are a fake. You breathe, you eat, you walk, you make money. You take a dream and give a dollar and give no hope."

"I survive," answers Nazerman.

"Survive? A coward's survival. And at what a price. No love. No passion. No pity. Dead. Sol Nazerman the walking dead."

Nazerman, once helpless, has done his best to make himself into a somewhat powerful figure in Harlem. The victim has become a victimizer, and he has constructed a persona and worldview appropriate to the role he has assumed. Money is all-important; human life is worthless. In the first third of the film, we witness a typical morning in the life of Sol Nazerman as the disenfranchised, the hopeless, the detritus of modern life move through his shop in a seemingly endless flow. Here Lumet establishes the degree to which Nazerman has trained himself to disregard their humanity. People do not matter. Perhaps nothing matters, ultimately. But money is an immediate concern. Everything can be translated into dollars and cents. Nazerman sits behind a protective screen that separates him and his cash supply from the world at large. Nearby he keeps his receipt spindle. The pawn tickets pile up as the morning develops, a visual reminder to all who enter that everything has a price in the world of Sol Nazerman.

An immigrant who lost his wife and children to a Nazi death camp, Nazerman has constructed a worldview, a private version of reality, that he thinks will allow him to function, if not prosper. His pawnshop is little more than a front for organized crime. When we meet Nazerman, he does not think of himself as a criminal, but crime does not repel him. It is the way of the world. Nazerman thinks the nightmare he has lived through has prepared him to cope with modern life: he cannot afford to think, remember, or feel anything for anyone aside from himself. He knows all too well the stink of the world and wants to keep it at a distance. Like many of Lumet's future protagonists, Nazerman is on the brink of self-revelation. He is about to be tested, and in the process he will discover much he does not know—or at least does not acknowledge—about himself as a person. The film is some two hours long. In all, the memory sequences account for less than 10 minutes of that length. No doubt it is to Lumet's credit that so little footage, relatively speaking, remains so vivid in the minds of his viewers.

Perhaps the greatest risk run by Lumet in terms of the flashback sequences is to be found in Nazerman's first recollection of the death camps. Early in the film, as Nazerman prepares to close his shop for the weekend, Ortiz moves toward a wall calendar. He starts to change the date to the following Monday, 29 September. Nazerman stops

The character Sol Nazerman works in his pawnshop. The Museum of Modern Art/Film Stills Archive.

him. In the first moments of the film, we learned that Monday would have been his twenty-fifth wedding anniversary, but nothing much has been made of that since, and, at this point in the film, we have only the faintest inkling of what he has suffered during the war. Both Ortiz and the viewer are puzzled by Nazerman's making an issue of changing the page on the calendar, which is surely Lumet's intention. The explanation lies ahead in the first extensive series of flash frames in the film. These flash frames are jarring; and on first viewing, only barely decipherable. They punctuate a sequence of some two minutes as Nazerman closes up the shop, walks to his car, gets behind the wheel, starts home, and (by this point so badly shaken that he can hardly drive) nearly strikes a pedestrian who has stepped into the street.

After locking a folding security gate, Nazerman proceeds toward his car in darkness. Somewhere, out of frame, a dog is barking. Inexplicably, four flash frames—each lasting only one-sixth of a second on the screen—are intercut with footage of Nazerman walking through this menacing Harlem neighborhood. After two or three, we recognize a dog on the screen, perhaps a German shepherd, approaching us, and the legs of a man walking—perhaps running—beside the animal. By the fourth flash frame, the head of the dog fills the screen, and the man's legs are beyond our field of vision. Perhaps he was never there.

We assume that this is the same dog we have been hearing, for the barking continues even more persistently. The camera closes in on Nazerman, who looks offscreen—toward the barking? Our uncertainty is apparently clarified through a subjective shot. Behind a schoolyard fence, a group of boys are beating one lone youngster. Another four-frame image appears, of Nazerman's face, or someone else's, filled perhaps with terror. The schoolyard returns. The beaten youngster has broken away and is scrambling up the fence. We see beads of sweat on his face, and sense his panic. Nazerman's face, or someone else's, reappears. Perhaps it resembles the face we have seen earlier only because it lasts so briefly.

The boy on the fence has been caught, and is being pulled downward by hands attached to a body we cannot see. It is daylight now, a different time and place, but the sounds of the gang and the dog's barking continue. The person on the fence changes—a man, not a boy, and a white, not black. He slides to the ground as if he lacks the strength to support himself. Now we see a lone Nazi guard, apparently waiting for help. A group of apparent prisoners fills the screen. Among them is someone who might be Nazerman, or who *might have been* Nazerman. His head is shaved. He is more muscular than Nazerman, but the look of terror on his face resembles Nazerman's when he first looked off camera. The resemblance is reinforced by quick cuts between Nazerman's face and the face in the camp—yes, apparently both images are Nazerman. He looks as though he might be about to scream.

Instead, we hear the barking dog, and see that it is an attack dog, part of the prison patrol. We see it, not through Nazerman, the prisoner's eyes, for he is looking offscreen, away from the charging animal; the prisoner is back on the fence, no longer trying to escape, but to put himself beyond the dog's reach.

In a flurry of cuts, the dog and its handler approach the prisoner, who lacks the strength to hoist himself. The handler seems to give orders—to the dog, to the man? It is unclear. The dog is unleashed upon the prisoner. Quick cuts take us from the dog's perspective to that of the prisoner. We understand what is happening now. Shots of the other prisoners also yield more information. Nazerman, and perhaps the others, are wearing Stars of David, and washed-out prison garb, and they are in a compound. For a moment, the present Nazerman appears, and though there is no doubt now that the prisoner is Nazerman at some earlier time, the difference between them is decided. Almost immediately, we return to the body virtually impaled on the wire.

Nazerman turns away in the dark, as if turning from the past. Shaken, depleted, perhaps even frantic, he resumes his walk though the streets of Harlem toward his car. The film seems to have slowed diametrically. In fact, the pace of the cutting is still reasonably fast but it appears slow compared to the flash frames we have witnessed. Nazerman puts his hands on the hood of his car, resting his weight. He looks as though he might be about to vomit. A flash cut appears, for one-sixth of a second, of the prisoner impaled. Nazerman enters his car. Again, we hear the dog's bark—from the school yard or the compound. Suddenly, Nazerman is driving. We see him from a passenger's perspective and we can tell, even from the back seat, that Nazerman is not fit to be driving, that he is shaken and fleeing blindly, thoughtlessly, savagely. We see a pedestrian step off the curb before Nazerman sees him. We hear the sound of brakes. Just as we think the car has run over the pedestrian, the last of the flash frames appear— the prisoner again, the compound, the wire fence, for one-sixth of a second. The pedestrian has jumped back. His hands are on the hood. He screams at Nazerman, who listens impassively or who may not hear him at all. The man moves on. A car honks, and Nazerman enters the flow of traffic. The scene shifts to Mendel's apartment and present action resumes.

Rosenblum has commented on the importance of this sequence to the film. Lumet intended to communicate not simply biographical information about his main character; he was trying to alert his audience to what Rosenblum has termed "the beginnings of a memory voyage." To a contemporary movie audience, the sequence is manageable, even commonplace. But at the time, Lumet and Rosenblum were sailing in largely uncharted waters. They had toyed with montages in *Fail Safe*. There was precedent for flash frame work in contemporary European film and for including flash frames in extended montages if one looked to cinema history. Russian film director Sergei Eisenstein had mastered such techniques as early as the mid-1920s. There was precedent as well for memory intruding on present action—most recently, in *Hiroshima, Mon Amour*. Still, this was American filmmaking, a commercial endeavor. Who knew what the movie audience would make of this?

What would it take to make Lumet's point? Rosenblum has discussed how much was done in the spirit of experimentation.

> How long should an initial flash last in order to suggest the percolation of memory? Eight frames, a third of a second, seemed (incredibly) to linger too long. But four frames were impossible to read. Would viewers become irritated by cuts they couldn't make out, or would they experience just the sense of anticipation we wanted? Back and forth we went from eight frames to six frames to four frames to eight frames, experimenting, screening, recutting, until every shot went through the Moviola in a comprehensive selection of lengths, and the entire flashback sequence seem to have experienced exhaustive permutations. Even when we had finally settled on our formula, Lumet feared that no one would understand it, and as a precaution he worked out a backup plan for editing the film in a more traditional way—a simple procedure whereby the story would dissolve from the black boy on the schoolyard fence to the dazed prisoner on the concentration camp fence and stay in the past until the memory scene was completed. Only the initial screenings convinced him that the experiment had worked, and worked in an exponential way.[5]

The flashback material in *The Pawnbroker* becomes more complicated technically as the film proceeds, and more challenging to the viewer. Lumet surely felt that if he could involve the audience in the material early on, and move his viewers to try to comprehend Nazerman's "memory voyage" through the first sequence in the death camp, they would be prepared to deal with more sophisticated presentation as the film approached its climax. One of the best examples of sophisticated editing is late in the story, as Nazerman rides the subway at night. Badly shaken by recent events, Nazerman's darkest memories of helplessness are evoked. Aboard the train to the death camp, his son slipped from his shoulders and suffocated—or perhaps was crushed—on the boxcar floor, while Nazerman pinned elbow to elbow with other prisoners, was unable to save him. Lumet and his editor do two particularly daring things in this sequence. The first has to do with a panning camera. Nazerman enters a subway car and leans against a pole at its center. We see then what he sees. Lumet's camera seems to sweep over the faces of the other passengers, most of them turning in

Nazerman's direction. There are so many faces, so many expressions. What do they want from him? Why are they looking at him? Or does he only think they are looking at him, perhaps turning to him for help?

Lumet and Rosenblum were betting that by this point in the film the audience would identify any flash frame with Nazerman's memories intruding upon the current action, and with that in mind they begin to intercut this panning camera work with Nazerman's memories of prisoners in the train car taking him to the death camp. Though the initial flashes seem shorter than any we have seen, they are not. They are flash frames from footage taken with another panning camera. Eventually we understand. One sweep of faces on the subway car recalls an earlier sweep of faces on the way to the camp; one survey of the helpless brings to mind another. That this is intelligible at all is to Lumet's credit, for a panning camera could easily have confused his audience, much less two panning cameras, with the second camera offering so much information in short snatches. Lumet and Rosenblum finally settled on a variation of the "mathematical cutting" they had used in *Long Day's Journey* to produce this stunning sequence. Each flash frame is progressively (and mathematically) longer than the previous one, four frames longer, to be precise. The first flash is four frames, the second, eight, the third, twelve, and so on, until the last flash frame, at 28 frames—that is, just a little over a second of screen time—seems to be a portrait of Jewish families, depleted, dehumanized, approaching their extermination.

The climactic events of the film—Nazerman's silent scream over the corpse of Ortiz, and the plunging of the pawnbroker's spike through his own palm—are dramatic indeed. If we were to disregard the memory material, they would be overwrought, histrionic. Unless we are aware of Nazerman's past, none of this makes sense, for there is no one in Nazerman's current life—neither Ortiz, nor Rodriguez—who could move him to such catharsis. What finally moves him comes from his past, for his reengagement with life can only come about once he has confronted a past long denied. One of the beauties of Lumet's flashbacks are their symmetry. The memory material becomes progressively complicated—until the very end. Then, in the final flashback sequence, it becomes quite simple. To appreciate this symmetry, we have only to look at the opening moments of the film. This action is not completed until the film's climax, when the two sequences bring us full circle.

Screenwriters Friedkin and Fine had suggested that the film begin in the style of the postimpressionist painters, but Lumet chose instead to put the first images we see in slow motion and without dialogue. Before the titles or credits, there are silent images of a family picnic. Children call to one another, though we cannot hear them. They move gleefully through the lush setting, stirring butterflies and the grass. They may be chasing butterflies. A young woman is also present, and an older man, an Orthodox Jew, by his dress and general appearance. Then a younger man enters the frame, Sol Nazerman but younger, broad-chested, almost moon-faced. The children run toward him. He takes them in his arms, a boy and girl, and spins them around with delight. As the camera comes closer to the boy's face, it is as if his father has inadvertently frightened the child with the exuberance of his embrace, for the child's glee turns to wariness, then fear. The motion slows. The child seems to see something out of frame. The father lowers the child, and looks out of frame as well. The action shifts. There is sound and a different light. We are in a different place and time, in a backyard on Long Island. An old man—possibly the old man we saw in slow motion, not the younger one, surely—is in his suburban backyard. Apparently he lives with his sister-in-law and her two teenage children, a boy and a girl. The woman mentions something about her "poor sister Ruth" and an upcoming anniversary—"Sol, it's been 25 years?" What she really seems to have on her mind, though, is a vacation to Europe. She is trying to get him to pay for a summer vacation overseas. Two flash frames appear during this sequence, one seemingly from the opening material. It is only four frames long: a young woman waves. The second comes at the mention of the anniversary. This flash is longer, nearly a full second, and, despite its brevity, it appears false, like slow motion. This time we know what we are seeing. The young woman from the silent opening waves.

These are the only flash frames Lumet uses until the close of business on Friday when Nazerman witnesses the school yard attack, and they are easily forgotten until then. They do not make much sense as we watch them, but neither do they distract us. The increasing complexity of the "memory voyage" culminates with a return to this same material—a sequence which in its beautiful simplicity completes the spiritual journey into Nazerman's long-repressed pain. Shortly before the robbers enter the pawnshop, a man brings a butterfly collection to Nazerman. Three shots follow: a flash frame, lasting one-sixth of a second, of Nazerman's children; Nazerman's face in the pawnshop, a shot that lasts about a second; and finally, a dissolve. To suggest that what we are about to see will culminate the other memory material, Lumet chose a long, slow dissolve, the most familiar and standard of Hollywood devices to alert the viewer to an oncoming flashback.

Ralph Rosenblum describes what we see next, as the dissolve leads backward in time:

> Steiger's children are running in slow motion through the field of high grasses, reaching for butterflies. Intercut with glimpses of the other members of the family is a new element. German soldiers arriving on two motorcycles with sidecar. Pieces of the silent picnic flit by punctuated regularly by an ominous DING! on the soundtrack. A momentary flash to the drained and beaten pawnbroker before the young Sol puts the children behind his back in a frightened protective gesture. A last close-up of the German soldiers looking down on their prey gives way to Jesus's three hoody friends entering the pawnshop to steal the five thousand dollars. . .[6]

That Lumet should have chosen a dissolve here is appropriate to the dramatic development of the story. Memory is not simply intruding on Nazerman, nor on the audience by this point. Memory now is there for the taking, there to be embraced in all its beauty and horror. The past is finally available to Nazerman in a form that will allow him to apply it meaningfully to the present.

CHAPTER TWO

Lumet's Middle Work:
Murder on the Orient Express, Serpico, Dog Day Afternoon, Network, and *Prince of the City*

If one had to pick a single film that established Lumet's international reputation as a first-rate director, that film would probably be *Murder on the Orient Express.* Lumet had been directing films for nearly 20 years when the film appeared. Virtually all of his films were respected, and some were highly touted, both in this country and abroad. Still, it was *Murder on the Orient Express* that fully established Lumet in the international film community. The film won Best Picture, Best Actor (Albert Finney), and Best Actress (Wendy Hiller), taking three out of seven British Film Awards in 1974. Though in this country it won only Best Supporting Actress for Ingrid Bergman, it was nominated for six Academy Awards, more than any of Lumet's films. But its importance in Lumet's career exceeds such cachet.

Murder on the Orient Express would become one of the most successful overseas ventures of the period, one that brought an American director and actors together with European actors and crews, and American with British distributors. Two relatively modest British producers initiated the project, Lord John Brabourne and his partner Richard Goodwin, and saw it through to completion. During production, the budget continued to climb, undoubtedly to the consternation of financially interested parties. Coming in somewhere between 10 and 12 million dollars, it was by far the biggest film that Goodwin and Brabourne had ever produced. Their willingness to find ever more money to put into the filming paid off. To date, it remains one of the most financially successful productions in British movie history.

Three traits above all recommended Lumet for the project. First, he was known as a director eager to serve the material he was given. He was also known to work quickly. He shot the film—which entailed location work in three countries with a variety of crews—in only 42 days. Finally, since *Twelve Angry Men,* Lumet had enjoyed a reputation as an actor's director. *Murder on the Orient Express* put to rest any lingering doubts on this subject. There is not a flawed performance in the film, and rarely does even an "actor's director" have the chance to work with so many major stars on one project. The cast of the film includes Sean Connery, Albert Finney, Lauren Bacall, Ingrid Bergman, Jacqueline Bisset, Jean-Pierre Cassel, John Gielgud, Wendy Hiller, Anthony Perkins, Vanessa Redgrave, Dennis Quilley, Rachel Roberts, Richard Widmark, Michael York, Colin Blakely, and George Coulouris.

Perhaps the greatest testimony to Lumet's directorial skills came from Agatha Christie herself. Christie had persistently voiced her objections to what filmmakers had done with her novels, and the producers took the daring step of allowing Christie to see a rough cut of the film before its release. Christie was in her eighties, suffering badly from a broken hip. In *The Mystery of Agatha Christie,* Gwen Robyns describes the uneasy mood of the evening:

> It was an anxious little party of E. M. I. executives who waited outside their own private cinema while the film was shown. When the door was opened Dame Agatha walked out tardily on the arm of her husband as her hip still troubled her. Finally she reached Nat Cohen (Chairman and Chief Executive of E. M. I.) and John Brabourne, who were waiting to greet her. She looked up into their faces and said very slowly and quietly, "I think it is a delightful film. This is one of the happiest moments of my life, knowing that at last one of my subjects has been put into a film that I'm delighted with."[1]

This was to be the last time Agatha Christie ever appeared in public.

The Christie novel from which the script was drawn was first published in 1934, in Europe under the title *Murder on the Orient Express,* and in this country as *Murder on the Calais Coach*. It was a significant success on both sides of the Atlantic, perhaps in some measure because it was so topical. Christie drew the story from two actual events. The first occurred in January 1929 when, during one of the worst winters on record, the Orient Express crossed the Turkish border and apparently disappeared. Six days later it was discovered moored in a huge snowdrift. The second event was the kidnapping of the baby of Charles Lindbergh, who had become an international hero thanks to his transatlantic flight in the Spirit of St. Louis. Barely two months old, the Lindberghs' baby was kidnapped from their home in New Jersey and held for ransom by Bruno Hauptman. The ransom was paid, but nevertheless, the child was slain. Hauptman was executed for the crime in 1933. Most of all, the story came from Christie's attachment to the Orient Express, the most luxurious and exotic means of travel in its time.

Set in 1935, the story offers Christie's Poirot the opportunity to deduce the guilty party from a limited number of suspects (specifically, passengers booked aboard a single coach car), once a murder is committed on the Orient Express. What a group of suspects they are: a wealthy and abrasive American divorcee (Lauren Bacall), a young man with homicidal tendencies (Anthony Perkins), a sleeping car conductor who seems decidedly suspicious (Jean-Pierre Cassel), an aged Russian princess (Wendy Hiller), a Teutonic maid (Rachel Roberts), a Pinkerton agent (Colin Blakely) who is as ineffective as he is inconspicuous, a car salesman from Chicago (Dennis Quilley), a ramrod stiff Ghurka commander (Sean Connery) who is returning from a tour of duty in India, his mysterious traveling companion (Vanessa Redgrave), a breathtakingly beautiful Hungarian countess (Jacqueline Bisset) and her diplomatic husband (Michael York), a prototypically British "gentleman's gentleman" (John Gielgud), and a clearly deranged missionary (Ingrid Bergman). The murder is committed on the second evening of the three-day journey to Calais. Ratchett (Richard Widmark), a wealthy art collector, is found dead in his sleeping car. He has been drugged, then stabbed with a dagger 12 times. When the train is snowbound in Yugoslavia and no one can leave, Poirot (with the viewer, of course) culls through the possible suspects, trying to determine motive, capability, and opportunity, as well as their relationships—if any—to one another.

Their relationships to one another are gradually uncovered as the train and its passengers await rescue from the snowdrift. Poirot dis-

Poirot examines his suspects in *Murder on the Orient Express*. The Museum of Modern Art/Film Stills Archive.

covers that they are connected through the kidnapping of Daisy Armstrong, a child taken from her Long Island home five years earlier. The kidnapping resulted in her death, a tragedy that shook the Armstrong family and its employees. The child's grieving mother, Sonia Armstrong, later died giving birth to another child, who was stillborn. Unable to cope with his grief, her husband, Colonel Hamish Armstrong, died as well, and a maid falsely accused of participating in the kidnapping took her own life. Poirot, it turns out, is ahead of the viewer, for while the audience has been looking for the guilty party, Poirot has deduced that there are guilty parties instead. Mrs. Hubbard, the brassy divorcee, is revealed to be the mother of the dead Mrs. Armstrong. The Russian aristocrat is revealed to be her godmother. The Hungarian princess is Mrs. Armstrong's younger sister. Mary Debenham, the fiancé of the Ghurka Colonel, was Mrs. Armstrong's secretary while the Colonel was Armstrong's comrade-in-arms. Beddoes, the butler, was Colonel Armstrong's manservant. The conductor was the father of the wronged maid who took her own life;

the Pinkerton agent was the maid's fiancé; the car salesman was the Armstrongs' chauffeur. Gretta Ohlsson, the deranged missionary, was Daisy Armstrong's nurse. Each of the suspects, we learn, has in effect committed the murder of the person they believe responsible for the kidnapping, Cassetti. Now calling himself Ratchett, Cassetti was a mafia kingpin. Although he was behind the kidnapping, he escaped unnoticed by the authorities as they captured and punished the kidnappers themselves.

Recognizing that justice has yet to be served, Mrs. Armstrong's mother, a famous actress, had booked all available spaces aboard the coach when she learned of Cassetti's passage. She has coordinated the trip, staging the events as though producing a play. Serving in effect as a jury condemning a criminal to death, the twelve interested parties have been given the opportunity to see that Cassetti receives his due. They had intended to make it appear to authorities in Calais that Cassetti had been murdered by a rival mafioso. But neither Mrs. Hubbard nor the others had counted on renowned detective Hercule Poirot being forced into their midst by a train line official, Mr. Bianchi (Martin Balsam), who was trying to accommodate his old friend's travel plans.

Christie was particularly fond of isolating her characters in out-of-the-way locations, of bringing apparent strangers together in one spot, having a murder committed, then eliminating the suspects one by one until, in the final moments, the guilty party is revealed. Next to *Murder on the Orient Express,* her best-known book to American audiences is surely *Ten Little Indians,* brought to the screen in 1945 by René Clair as *And Then There Were None.* There she placed a group of strangers on an island they cannot leave and literally eliminates them one at a time. As any Christie reader can attest, to play along with her detectives and discover "whodunit," we must first learn about the characters' pasts and determine what links them, for though they may be strangers to one another, they are apt to have some common relationship. In the process of determining this, we generally discover that all of the characters are guilty of something. Each has a skeleton in his or her closet, something in the past to hide. Christie's work is a double-edged sword. Though guilt is wide-spread, justice is generally served by the end of the story; blame is laid where it belongs. Insofar as blame is rightly assigned, our faith in the world's moral order is to be renewed. Civil authorities may fail in their duties to apprehend the appropriate wrongdoers, but not Christie's detectives. By the story's end, we have proof that there is justice in the world.

Christie's groups, often enclosed and isolated, offer us a micro-cosmic view of society, combining characters from various social tiers and walks of life, who come with many of the virtues and vices found in society at large. A savvy reader knows that any crime committed early in the book (short of murder) is sure to be a red herring. Murder is Christie's subject, and within pages the first one will be committed. A murder is required, since it poses the ultimate threat to society; it is the one crime for which there is no possible restitution, save appre-hending and punishing the murderer. Christie was toying with these suppositions in her *Murder on the Orient Express* (as it turns out, every-one is not simply guilty of something; everyone is guilty of the same crime), and much of the book's charm has to do with the aura of playfulness she brought to it. Lumet seems to have understood this, and it shows in his direction. The actors exaggerate their perfor-mances just enough to remind us that they are playing parts—as are the characters on the train. But not once does Lumet allow them to descend into caricature—not even Finney's portrayal of Poirot, a char-acter so extreme that he invites overexaggeration. In a 24 November 1974 *New York Times* review, Vincent Canby praised Albert Finney in particular: "The performance is made up of the sort of wildly theat-rical overstatements that heretofore only Laurence Olivier, Marlon Brando and, occasionally, Maggie Smith have gotten away with. It's [Finney's] a performance of exaggeration which is fun to watch both for the goals achieved and the risks taken. Though to a less extent all the other stars come on and take similar risks."

Lumet seems to have also understood the need for playfulness in his camera work. Lumet has said, "Stylistically . . . it was very tough for me to do. I've always had a problem with gaiety. I tend to get heavy and this was Agatha Christie, and it dictated a certain style, which was difficult for me to find since it went against my grain. I was in-deed the grimmest person on the set."[2] There is no way to detect that from the finished product. Perhaps no director since René Clair (with *And Then There Were None*) has found camera work so perfectly at-tuned to the tone of a Christie story. Working with veteran British cinematographer Geoffrey Unsworth, Lumet uses the private eye of the camera to give the viewer important clues from the outset of the film, to which Poirot will have only partial access. In the film's first moments, for example, we are with Poirot. The camera leaves Poirot to allow us a glimpse of two other characters, both pertinent to the action to come. We watch as Colonel Arbuthnot (Connery) joins his traveling companion Miss Debenham (Redgrave). Although later, aboard the train, they will appear to be acquaintances rather than lovers, here their passion for one another is unmistakable. Upon being reunited, they embrace. She tries to contain him, saying, "Not now, not now. When it's all over, then." We do not know what the "it" is, though we will later surmise "it" was the murder of Cassetti. The camera then shows us Poirot in the distance. He is too far away to have heard this exchange, but he seems to have seen the embrace. Later, as Mrs. Hubbard boards the train, she looks knowingly at the conductor, and he looks knowingly at her. She walks past. Behind her, Bianchi approaches the coach with Poirot in hand, instructing the conductor Pierre to find Poirot a berth. Pierre asks Poirot if he is Hercule Poirot, the famous detective. Pierre may have done this for Mrs. Hubbard's benefit, for the camera returns to her; the question has stopped her in her tracks. It should. She can hardly afford to have an outsider in their midst, particularly a detective.

The camera begins to link Poirot with the various suspects as soon as he comes aboard the train. We see Poirot not only making his way to his compartment, but also squeezing past Colonel Arbuthnot (who knows he is not part of the plan, and watches in dismay as he passes). Then we see what Poirot sees in the various compartments—the Hungarian princess being reassured by her husband (Bisset, York), the brassy Mrs. Hubbard (Bacall) complaining about her accommodations, Cassetti (Widmark) settling into a compartment adjacent to hers, Miss Debenham (we are close enough to Poirot's face to see that he may recognize her as one of the two lovers he has seen earlier). At the beginning of this sequence the camera is at the far end of the coach. Space is at a premium. The aisle outside the compartments is barely wide enough for a grown man to pass. We begin in long shot, then, as Poirot approaches, we see him in other focal lengths. By the time he confronts Mrs. Hubbard, he is directly before us at medium close-up range. We are close enough to see that Mrs. Hubbard's complaints are actually an attempt on her part to engage him in a conversation, one, we later surmise, in which she can begin to take his measure. Then Poirot pushes past us just as he has the colonel. But unlike Arbuthnot, we follow him, seeing more or less what he sees. And we remain close enough to him to get some inkling of his reactions. Just as the script offers us expository information at this point in the story, so does Lumet's camera. It invites us to share a fundamental supposition about the world with Poirot. Everything about the camera work suggests a world that can be finely observed and carefully considered, and it invites us to do a little detective work of our own. The end result of this cinematic strategy is to give us information that links characters visually in a limited, enclosed space. What is happening visually prefaces what will be true dramatically, for Lumet never lets us forget that we are cut off from the outside world, that we are aboard a train; well before Poirot solves the mystery, Lumet suggests with his camera that the truth is inescapable. The vast majority of the exteriors are "cutaways" to the locomotive engine, at first speeding us forward, later moored in the snow. Relying predominantly upon interiors at medium, medium close-up, and close-up range, Lumet's camera work keeps us aware of how little space is available to conceal the truth from the persistent Poirot.

This cinematic strategy comes to its conclusion just as the story line promises to reveal the guilty party. Christie's story suggests a distinction between moral and legal responsibility, and Lumet develops this distinction as he choreographs camera movement within the confines of available space. He establishes a position of authority at the far end of the train car. This space is initially occupied by Bianchi, then by Poirot. Poirot will move from this position as he gradually reveals the conclusions to be drawn from his investigation. When the mystery is finally solved, he will relinquish his position of authority to Bianchi, suggesting both the breadth and the limits of what Poirot's keen mind can accomplish.

All of the suspects are gathered in the snowbound dining car. The scene begins with the camera at the far end of the car. Our point of view is just over Bianchi's left shoulder. He is standing, addressing the other passengers, promising that Poirot is about to solve the crime and disclose the murderer. Before us are all 12 suspects, crammed into the frame, standing virtually shoulder to shoulder or sitting atop one another. Poirot is center screen, in the middle distance. He is near the center of the group, but clearly not a part of it. By this point in the film, he has discovered their individual relationships to the Armstrongs, but he has yet to make this information available to the audience, nor has he disclosed the nature of their relationships to one another. It is the first time we have seen the full group assembled. The camera now changes focal lengths as Poirot lays out the salient physical evidence. It is a fluid take, one of the longer in the film. First we see the evidence in close-up: a pass key, a decanter, a dagger. Foremost in the screen is a pile of documents, the passports of the various passengers. The camera gradually looks up from the evidence so that the suspects fill the screen. It then circles 60 degrees to the left. More suspects come into view as Poirot speaks. We see their reaction to the evidence he has gathered. Primarily, these are things that have been planted by the conspirators in an attempt to throw him off the scent. The camera reminds us that the evidence is less significant than Poirot himself, for it continues to circle clockwise until he fills the frame; then moves on, still clockwise and without a cut. It has now moved about 360 degrees. We have seen each of the suspects in the background. When Poirot says that the evidence points toward a murder performed by mafia figures, there is a general look of relief that seems to spread from face to face. This brings about a cut. Poirot is asked if it is his conclusion that Cassetti was killed by the mafia? Certainly not, Poirot says. With this, the camera returns to where it began in the scene, at the far end of the car where Bianchi has been, with Poirot once again in the middle distance and in the middle of the suspects. Once again, they are all in view as a group, and Poirot is visually separated from them. Lumet arranges the suspects in an acute angle configuration. The camera moves in on Poirot as he says that there was no mafia killer aboard. His back has been to the suspects. Now he turns to face the group. We see the conspirators from over his shoulder, reminiscent of how we first met them as he boarded the train. The camera pulls back as he suggests that Ratchett was murdered not by one assailant but by several. He walks toward the vortex of the configuration. The camera follows Poirot as he describes each character's relationship to the Armstrongs and, implicitly, their motives for murdering Cassetti. Each has had something to hide from Poirot; each has assumed a false identity of some kind. By deducing their true identities one by one, Poirot has reasoned his way toward the truth about the murder.

As Poirot discusses how each suspect gave himself away, flashbacks are intercut, to earlier conversations with the suspects that we have witnessed. Or is it the same footage we have seen before? These bits of earlier conversations are now presented at more extreme focal lengths and angles than we have seen earlier. The images are visually skewed, we gradually realize, but then that is Lumet's point: so was the version of the truth that the suspects were offering Poirot. This technique is complemented by Lumet's use of lighting. Poirot says in essence that in their previous interviews with him, each of the suspects attempted to keep him in the dark. Poirot says that as he approached the truth, "the light, as Macbeth said, flickered." As he says this, we become more aware of the overhead lights in the dining car, thanks to a lowering of the camera on its vertical plane. An enlightened Poirot is literally illuminated, in a way we have not previously seen.

Merely deducing the true identity of each suspect did not reveal the murderer however, Poirot explains. Who brought them together? Who masterminded this ritualistic execution, with such verve, such dramatic flare? After moving past Mrs. Hubbard a number of times in the scene, Poirot (and the camera) confront her. Mrs. Hubbard, also known as Linda Arden, is revealed to be a famous American actress. Poirot then begins to reconstruct the murder. Through flashbacks, photographed in normal camera range and focal lengths, Poirot reconstructs the murder as Hubbard has directed it: the drugging of Cassetti, the falsifying of evidence, the various characters putting on little performances in an attempt to divert Poirot's attention the night of the murder, the gaining of access to Cassetti's compartment through Mrs. Hubbard's. We switch back to the dining car and present action as Poirot pauses. He now physically occupies much the same space as Bianchi did at the beginning of the scene. It is the second time we have been in this position visually. Poirot is at the far end of the compartment, well-removed from the suspects. He is seeing the suspects from the same perspective from which we first viewed them, but they appear different now that we know who they are. The camera comes in until Poirot's face is presented in close-up. A flashback returns us to Cassetti's compartment as the various characters enter and stab him. The camera in Cassetti's compartment is positioned at an impossibly low angle. The compartment lights are out. Only a light from the adjoining compartment of Mrs. Hubbard, and a blue night light, make it possible to see. We seem to be seeing "through a glass darkly." Everything is visually exaggerated. The effect is almost Expressionistic. As the ritual sequence begins, we hear but do not see the dagger plunging into the body as the conspirators file through, each one announcing the death they are avenging. While the sequence is not particularly horrifying, the execution of Cassetti is a dark moment, and Lumet means it to be understood as such. Certainly that is how Poirot understands it: the "repulsive" murder of a "repulsive murderer," he terms it.

As the film returns to present action, Poirot walks forward until he occupies the middle distance, mid-screen. He is in much the same position as he was when he laid out the misleading evidence, but this is a somewhat different Poirot. No longer is he simply trying to solve the mystery of Cassetti's murder. He must decide which version of the murder to present to the authorities—the version that he knows to be false, that Cassetti was killed by a gangland assassin, or the version that the facts have disclosed, that Cassetti was killed by Mrs. Hubbard and her conspirators? A murder investigation demands that justice be served. Has justice already been served? What is to be gained by turning these passengers over to the authorities?

What has been for Poirot an intellectual exercise, now becomes a matter for metaphysicians. In which alternative does the greater good rest? Poirot sits. The camera comes in on his face. In close-up, he acknowledges that civil authorities invariably are drawn to the simplest and most obvious solutions, even when they are incorrect. Poirot sees the difficulty in either alternative he chooses. Sure of himself for much of the film, he now seems stymied. Apparently, even a mind as fine as Hercule Poirot's has its limits. He opts to leave the situation to Bianchi. Apparently, such matters are best left in the hands of those seeking ultimate truths, or businessmen more interested in simple expedience than in truth. In either case, Poirot is eager to wash his hands of the mess. The camera work now brings us back to the configuration with which we began this sequence: Bianchi at the far end of the train, Poirot in the middle distance, the members of the group crowded together within the frame. It is the third time we have been here—once, as Poirot explained the apparent murder, again as he explained the actual murder, and now a third time, as he relinquishes the floor to Bianchi. Bianchi gets right to the point. What train line official is eager for a messy murder investigation that may attract an uncharitable press? Bianchi asks for the falsified evidence. A snowplow has just broken through to the Orient Express. The passengers are about to be reconnected with the rest of the civilized world. It is the falsified evidence that will be given to the police. Officially, this will be presented as an underworld killing.

The film ends with the group reconfigured in a way that recalls our first encounter with them. The mother and sister of the late Sonia Armstrong stand side by side. The camera is behind and between them, locating us over their shoulders, inviting us to take our place in the receiving line alongside them. Each holds a glass of champagne. The other conspirators line up, preparing to appear before them one by one, to touch their glass of champagne to the mother's and daughter's, and move out of frame. Triumphant, the group seems about to disassemble. Poirot, having completed his job, has returned to his compartment.

SERPICO (1974)

Elements of *Murder on the Orient Express* are reminiscent of Lumet's earlier thematic concerns. Here the lone individual confronting the solidified group takes the shape of Poirot confronting Mrs. Hubbard and her eccentric cast of avengers; here, the guilt plaguing Sol Nazerman for surviving his wife and children takes the shape of seeking out and punishing the guilty party. There is also evidence of cinematic techniques in *Murder on the Orient Express* that we have seen earlier in Lumet's work. But the film may be best appreciated in terms of its place in Lumet's ongoing career.

Throughout his career, Lumet has directed films that are most remarkable for their intelligent efficiency, their professionalism; *Stage Struck* in the 1950s, *The Anderson Tapes* in the 1960s, *The Verdict* in the 1980s. *Murder on the Orient Express* is to be counted among them. Certainly Lumet owes no apologies for such work, though it would be a mistake to judge his career by these films alone. He is not, to be sure, an auteur, as Resnais, Godard, Bergman are. He has never claimed to be; but nor should his reputation rest solely on his skills as a technician, as someone who understands the job at hand and does it. Other films from this same period, such as *Serpico* and *Dog Day Afternoon,* seem more closely related to Lumet's earlier work than the more popular *Murder on the Orient Express.* They deal with the limits of what a reasonable person can accomplish. They also deal with acts of crime, and bringing criminals to justice. Cinematically, they too are photographed, lit, and edited in ways reminding us of the limited space available and the inescapable realities before us. In their way, they are equally authentic, and they certainly have more to do with the majority of Lumet's films to come.

Adapted from Peter Maas's book of the same name by screenwriters Waldo Salt and Norman Wexler (who received an Academy Award nomination for their efforts), *Serpico* brings several of Lumet's earlier thematic concerns together in one dramatic vehicle—the process of self-discovery, divorce from a solidified group during that process, a simplistic view of modern reality that gradually must be modified as the protagonist comes into his own, and the complexities of trying to take control of a pressing situation. Photographed on the streets of New York by cinematographer Arthur Ornitz (his finest work since *Requiem for a Heavyweight*), *Serpico* has a visual authenticity that reminds a viewer that the movie is based on actual events. Sergeant David Duke (the film's "Bob Blair," played by Tony Roberts) and Detective Frank Serpico (Al Pacino) really did go to the *New York Times* reporter David Burnham in the early 1970s with evidence of rampant police corruption and the failure of the authorities to do anything about it. These revelations were published in a series of award-winning articles that eventually prompted Mayor John Lindsay to form the Knapp Commission, beginning the most extensive investigation of police department corruption in New York's history. In Maas's book, David Duke plays only a supporting role to the more colorful Frank Serpico, and this is accentuated in Lumet's film. It is Serpico's story, from the moment he gets his badge at the police academy to the time he waits for a ship bound for Europe at film's end, an exile from the city, the profession, and the life he has loved.

Lumet completed the project in 71 of the 75 days for which it was budgeted, a yeoman's task when one considers the production problems. As the story unfolds and Serpico becomes increasingly alienated from the police department and the world at large, he lets his hair grow, acquires a beard, sports an earring, and dons a series of idiosyncratic costumes both on and off the job. To play the part within the allotted shooting time, Pacino began the film with shaggy hair and a full beard, then gradually turned himself into a clean-shaven, bright-eyed rookie. For this and other reasons, the film had to be shot out of sequence, working primarily from end to beginning. Except for one set (Serpico's apartment), the entire film was shot on location. This posed numerous shooting problems. The exteriors and interiors of several police precincts were used. Lumet had to gain the cooperation of the police and other city officials, a particularly touchy matter since his film cast both in a troubling light. The grand jury room in which several scenes were taken was only available when proceedings were not under way. The party scene finally had to be shot at the elaborate loft of Lumet's old friend, Sidney Kingsley. A garment loft could only be used on days when deliveries were not being made. And then there were the seasons to consider. To indicate the amount of time passing in Serpico's life and career, Lumet tried to change seasons visually. This was not always easy, especially when the season of the shooting (the dead of summer) was at odds with the seasons of the story. Finally, there was the script. The more Lumet rehearsed with Pacino, the more he realized that Pacino could spontaneously incorporate material that was not in the script he had been handed. In fact, Serpico was back in the country serving as a technical advisor on the project, and Pacino spent many hours talking to Serpico as he researched the character. Lumet has estimated that the finished movie contains about 40 percent of the structure in the Maas book that Wexler adapted into a screenplay. About 40 percent is dialogue supplied by Waldo Salt. The remaining 20 percent was improvised during rehearsal, then formalized in writing before the shooting began.

Serpico's initial taste of police corruption comes during his first days on the job. As a rookie cop working a beat with a seasoned veteran, Serpico is taken into a diner in which Charlie (Kenneth McMillan) lets the cops eat for free in return for overlooking his double-parked deliverymen. Less as a matter of principle, and more because he does not like the leftovers Charlie serves him, Serpico balks at this. A bit later, while working at the Twenty-first Precinct in lower Manhattan, Serpico and his partner interrupt a gang rape in progress. Serpico apprehends one of the rape suspects. At the precinct, the suspect is beaten during the interrogation in an attempt to make him identify his accomplices. Serpico refuses to take part in this, but neither does he interfere. He leaves the room, preferring to fill out arrest cards. A few days later, Serpico catches the rapist's accomplices. During booking, credit for the arrest is taken away from Serpico and given to a pair of plainclothes detectives. It would make the detectives look bad to have the suspects arrested by a foot patrolman who is not even assigned to their territory, he is informed. When Serpico protests, he is threatened with a trumped-up disciplinary action. Together, the incidents form the beginning of Serpico's rite of passage into the force. On the street, there is the law to be enforced, though when and how to enforce it are questions to consider. A policeman's world is tough. Serpico will have to be tough and flexible if he is to survive. One hand holds another—it is the way of the world.

Within the force, a fraternity exists in which pledges serve the brothers until they have earned the right to be served themselves. Loyalty to one's own is what matters, rather than abstract concepts of law. Neither lesson sets well with Serpico, but he is not prepared to buck the system. He transfers out of the unit, moving upward to the

Bureau of Criminal Identification, a stepping stone for a patrolman seeking a detective's gold shield. While working at BCI as a plain-clothesman, he meets Princeton-educated Bob Blair, a figure who will later play a key role in events. Blair is headed for the detective squad of a special unit working for the mayor. Serpico subsequently trans-fers to the Ninety-ninth Precinct. Shortly after he arrives he is handed an envelope containing 300 dollars. It is his cut, a welcoming gift from his brother police officers. Serpico finds Blair, who suggests they take the matter to Inspector Kellogg (John McQuade), the second highest-ranking official in the Department of Investigation. Over a swank lunch, Kellogg tells them to ignore it. Serpico takes the money back to his partner, who assures Serpico he will pass it along to the Police Benevolent Association.

Serpico realizes that he will have to continue taking such payoffs if he is to keep his place in the unit. The other policemen can hardly allow him to do otherwise. Unless he is as vulnerable to discipline as they are, he poses a direct threat to their well-being. With this in mind, Serpico goes to his superior, Captain McClain (Biff McGuire), who agrees to act on Serpico's behalf and get him transferred. McClain promises to go to his friend Inspector Roy Palmer, an official of a Bronx narcotics precinct. The precinct, McClain assures Serpico, is "as clean as a hound's tooth." Before Serpico has time to sign in, Tom Keough (Jack Kehoe), an old friend from Serpico's early days in plain-clothes, seeks him out. Together they shake down a gambling suspect for 200 dollars. The precinct is "clean" only in this regard, that while the payoffs in his former unit came from drug money, here they will come from gambling. Serpico's new partner, Rubello (Norman Ornellas), proclaiming himself Serpico's "paisano" (or brother), takes Serpico into the streets and shows him how the "collections" are made. When Serpico refuses his share, Rubello tells him he will hold it for Serpico. He will not tell the others. He will give Serpico time to change his mind. It is becoming a familiar scenario to Serpico: to refuse his cut, to try to stand aside from corruption, is to make himself a threat to the others. As Keough later says, "Who can trust a cop who don't take money?"

Serpico returns to McClain with news of what has just happened. McClain tells him he has taken the news to Commissioner Delaney (Charles White). According to McClain, the commissioner responded that he was "delighted a man of integrity has surfaced." The commis-sioner, says McClain, wants Serpico to stay where he is, to play along for now. The implication is that a full-scale investigation is in the offing. Serpico will play a part in this with the evidence he gathers. McClain assures Serpico that Delaney will reach out for him when the time is right. But time begins to run short for Serpico. Rubello is transferred. In his place, Serpico is partnered with Al Sarno (Ted Beniades). Sarno is less sanguine about Serpico's reluctance to accept payoffs than Rubello had been and unwilling to keep the matter confidential. Since his colleagues will soon know that he is not accepting illegal payoffs, Serpico must take some action. He calls McClain again, who tries to calm him, saying "Simply continue to wait." When Serpico presses his case, McClain informs Serpico that he has done all he can.

It is beginning to appear to Serpico that there is no cop at any level willing to deal with his revelations. When Bob Blair learns of this, he urges Serpico to circumvent the police department entirely. He suggests that they go directly to Jerry Berman (Lewis J. Stadlen), the mayor's right-hand man. This comes to nothing. Berman takes the information to the mayor's office only to discover that the city is anticipating riots in the ghetto during the summer; no politician in his right mind would risk alienating the police department with "a long, hot summer" on the horizon. Blair has put Serpico at high risk by taking him to Berman. Serpico realizes that the more people he talks to, the more he increases his own vulnerability. Serpico faces a curious paradox: the more people he involves, the more isolated he becomes. There is no strength in numbers, as he once believed. In this case, on the contrary, there is peril. Serpico is still a working policeman. If word leaks out that Serpico is trying to inform on the cops with whom he works, his life will be worthless.

Even his best friend Bob Blair has failed him, Serpico believes. Rumors have begun to spread within the department. Someone, rumor has it, is eager to inform on the collection of bribes and their distribution. Serpico is confronted by a group of his fellow narcotics detectives, led by Keough. The point of the confrontation is clear: any cop who refuses to take money has no place among them. Serpico returns to McClain yet again. He has waited a year and a half to hear from Delaney, he explains. Time is up. Serpico is going outside the official chain of command. Shortly thereafter, Serpico returns to the precinct. Palmer (Bernard Barrow) puts him before two inspectors from City Hall. The inspectors have been sent to learn to which officials—if any—he has spoken. Serpico suspects that the inspectors are part of a political cover-up, that McClain has been lying to him all along. Delaney is not about to conduct an investigation. He has simply been trying to keep Serpico contained.

Word soon spreads that Serpico is the officer who has gone to the authorities. He is then urged by veteran police official Sid Green (John Randolph) and District Attorney Herbert Tauber (Allan Rich) to testify before the grand jury. He is assured that going to the grand jury will prompt an investigation that will extend to the "highest levels" of city government. It is not just the police Serpico is indicting, after all, it is much of city hall. A grand jury is the best way to go about this, and to get the grand jury to act, Serpico must tell his story. Serpico realizes that he has no more reason to trust Green and Tauber than any other official with whom he has dealt. So far, "the system" simply has not worked. Yet what choice does he have? His allegations are now a matter of record. He has cut himself off from his brother policemen. He is alone, no matter what he is told. Responds Serpico, "And meanwhile, where am I? I'm out there alone, who gives a fuck about that? You know that I'm totally isolated in the department? I haven't a friend!"

When the policemen in the Bronx precinct learn Serpico is scheduled to testify, Tom Keough alerts him that his life is in danger. To complicate matters for Serpico, the grand jury investigation for which he is risking his life is turning out to be so superficial as to be meaningless. What the district attorney intends to do is largely what Delaney had in mind, Serpico realizes. Tauber is interested in making a few showy indictments at the lowest possible levels of the police force. The high officials who have turned a deaf ear to Serpico's allegations are to get off unscathed.

Serpico transfers to a Manhattan precinct run by Inspector Lombardo (Ed Grover). Lombardo is as decent a cop as Serpico has met since graduating from the police academy. When Lombardo discovers that there is corruption in his own precinct, he goes with Serpico to their superior, the Chief of Police (E. Emmet Walsh). When the Chief refuses to take action, Lombardo, Serpico, and Blair go to the *New York Times*. Shortly after the story appears, Serpico is transferred back to a narcotics division, this time to the Eighth Precinct in south Brooklyn. There he learns that payoffs are by thousands rather than by hundreds, as they were in the Bronx. Set up by his partners (among them F. Murray Abraham, in a bit part) during a routine drug bust, Serpico is shot in the face and nearly killed. As the film reaches its conclusion, the Knapp Commission is formed, Serpico testifies, and finally quits the police department. A final screen title tells us he lives in Switzerland.

Over two hours in length, with more than 100 locations and speaking parts, the film is a modern urban epic—but it is also a personal film, a character study in self-revelation and a growing understanding of the world's corruption, as well as the limitations of the individual in dealing with it. In the film's first moments, we are with Serpico at his graduation from the police academy, listening to the commencement address. "To be a police officer means to believe in law, and to enforce it impartially, respecting the equality of all men, and the dignity and worth of every individual. Every day, your life will be on the line. Also your character. You'll need integrity, courage, honesty, compassion, courtesy, perseverance, and patience. You men are now prepared to join the war against crime and put the theory you have learned into practice in the streets." Serpico is every bit that police officer, we are to understand. He believes in the law, is compassionate, patient and steadfast. Lumet makes these points clear, particularly during the initial episodes of Serpico's tour of duty. But insofar as Serpico believes in such ideals, he is also naive, a point Lumet also makes. The world in general, and the police force in particular, make these ideals difficult to "practice in the streets."

Midway through the film, after Blair's friend Jerry Berman has been unable to move the Mayor to act, Serpico declares that the whole system is corrupt from top to bottom, then accuses even Blair of betraying him. Blair says, "You know, Frank, you're behaving like a goddamned child. . . . You come looking for help, whining, mealymouthed with your humble pie act and your saintly, injured innocence. Who told you the department or the whole world was some kind of fucking Boy Scout camp? What do you expect [me to be], for Christ's sake, a magician? Big daddy? White knight rides in on a horse, snaps his fingers, the whole dirty world turns virgin white?" Blair's words are said in the heat of anger, and they overstate the case, though perhaps only slightly. For the first half of the film, Serpico's vision of the world is almost childlike. An otherwise savvy character, Serpico's world is divided to a surprising degree into good guys and bad, with himself in the former role. The film is half-finished before he begins to acknowledge the depth and breadth of the corruption he is up against. Believing in the beginning that truth is on his side, and that it will allow him to triumph, Serpico assumes that he merely needs to take what he knows to someone in authority, a white knight, as Blair has put it, a big daddy. That has not proven to be the case. Indeed, the film is mounted so that the audience perceives the extent of the corruption long before Serpico does.

That Serpico should remain "a saintly, injured innocent," so long reminds us that innocence on the streets is tantamount to ignorance. It is only with knowledge of the limits of his own capacities that Serpico can begin to properly define his role in relation to a corrupt world. But to do that, he must first be separated from family, removed from any sense of fraternity with his colleagues and from his lover. As in later Lumet films, self-knowledge comes only with the shattering of one's illusions about the world. Only once the individual is standing alone can he begin to find his way.

In their treatment of Serpico's earliest days in the police department, screenwriters Salt and Wexler remind us of the degree to which the police are a solidified group, a surrogate family in which father figures initiate the young, and your partner is your brother. Serpico's official orientation during his first day of work amounts to one sentence: "Grab yourself a locker; any questions, the older guys'll fill you in." But to act according to his principles and beliefs, Serpico discovers, is likely to put him beyond such bonds. The only high official who really helps Serpico is Captain Green, a Jew in a world of Italians and Irish, a man who has spent more of his career catching crooked cops than catching street criminals, and he is as meaningful a surrogate father figure as the film can envision for Serpico. Green defines himself as an outsider. His name, he says, is an obscenity in precincts throughout the city. When Serpico complains that he is all alone in the department, and without a friend thanks to the allegations he has made, Green gives him some potent, paternal advice: standing apart from the group is the price you pay for doing what is right, he explains.

When we meet Serpico at his graduation from the police academy, he is one face in a sea of blue uniforms. This is paralleled by our last view of him. In the graduation scene, he is scrubbed and polished, wholesome looking. At the end, he sits slumped. From the distance at which we view him, he might be a hippie, a street bum, or one of the homeless, but in any case he appears to be one of the disenfranchised. The camera begins at relatively close range on a seated Frank Serpico with his dog and luggage. He is on the street. Lumet has photographed the image with a zoom lens. The shot is a reverse zoom, and as the focal length becomes smaller and the image wider, Serpico's lone figure is cast against an ever larger blue background. When the focal length is short enough, we see that the blue is the hull of the ship he is about to take to Europe. Cinematic motifs mark key stages in Serpico's isolation from the profession he loves.

Lumet has often been identified with "the New York school of film-making," a loosely defined group of directors including John Franken-heimer, Delbert Mann, and younger directors such as Martin Scorcese who specialize in gritty visual images and films that strive for a sense of spontaneity. Two-thirds of Lumet's films have been shot in New York City, and there is certainly much about his work that earns him a place in the group. The aura of authenticity Lumet achieves in *Serpico* has to do with his camera work and editing, as well as his sense of the city. But his "New York" films are more stylized than is generally acknowledged.

There are a number of motifs that recur in *Serpico*. The film begins at night in a prophetic rain. There is very little sunshine in the film; particularly in the second half, many of Lumet's exteriors have an overcast quality, as if the figurative clouds hanging over the head of Frank Serpico are being manifested just beyond the frame. There is very little sense of open space. We rarely see a skyline. The streets of New York City become a virtual maze in which Serpico finds himself trapped. This is true of the interiors as well. Lumet keeps the camera low on its vertical plane, making Serpico's basement apartment increasingly confining as the film continues. Elsewhere Lumet often keeps walls, doorjambs, and ceilings in view, to suggest that the hero is boxed in. In terms of the developing plot, such a cinematic strategy makes sense, as if each of Serpico's attempts to extricate himself succeeds only in putting him back in equally confining space.

Only sparingly do we see Serpico inside a car (though, he owns or at least has access to one, he seems to prefer his motorcycle). Generally he is on foot in the streets of New York, or inside a building. In cars Serpico is physically closest to his fellow policemen. But when physically closest to them in the frame (for example, when his partner refuses to investigate a gang rape in process, or in his interview with Captain McClain early in the film, or when Serpico confesses to Sarno that he has not been taking his share of the money, or on his way to a drug bust in the final sequences), he is furthest apart from them emotionally and spiritually. This comes to a fitting conclusion when Serpico and Blair are reunited late in the film. They ride together in the backseat of a car. Serpico has decided to go to the *New York Times*.

Blair agrees to help him. Unlike what we have seen previously in automobiles, Serpico is reaching out for a brother and apparently finds one. Lumet photographs the sequence primarily in one-shots, however, isolating the characters from one another, and this suits the mood of the scene. Serpico has decided to go to the *New York Times* not because he thinks he can effect change but because his life is in danger. It is less a revelation than a last will and testament; if murdered, he explains, he wants "something on the record." Although he is willing to help, Blair thinks that going to the newspapers may turn out to be just one more fool's errand. As Lumet photographs their ride, the sequence is marked not by triumph but despair.

Lumet's use of vertical space is interesting as well. Serpico seems to be in motion for much of the film, even at night in his home when he is kept awake by his troubles; but the plotting of the film reminds us that, for all his activity, Serpico is accomplishing painfully little. Much of the movement is at street level. But when he climbs upward or descends, the motion generally precedes another bitter lesson about corruption in the world. The final ambush comes after he has climbed the fire escape of a tenement, entered the building from its rooftop, then descended a staircase to a landing. Once he climbs the precinct stairs late in the film to book a mafioso loan shark, Serpico sees that he has been deserted by the other narcotics policemen, who prefer defending a cop killer to accepting Serpico as one of their own. After accompanying Captain Lombardo on a bust that entails descending a fire escape on the side of a building, Serpico and Lombardo go to the police commissioner, and Serpico learns that he has now exhausted every official avenue available to him—he will have to go to the newspapers. Once the story appears, we see Serpico descend into a subway entrance with the paper in his hands; in the next sequences, the appearance of the story sets events into motion that nearly cost him his life. Something of the spirit of this strategy is to be found in the few scenes that employ open spaces. Key stages of Serpico's education in the ways of a corrupt world are signaled by scenes set outdoors in daylight in deserted locations. The meeting in which Blair suggests to Serpico that he go to Kellogg is set outside in a deserted stadium at midday—but the meeting with Kellogg only serves to alert the higher-ups that Serpico is a threat. The meeting in which Serpico is confronted en masse by the other narcotics detectives is held in an open field, with Yankee Stadium visible in the background. His final encounter with Captain McClain is held out in the open as well. The more open the space, the tighter the trap.

At one point in the film, Serpico tells Captain McClain that he was baptized a Catholic. Significantly, there is a baptismal quality to the film's beginning that exceeds the auspices of any holy order. The only rain we see in the film is to be found in its opening moments. The film begins at night in the rain as an ambulance speeds Serpico to the hospital. This raises a continuity question: Serpico is wounded in the afternoon. How much time could have passed before the ambulance arrived? To which hospital was it taking him? But insofar as the scene raises continuity questions, it may do so in favor of dramatic and artistic concerns. Set up by his partners in the Eighth Precinct in Brooklyn, Serpico has just been shot in a drug bust. We follow him into the hospital where a religious medallion hanging from his neck by a gold chain is severed by emergency room attendants. Intercut with this sequence is Serpico's graduation from the academy; the commencement speaker's voice is heard sending the cadets into the streets where they can put into practice what they have just learned in theory. In both cases we are witnessing the final moments of a learning process, a baptism of sorts.

Vincent Canby dubbed Lumet's Serpico "the Saint Francis of Copdom," and there is something saintly in the image of Serpico in the back of the ambulance. With his long, dark hair and beard, with his head turned and a bullet hole visible in his face, bloody, he is reminiscent of holy pictures of Christ on the cross. This is also true of the way Serpico is photographed in his hospital bed. But it is also ironic. Serpico is not a sacrificial figure who redeems fallen man through the pain that he suffers. On the contrary, Lumet has said repeatedly that the corruption he was trying to explore in the film extends so completely from top to bottom in our society that no conventional hero can hope to overcome it.

DOG DAY AFTERNOON (1975)

Even more than *Serpico, Dog Day Afternoon* asks us to consider the degree to which there are no longer simple, easy answers to account for the world in which we live. The film is darkly comic and deadly serious; and while it is generally considered one of Lumet's strongest films, at the time of its release it baffled some critics, though not all— it did receive a great deal of praise. Nevertheless, its contradictory tone, paired with its aura of spontaneity, and its attempt to find a mode of cinema verité appropriate to its times, was occasionally met with dismay. Writing in the 23 October 1975 *Rolling Stone,* John Landau said the film "fails on all levels, especially in its construction. . . . Everything suffers from lack of development. . . . Frank Pierson has written the kind of stream-of-anecdotes script that needs a more creative and adventurous director and a greater use of locations. It's misplaced in a film that covers less than a day's worth of time and a block's worth of territory."

John Simon was less troubled by the apparent lack of script development than by the mix of tones. He wrote in *New York* (29 September 1975):

> The real problem is those jarring, warring types of comedy that suddenly veer into seriousness, and the blurry values of Lumet and his scenarist, Frank Pierson. It is always hard to mix comedy and drama, and particularly so when there is no clear moral attitude at work. It is impossible to tell whether these underprivileged and maladjusted veterans are ultimately treated with compassion or ridicule, whether homosexual marriage is accepted or made fun of, whether the law enforcers are viewed as put-upon, befuddled creatures attempting to do their best, or brutish villains, whether the hostages are little people doing their utmost in trying circumstances or a variety of buffoons and poltroons either lighting up indecently in the spotlight or just turning yellow.

Andrew Sarris, writing for the *Village Voice* (29 September 1975), felt the film never found the proper balance between the "complex pathology" of its characters and their "simple virtue." In a review on 22 September 1975, the *New York Post*'s critic Frank Rich thought the film suffered from both its mixture of tones and its freewheeling script structure.

> *Dog Day Afternoon* is an aimless exercise in professionalism. It looks like a pickup game of filmmaking, and, however much fun it might have been for its participants to play, it doesn't qualify as a spectator sport.
>
> A point of view is needed and so is a dramatic strategy and neither the screenwriter nor the director has bothered to devise them. As a result, *Dog Day Afternoon* is part comedy, part pathos, part suspense melodrama, and part love story, and the parts just sit there, ill-formed and unconnected, waiting in vain for someone to come along and make them into a whole.

Among reviews praising the film, Judith Crist's remarks in the 4 October 1975 *Saturday Review* explained it best. How could one tell this story without an uneasy mix of comedy and drama? How should it be shot if not with camera work that seemed to fly by the seat of its pants? Of course things tended to seem spontaneous, confused; for Lumet, Crist said, has used a failed robbery in one block of a New York City neighborhood to distill in one incident the absurdity bordering on madness that was overtaking the country. And where better to do that than in Brooklyn, New York? "It is in the streets and small shops and neighborhoods that the major madnesses of our time take place," Crist remarked.

To illustrate his feel for the street life of New York City, Lumet tells a story about making *The Pawnbroker* on location in Harlem. The time came to film the shooting of Jesus Ortiz.

> "For that scene . . . we had three hidden cameras outside the shop. When the shots went off inside the pawnshop, neighborhood people were walking by. They were unaware that a movie was being made. We just decided to fire the gun and let it happen. Whether it's through my knowledge of the city or something else I can't explain. I had the confidence to know something extraordinary would happen—and it did.
>
> "As soon as the shots went off, everybody disappeared, which, of course, is perfectly logical in that neighborhood. I had a police car standing by, we cued it, and as soon as it came in, so did the people. They knew if they showed up after the police, they wouldn't be called as witnesses. We were able to get the entire sequence in one take."

Lumet shot most of *Dog Day Afternoon* in the Park Slope section of Brooklyn. He did this in a remarkably short time, slightly less than six weeks, and nearly half a million dollars under budget. That he knew the right people to call contributed to this. The Beame administration proved to be slightly less organized than the Lindsay administration in assisting filmmakers, but no less eager to help Lumet. At one point he convinced them to change a bus route because his equipment was picking up its sound. Lumet's speed also stemmed from his sense of New Yorkers. Most of the film takes place inside a bank, in the street that it fronts, and in the barbershop it faces. Inside the bank, two gunmen hold eight people hostage while outside the street gradually fills with plainclothesmen, squadrons of uniformed police, SWAT teams, members of print and television media, FBI agents, and hoards of onlookers. Lumet only used 400 extras, a fraction of the number of people we see in the finished product. Lumet knew he could get by with that number since he knew that as people began arriving home from work, the whole neighborhood would turn out and join the production for free.

Lumet also cast the film with actors he knew would give first-rate performances even under trying circumstances. Al Pacino (Sonny Wortzik) and John Cazale (Sal) are sure to most attract a viewer's attention, but the supporting players are wonderful as well: Charles Durning as Eugene Moretti, the police sergeant who tries to negotiate the release of the hostages; Chris Sarandon, as Sonny's homosexual lover Leon; Penny Allen as the head teller Sylvia; Sully Boyar as the bank manager Mulvaney; and Susan Peretz as Sonny's wife Angie, just to name a few. Perhaps the most brilliant performance per minute of screen time belongs not to Pacino but to Judith Malina, who plays Sonny's mother. Malina was Pacino's idea. He knew her work from the Living Theater in Brooklyn. So did Lumet, but the last time Lumet had seen her perform was eleven years earlier in *Medea*. When Lumet learned that the number for the Living Theater had long ago been disconnected, he sent a production assistant to the theater's address. The assistant found an old man there who eventually came up with a number for Malina in Vermont. Lumet called and hired her over the phone. For all intents and purposes, she had quit show business. Lumet had no way of knowing what to expect. All he knew was that she seemed to have fallen on hard times. He had to pay her bus fare from Vermont to the city.

Based on a *Life* magazine article by P. F. Kluge and Thomas Moore (that incidentally described Sonny Wojtowicz as having "the broken-faced good looks of an Al Pacino"), Frank Pierson's Academy Award-winning screenplay focused initially on Sonny's botched bank robbery. But the real concern of the finished film is Sonny's broken dreams, and by implication, our own. Lumet chose to bring the script to the screen as a character study, defining Sonny through his relationship to his wife and mother, his partner Sal, his lover Leon, his police antagonist Moretti, the women he holds hostage; or, more accurately perhaps, by defining Sonny as separate from these relationships, for he is alone, and increasingly helpless. Although he maintains the hope of salvaging himself and his partner from a bank robbery gone awry, we see—even if he fails to—that events acquire a momentum of their own and that he is powerless to direct them.

At one point in the film Sonny exclaims that all the media attention devoted to the hostage situation will only turn the event into a freak show. In fact, that turned out to be true of the actual robbery. What might have otherwise been worth a few seconds of broadcast time on a local news program about the holdup of a Chase Manhattan branch office on a hot day received national coverage thanks to the fact that one of the robbers wanted money to pay for his male lover's sex-change operation. Lumet's *Dog Day Afternoon* meant to be the story beneath that media coverage. Sonny is put before us as a modern day everyman more than as a hardened criminal. He is looking for a way out of the circumstances in which he finds himself. He is struggling against the realization that his life has taken turns he has been unable to control. His mistake, to paraphrase Lumet's comments about *Serpico,* is to look for this in simple, easy answers.

It is no accident that Lumet devotes considerable attention to the crowds of onlookers who threaten to take Sonny's side against the police. To them, the police are representative of a system that has failed to work on their behalf. This is post-Attica, post-Watergate America. The Kennedys, Robert and John, have been felled by assassins' bullets, as has Martin Luther King. The war in Vietnam has not only been lost, but also waged at a dear price. Raymond Chandler once remarked that urban crime reminds us of a darkness in our streets that has nothing to do with the absence of light. Lumet's America is one where that darkness has come to our streets. We no longer believe that mysteries can be solved by Philip Marlowe, or by any other Herculean detective. We have no faith that solving the crime will restore moral order. There are not many illusions left. The bloom is off. America has entered its dog days. The law-abiding citizen and the bank robber have an enemy in common.

Lumet has said that one of the reasons he likes making films in New York is because he feels so comfortable there, that he enters a project thinking he will be shooting in an area that holds no mysteries for him. The wonderful opening montage of *Dog Day Afternoon* would seem to be testimony to how right he is about this. Some 30 shots appear in just under three minutes. Many of the takes are short, and some are disconcerting, thanks to the camera movement. The longest takes are to be found toward the end of the montage, as the camera locates the getaway car of the would-be bank robbers and allows us to see them outside the bank just as it is closing at three o'clock. Only about one-third of it is shot with a stationary camera. There is a general sense of movement, with the camera moving right to left, left to right, sometimes zooming out, sometimes moving along the street in a vehicle and photographing what it sees on the sidewalk, sometimes moving in the same direction as the action it follows and sometimes moving against it.

A slow, reverse zoom shows us a launch pulling out of a slip, the screen fills with inviting blue water, then we see a luxury liner to its side that dwarfs the boat. Then, as the focal range shortens, concrete and buildings along the wharf enter the frame, while in the far distance we can see the Manhattan skyline. A dog rummages through garbage; when more garbage is tossed onto the heap, the dog moves on and the camera tilts up, following the panting dog as it moves toward street people suffering the heat. A swimming pool, a smaller version of the blue water we have seen earlier, comes on screen, but behind it is the Manhattan skyline. A garbage truck passes before us moving screen-right to screen-left; as it passes, we see two street workers, one with a jackhammer, the other with a shovel, at work in an intersection. A well-kept Brooklyn neighborhood, complete with manicured green lawns, appears momentarily and we see a home owner in the middle distance watering his lawn. A man standing outside a run-down urban building hoses garbage off the sidewalk as though he is a suburbanite watering his lawn. An expressway tollbooth with a sign demanding 50 cents in return for passage appears—a bus is passing through. A jet airliner passes over the tollbooth (later in the film, awaiting the bus that will take him to a jet waiting at the airport, Sonny will say, "Where's that goddamn jet? They're always screaming overhead when you don't need them, you know?"). Well-practiced players volley tennis balls on a city court; construction workers hoist a main girder at a building site. The camera pulls back; a cut to the beach—the cut is quick enough so that the receding camera at the building site seems inexplicably to disclose two people sitting in white sand beneath a sun umbrella. A series of umbrellas seen from overhead shade the outside tables of a restaurant. We return to the beach—a boardwalk—then to the city, where a skyscraper in the distance is reflected in a pool of water (not blue this time, but dirty). A man lies prostrate on the street—he may be wounded or destitute, perhaps dead, but his posture suggests that he is sunning himself on a beach. Employees from office buildings walk along the sidewalk; a heavyset young woman, a child's hand in each of her own, comes out of a building—later she will be identified as Sonny's wife, with their children—and as she walks in our direction the camera pulls back to show the marquee of a revival movie house advertising *The Thing* and *A Star Is Born*, while in the foreground a teenage girl gooses the boy who walks with her. Traffic slows toward gridlock on an expressway. A trucking camera picks up a pedestrian walking along a garbage-littered street, while in the background a sanitation truck appears about to deposit garbage rather than collect it. A panning camera moving left to right passes a vegetable cart—it is stationary, but the moving camera makes it appear pushed by a street vendor in the opposite direction. A speedboat at the beach moves left to right across the screen. A mounted camera moving right to left passes two women on a bench; that same mounted camera, still moving right to left, passes pensioners sitting curbside in their folding beach chairs. A Dannon Yogurt truck pulls away from the curb, appearing out of the lower right corner of the screen, while on the left is the branch office of a bank. Before it we see one parked car. As titles and credits begin to appear, the pace of the montage slows noticeably; we see a cemetery overcrowded with headstones while, in the distance, we see the same Manhattan skyline. Perhaps it is the same cemetery, this time seen from an angle that shows us much more impressive markers, though here too there is overcrowding: in the distance we see Manhattan skyscrapers that seem to be simply taller and more impressive markers still; a billboard clock shows us that the time is 2:57—it is an advertisement for Kent cigarettes, and a giant, sparkling white pack of Kents belies the warehouse roof to which the billboard is anchored. We return to the bank where an aging black guard is lowering the flag while, insectlike, a street sweeper moving along the street and pushing garbage ahead of it has to swerve to miss the parked car we have seen earlier. We get a closer view of the parked car (there are three men inside) and the driver emerging (this is Stevie, played by Gary Springer), and the moving camera follows him as he walks toward the bank, turns to face the men in the car, nods. The story begins.

The editor of the film was Dede Allen who was later to work with Lumet on *The Wiz* and whose cutting of *Bonnie and Clyde* remains a textbook study of editing at its best. This tone poem to the city in the summer is worthy of study as well. But the montage is more than an exercise in shooting and cutting. It establishes some of the basic motifs of the film. Thematically, it gives us not only a sense of the life of the city, but also of the disparity between its "haves" and "have nots," between those who have the time and money to play in the heat and those who are left to swelter in it. If one man suns himself on the beach, another lies prostrate on the sidewalk in the sun; if one man waters his lawn, another uses a hose to keep the garbage on the street away from his door. In addition, the montage sets up some of the basic cinematic patterns of the film—a camera that will often move laterally, from right to left or left to right, sometimes in sync with the movement of the drama it is recording, sometimes at odds with it. Spatially, the montage takes us from a spacious, natural image (the vast expanse of blue water) through a series of shots reminding us that city dwellers make the best possible use of the limited space available, and ends on the street with three men in a car about to enter another confined space. It is in a still more crowded vehicle that the day will finally end, with Sal dead and Sonny surrendering. This is in keeping with the dramatic structure of the film. Sonny feels trapped by the circumstances of his life and thinks that his way out is to hold up a bank. But as the film progresses, he only succeeds in putting himself in increasingly smaller entrapments.

The film begins comically as the holdup gets under way. First Sal gets out of the car and enters the bank, then Sonny. Sonny is carrying the sort of box one gets at the florist with long-stemmed roses, inside which is a rifle. (Ironically, the bank's policy is to send a dozen red roses to any teller who has been through a holdup.) Stevie enters next. The camera then sweeps up the aisle to the manager's desk where Sal has taken a seat. Sal takes an automatic weapon from his attaché case. The manager, Mulvaney, sees this and handles the situation with admirable poise. He has been talking on the phone. He ends the conversation. So far so good. But then the camera returns to Stevie. He approaches Sonny, who is stalling for time. Sonny is waiting for one last bank customer to finish up her business and leave. Sonny has his back to the tellers and from their vantage point, he must appear to be filling out a withdrawal slip. Stevie confides that he is having second thoughts about holding up the bank; he is getting "really bad vibes." Sotto voce, Sonny does his best to explain to Stevie that it is too late to back out, but Stevie is insistent. Sonny finally shoos him away, back to his lookout post near the door. When the last bank customer leaves, Sonny approaches the tellers and clumsily tries to free his rifle from the flower box. Freeing the rifle puts Sonny in a flurry of wasted motion. He is almost unsuccessful, and when he finally gets the weapon in his hands, he has lost whatever poise he might have otherwise maintained.

No sooner does Sonny get his rifle out than Stevie demands his attention again. Stevie wants to leave, and he wants to take the getaway car with him. Sonny has to coax him into taking the subway. "We need the car," Sonny tries to explain. Thus far, we appear to be dealing with bunglers. Sal has a threatening edge, but the robbery itself is going so badly that surely we are meant to laugh at it. Yet it is not filmed as a comedy or cut like comedy. We are too close to the characters too often, and the camera moves around too much. What we are watching is almost like newsreel footage. But as events progress, Sonny seems surprisingly schooled in robbing a bank. The first sign that he may know what he is doing comes when he sprays the lenses of the videotape surveillance camera. He subsequently notices a "spark" key Mulvaney is about to use to gain access to the vault. Sonny says it will trigger an alarm if the vault is opened. A bit later he will say, "Look, I worked in banks. I know alarms." With that statement, things begin to fall into place. No wonder he seems knowledgeable.

Sonny can tell marked from unmarked cash. He knows how to take cash out of the drawers without tripping the silent alarms. He knows to destroy the register in which a record is kept of the cash on hand. Not much is funny now. Occasionally Sonny's reactions seem out of keeping with what we might expect from a bank robber. For instance, when he threatens Mulvaney, he says, "I'm a Catholic and I don't want to hurt anyone." Surprisingly, Sonny is cowed by the head teller when she tells him not to swear in front of the girls. She almost persuades him to let the tellers go to the bathroom before Sonny locks them up for safekeeping. And Sonny has mistimed the robbery. There is only 1,100 dollars. The rest of the money had been picked up earlier that afternoon. All in all, though, what made us laugh at the beginning of the robbery seems to have been the result of temporary jitters.

Then the phone rings. Mulvaney picks it up. He says the caller has asked for Sonny. Stunned, Sonny takes the receiver. We learn that the police are on the other end. It is Detective Sergeant Moretti, demanding his surrender. Soon police cars arrive. Sirens are heard. People in the street begin to scatter. Sonny seems defeated. When the bank employees ridicule Sonny for how he has bungled the robbery, he refuses to focus on anything but the near empty safe. He thought he could rob the bank thanks to his knowledge of banking procedures. He attributes the failure to "Jack," someone "downtown," who gave him "the wrong information"—the money was suppose to be delivered,

Jack had said, not picked up. But even if Sonny is without sufficient knowledge of the bank to hold it up properly, he knows enough about human nature to see a possible way out of this, he believes. The bank employees stand between him and utter failure. So long as he has them as hostages, he may have a means of making a getaway, of regaining control of the situation. None of this is well considered. Sonny is too rattled. Still, he knows he has the hostages. The cops have no interest in preserving the lives of the hostages, he explains, but they can't afford to have news of dead hostages appear in all the papers. Witness Attica, says Sonny, where 42 inmates were killed, the innocent along with the guilty. "There's a way out of this," he reassures Sal. "I know a lot about a lot of things," he says to Mulvaney.

Quickly it becomes clear that if he is to take control of the situation, Sonny will have his hands full. There are the tellers, to begin with. Several are on the verge of hysteria. Also, there is Sal. To get the attention of the police, Sonny has threatened to kill the hostages and throw their bodies out onto the street if he does not get what he wants. Sal has taken him seriously. Sal is ready to do just that. (What we do not know at this point is that Sonny has made a suicide pact with Sal in case the robbery fails. Apparently the pact was made seriously. Sonny's homosexual lover Leon will later complain of Sonny's obsession with death, suggesting a suicide pact of their own.) Then, too, there is Howard, the guard, who suddenly slumps over. An asthmatic, he is having an attack.

Of course, Moretti does not have control of things either. Moretti has made a tactical mistake. Had he waited to apprehend Sonny and Sal until they came out of the bank, he would not be facing a hostage situation at the moment, and he is in danger now of compounding that mistake. As Sonny tries to organize matters inside the bank, outside the streets are filling with more police from other units. A helicopter is flown in. Although the jurisdiction is Moretti's, the FBI has involved itself, sending in Agent Sheldon (James Broderick). The news media, print and television, are all over. They ignore the police barriers, and television helicopters are sure to be confused with those of the police. Only a few of the police seem to understand that Moretti is in charge. And too, Moretti has the onlookers to consider. The onslaught of police has drawn much of the neighborhood out of their businesses and homes. They are eager for a spectacle. The crowd is growing larger as the situation goes unresolved, and the police seem to be making no organized effort to contain them. Soon the onlookers

Al Pacino stars in *Dog Day Afternoon*. The Museum of Modern Art/Film Stills Archive.

will outnumber the police so greatly that the crowd will become as significant a threat to the public order as the robbers behind the doors of the bank. Worst of all, communication is poor between the various factions involved. Nothing is being coordinated. The ramifications of this are brought home to us when Moretti tries to open negotiations with the robbers. He asks Sonny to release one of the hostages as a sign that Sonny is bargaining in good faith. Sonny chooses the asthmatic guard, who appears to be in need of medical attention. But Sonny releases the guard onto the street before word of the agreement spreads through the approximately 250 policemen outside. They assume the guard is one of the robbers and, despite the show of a white flag, nearly gun him down on the sidewalk. Ominously, still more police are arriving. Clearly what is needed is fewer police, not reinforcements. The more complicated the hostage situation becomes, the more variables there are to deal with and coordinate—and the more chance there is for some grievous mistake. Still, neither Moretti nor his minions seem to know how to do this.

Moretti finally entices Sonny out into the open, into the middle of the street, intending to show him what he is up against. Astute, Sonny sees something else as well—the hoards of news media, and the expanding crowd of interested bystanders. When Moretti is unable to keep several policemen with drawn guns from approaching Sonny, Sonny turns to the crowd. The police want to kill him so badly they can taste it, he tells the crowd. This will turn into another Attica, Sonny warns them. The police will act indiscriminately, killing the innocent as well as the guilty. Soon Sonny is leading the crowd in a chant of "Attica, Attica," strutting before them like a rock star. The police turn to look at the massive throng of civilians at their backs, then begin to draw their guns. Moretti tries to get them to holster their weapons, but there are too many police and civilians, and too much tension in the air. Encouraged by his public reception, Sonny continues to work the crowd. The situation is turning into chaos. This is just the point Sonny means to bring home to Moretti, of course. If Moretti's attempt has been to show Sonny that he and Sal are severely outnumbered, Sonny means to show Moretti that Moretti cannot let anything happen to the hostages. To many in the crowd, the police are the symptom of a failed and unjust America. There could easily be a riot that police could not control, with media present to cover it. It is not in Moretti's interest to let a bungled bank robbery erupt into a full-scale urban crisis, one that will appear in newspapers and on news shows throughout the city for days.

We learn about Sonny's life in fragments. Sonny is an unemployed Vietnam veteran, who has spent some time in prison, Attica perhaps. He has a wife and two children to support, and he pays his parents' rent. Sonny's lover Leon wants a sex change operation, and Sonny is trying to pay for it. As we watch him interact with his mother, wife, and lover, we have a sense of Sonny's dilemma. To each, he reaches out for comfort, but his attempts are futile, for they are less interested in Sonny's plight than in how it effects them personally. Angie complains that he has failed her as a husband. Leon accuses Sonny of driving him to a suicide attempt. Sonny's mother accuses him of ruining his life by marrying Angie. In a telephone conversation with Leon, Sonny tries to confide some of the strain he is feeling, but Leon refuses to listen. Leon hears this as an accusation. He says he refuses to let Sonny use him as a scapegoat for the mess in which Sonny finds himself. Rebuffed, Sonny says, "I'm not puttin' this on anybody. Nothin' on nobody. I did this all on my own, all on my own." But that is not the case. The cumulative evidence points in another direction. Sonny is in over his head. Leon has been coerced by the authorities to talk Sonny into surrendering. When he broaches that subject, Sonny says, "I'm not going to give up because, what have I done here so far? You know what I mean? I've gone so far with this. I mean why should I give up now? I can't give up."

There is much going on inside the bank that emphasizes the pressure Sonny feels, the sense he has of holding things together single-handedly. Here, as on the outside, Sonny feels alone, overpressured, given responsibilities without the power to see them through. A diabetic, Mulvaney needs a doctor. Sal threatens to go on a killing spree virtually every time Sonny is beyond his line of sight. The bank personnel seem to be looking to Sonny to take charge of a situation that may ultimately prove to be unmanageable. As tensions grow and a nearly fatal situation erupts, Mulvaney demands that Sonny "get the ball rolling" and bring the siege to an end. Sonny replies frantically, "Yeah, we're going to get the ball rolling, what do you think I'm doing? I'm working on it, right, what does it look like? You think it's easy? You know I've got to keep them [the police outside] cooled out. I've got to keep all you people happy. I've got to have all the ideas and *I've got to do it alone*. I'm working on it. You want to try it?" (emphasis added).

Sonny's feelings of powerlessness are tempered only by his possession of the hostages. Only the thought of what they may mean to him seems to bolster his spirit. There is much that recommends Sonny, including his ability to improvise (witness his playing to the crowd outside) and how brazenly he bluffs. "Everyone's a con man," he says later in the film. Holding up the hostages to Moretti in the beginning seems to have been largely a matter of stalling for time. But as Sonny sees that Moretti is taking him seriously, a vision of freedom begins to take shape in Sonny's mind. For once, he may have some power after all. He may have, at least, some power as an individual to bring about the turn of events he wants. As he says to his partner, "Sal, Sal. We can do it. Sal. Sal. Look, we got 'em. We got the hostages. You know, we've been looking at this the wrong way. They'll meet our demands. They're going to give us anything we want. I'm flying to the tropics. Fuck the snow. . . . Sal, *I can make it happen. I've made it happen so far. I can make it happen*" (emphasis added). A plan forms. In return for the hostages, Sonny demands to be taken to the airport. There a plane is to be waiting. He asks for safe passage to the foreign country of his choice.

"I can make it happen" becomes a recurring phrase as the afternoon wears on. But can Moretti also "make it happen"? Moretti inadvertently allows a rogue SWAT team to try taking the bank by force. The boyfriend of one of the bank tellers breaks through the police barricades and tries to accost Sonny as he steps onto the sidewalk. As the negotiations wear on toward evening, Sonny begins to doubt Moretti's intentions, his ability to control the present situation, and his authority to meet the demands Sonny has made. Sonny continually taunts Moretti by demanding to deal with someone else, to find someone in charge. In part, this is only a negotiating ploy. But as his patience wanes, Sonny starts to convince himself that Moretti is all that stands between himself and success. Perhaps, thinks Sonny, it is only a matter of finding someone to deal with who is at a higher level of police authority than Moretti, someone from the FBI who will meet his demands, someone who is smarter than Moretti and whose powers are more encompassing, someone who will not only listen to reason but also act accordingly. FBI Agent Sheldon replaces Moretti as the chief negotiator. He promises Sonny that a bus is on its way, that a plane is waiting at Kennedy airport. But he also tells Sonny to "sit tight," to let them handle Sal, that no harm will come to Sonny. This suggests a trap, perhaps an ambush, and when the bus arrives, Sonny thinks he knows what Sheldon is up to: he recognizes the civilian driver (Dick Anthony Williams) as a plainclothes policeman. Sonny says that he, not Sheldon, will choose who makes the drive to the airport. Sonny chooses Murphy (Lance Henriksen), one of the FBI agents, to be his driver. Sonny will also decide how he and the hostages leave the bank—he demands that the city police be put out of reach of the bus, and he surrounds himself with a circle of hand-holding hostages as they enter the bus. When Sheldon accedes to these demands, Sonny thinks he may actually be in control of the situation, and he seems as surprised as anyone. "We did it," says Sonny, as the engine is started. "I'll be a sonovabitch, we did it."

He repeats this again at the airport, with still more amazement in his voice. As the bus pulls onto the tarmac, Sonny says, "Oh fuck, we did it, we did it. . . . Sal, we did it, huh? I'll be a sonovabitch, we did it." But Sonny is not in control at all. He has been set up. Upon relieving Moretti, Sheldon has taken steps to remind Sonny that he is trapped. Sheldon has turned off the air conditioning in the bank, and shut down the lights. "No more favors," he tells Sonny at one point. Sonny thinks their arrival at the airport marks the success of their escape, but the opposite is true. Sitting shoulder to shoulder in the car, he is more trapped than ever. As the car approaches the waiting jet, Murphy uses a revolver that has been concealed in the dashboard to kill Sal, then the police close in and apprehend Sonny. As Sonny is manacled and read his rights, we see what he sees—Sal's body being taken away on a gurney, the hostages linking arms as they are escorted into the terminal. Screen titles are superimposed over the final images of the airport. They tell us that Sonny is serving a 20-year sentence in federal prison, that his wife is still on welfare, that Leon is living in New York City as a woman.

Lumet's use of space is particularly interesting in *Dog Day Afternoon*. The film can be divided into five sections, each corresponding to a different stage of Sonny's attempt to take control of events and free himself. The first stage of this attempt is the bank robbery. With his share of the money, Sonny hopes to stabilize his relationship with his lover by getting Leon the operation he wants, and to meet his other obligations. The second stage begins not long after Sonny's discovery that the police are waiting outside. Sonny and Sal are cornered, but Sonny begins to see a possibility of escape by using the tellers as hostages. That this will escalate his crime from armed robbery to kidnapping is of little concern to Sonny—he cannot see beyond his need for escape. Says Sonny to Mulvaney and the other bank employees, "Now listen everybody, I know we've got a problem here, right? But there's a way out of this thing, I'm tellin' you, there's a way out. Now all you gotta do is cooperate with me. Stay cooled out and we're gonna get out of this thing, all right? Nobody'll get hurt if you listen to what I say. First off, we'll do things a step at a time." Sonny means to act as though he will trade the lives of the hostages to the police for his freedom, but first he must come up with a plan of some kind; once he has a plan, it will only be a matter of doing things "a step at a time."

The third and longest stage begins as Sonny leaves the bank for the first time since the robbery began, walks into the street, and discovers the crowd and the press, both of which can be used to manipulate the police and Moretti. But Sonny comes to doubt Moretti's effectiveness. How can he wrest control of the situation from Moretti if Moretti himself is not in control? He needs a person in charge. The fourth stage introduces such a person in Sheldon. By elevating tensions, Sonny has contributed to Moretti's failure and the intervention of the FBI, something he will live to regret. Both Sheldon and Murphy have been present in the film nearly since the beginning. Lumet has kept them in the corners of the frame, however, apart from the central action. (Murphy has been silent; Sheldon has had less than two full pages of dialogue.) When Sheldon presents himself to Sonny as an official negotiator, Sonny says, "Oh good. About time. Maybe we can get things started." Sheldon appears in the street, by himself, taking Moretti's place. He has a bus on the way; the plane has been readied; he can get Leon to speak with Sonny by phone. Sheldon accomplishes many of the things Moretti has been unable to do. Sheldon also presents himself as a more reasonable man than Moretti. Sheldon is as professional as Moretti is sloppy, as methodical as Moretti is disorganized. But he is also cold-blooded. Sonny recognizes this within minutes of meeting him. He senses he is about to be double-crossed, but he doesn't realize that Sheldon has anticipated this. The undercover policeman driving the bus is apparently a decoy to which Sonny is meant to object.

The fifth and final stage takes place at the airport, with Sal's death and Sonny's capture. It puts us back in an automobile, where we first met the robbers, and it completes the pattern that has marked the plot's development, in which each of Sonny's attempts to break free only entrap him further. Each of these central stages of the plot has its own dominant cinematic patterns. The first stage is marked by an uneasy mix of cinematic tones, of composed and (seemingly) uncomposed images. The action begins in late afternoon. The robbery is filmed in natural light coming through the plate glass windows of the branch office, combined with the fluorescent lights overhead. The camera moves the length of the bank, from the front door that faces the street to Mulvaney's desk and the vault at the other end. It seems to be doing its best to track with the action in an area that is filled with obstacles—desks, tables, waste cans, and the like. It seems as if the action is being shot with only one camera, and with handheld camera work, for the initial sequences are marked by relatively long takes punctuated by cutaway shots, and by a camera that is not always successful in keeping the action in frame. Also, much seems to be happening too quickly. The kind of cinematic choreography Lumet employed in *Murder on the Orient Express* is nowhere to be found. The sense of reasoned, careful scrutiny we have found in the cinematography of earlier films, as such *Twelve Angry Men* or *Long Day's Journey,* where the camera seems to sit in judgment on the characters, refining and circumscribing the action with care, is missing here. The camera work in the beginning of *Dog Day Afternoon* seems to be as unrehearsed as the robbery itself. Nor is there a sense of an editing plan. It feels like raw footage—but of course is not—something approaching 16mm, documentary footage (early work by Don Pennebaker, for instance, or the Maysle brothers), perhaps shot with a filtered lens in the normal range of focal lengths. At least that is how it appears until Sonny enters the vault, when this sense of immediacy and spontaneity is broken. The vault is visually framed as if by a proscenium arch. Sonny is on the left, the teller in the middle, Mulvaney on the right. We cut from Sonny to Mulvaney to the teller. Everything seems to have stopped in its tracks. The action gets under way momentarily as Sonny heads toward the cash drawers with Sylvia, the head teller, but it never quite regains its momentum. Only as Sonny begins scurrying around the bank, trying to gather what money he can, does it pick up its pace. Then, as before, the camera cannot quite keep Sonny in frame. He seems to be moving about in unrehearsed and uncoordinated patterns.

Then Mulvaney holds out the phone. The police are outside. The camera dollies in slowly on Sonny, fixing him in the frame, putting his back against a pillar of the bank, watching him slump to the floor once he gets the bad news. To this point, we have seen Sonny primarily in long shot range, at or slightly above eye level. Now we look down upon him. The camera pulls back and we see Sonny in the distance from a lower angle. The ceiling is visible in the frame. Its fluorescent lights are harsh on the eyes.

The second stage is defined by greater reliance on a stationary camera inside the bank, and greater interest in the camera's vertical plane. Thanks to a periodic lowering of the camera angle, we become more aware of ceilings, walls, and windows. It is not unusual in this stage for a shot to begin before Sonny enters the frame, or for the camera to follow Sonny, then cut away from him. This slows the pace of the film, relative to the first stage, but it also corresponds to Sonny's new position in the situation at hand. Sonny has yet to set foot beyond the bank; its walls and employees are his protection. At this point, that is all Sonny knows with certainty. The camera keeps reminding us of the physical presence of the building itself, just as it tends to keep the bank personnel in the corners and rear of the frame. It also reminds us that Sonny is in a confining space, however, that the same walls which keep the police at bay also enclose him.

The third stage is prefaced by Sonny's release of the bank guard. Whatever rhythm and pace the film has established in the second stage are suddenly disrupted. The action is suddenly dizzying, though the editing more than the camera work creates this effect. The policemen become indistinguishable from one another. We cannot tell with ease who is doing what to whom, or why. Action seems to move in all directions in the frame. The cuts are hard to follow; the patterns of the moving camera suggest confusion and disorder. The editing is reminiscent of Dede Allen's handling of the Joplin Ambush in *Bonnie and Clyde*. From the moment Howard, the guard, leaves the bank until Moretti restores order takes roughly 45 seconds of screen time. There are some 25 shots in this sequence, five of them lasting a second or less. This pattern establishes the foundation for the third stage, as Sonny goes out into the streets and has his first encounter with the crowds and police. This is the first time we have seen Sonny in an exterior setting since he entered the bank, and in natural light. Sonny seems to bask in it, particularly as he begins to incite the crowd. To give a viewer Sonny's sense of how near the situation is to chaos, the patterns we have witnessed earlier come together. This effect is achieved through a combination of moving, tracking, documentary-like camera work and editing patterns that jar the nerves and jolt the eye. Just as the camera had followed Sonny up and down the length of the bank, it now follows him right to left and left to right as he struts outside the bank, pacing its width, playing to the crowd. He is Mick Jagger-like, bouncing on the balls of his feet, a hand on one hip and an elbow out. Everything about him says that he is adopting an attitude for public perusal, and the way the sequence is cut shows us that his pose is successful. The cuts come quickly, moving us from Sonny to Moretti to the police to the crowds, and combinations of them.

Sonny is in motion for more than two-thirds of the film's duration, and by this point in the film we can see Lumet's intention. Inside the confined space of the bank, Sonny will move primarily from front to rear, from rear to front; outside the bank, he will move from right to left and left to right. In both cases, the moving camera usually follows him. But it is primarily outside the bank—that is, in the space the police have claimed as their own—that the cutting is montagelike and the action seems to border on frenzy.

Defined by the entry of Sheldon, the fourth section of the film brings relative calm to the street. But its lighting tends to be disconcerting, making even smoothly edited, contiguous footage hard to watch. One of the first things Sheldon does when he takes over from Moretti is to have the lights shut off inside the bank. Hours have passed since the robbery began. It is dark by this time, and Sheldon has put up spotlights outside the barber shop that shine directly on the bank's facing. This puts Sonny more than ever in the limelight. He has already been a media figure for several hours and television stations are covering the holdup live. But it also makes it hard for Sonny—and us—to see with whom he is dealing. That Sheldon should construct a setting in which Sonny is to be "blinded" is appropriate. Moretti's tactic has been to overcome the robbers with a show of force. It has not worked. Sheldon's is more insidious, if also more effective. He means to weaken Sonny by making it hard for him to see.

Neither the editing nor the moving camera work is hard to follow in the fourth stage as Sonny negotiates with Sheldon. But they remind us visually that Sheldon wants to keep Sonny in the dark for as long as possible. When the lights go off inside the bank, Sonny comes to the door and shouts for Moretti. A voice is heard in the distance. A figure standing before the barbershop across the street steps forward. Sonny recognizes that it is not Moretti before we do. The blinding effect of the spotlights is signaled as Sonny puts a hand before his face, squints, and calls out Moretti's name, then asks who it is. Sonny's primary pattern of movement when dealing with Sheldon outside the bank in this meeting is not side to side, as it has been with Moretti, but rather back to front and front to back. It is as if Sheldon's presence has redefined the division of territory; in fact, Sheldon, unlike Moretti, succeeds in getting Sonny to let him inside the building momentarily. Sheldon demands to go inside to inspect the hostages for himself: "I have to see," he explains to Sonny, unblinkingly. Sonny squints, putting his hand before his face, trying to take the measure of Sheldon. "I have to see," Sheldon repeats.

Turning off the electricity in the bank has activated an emergency lighting system, a half-dozen spotlights mounted high on the walls. This often puts "hot spots" in an otherwise darkened frame, making the image uncomfortable to watch. This is true of Lumet's exteriors as well. Lumet has used a filtering system on his camera that surrounds any point of light with a halo that radiates harshly from its center. This is used to particular effect in the fifth stage, during Sal's death and Sonny's capture. The rotating lights of the squad cars, their headlamps, the streetlamps, and the plethora of lights along the runway contribute to our sense of unease as the bus is loaded and proceeds to the plane. What illuminates the action also serves to obscure it, and has another effect as well. Spatially, we should have a sense of release. For the first time since the film's beginning, we are out in the open, beyond the walls of the bank, away from the street where the siege has occurred. That sense of release is denied us, however. The camera tends to show us what is happening in the automobile rather than in the territory beyond it; what we see beyond it is hard on the eye. Together, this effectively reduces our sense of space to its lowest level yet.

The fifth stage is the only one where a stationary camera predominates, and where the cutting is consistently rhythmic. One of the last times we see Sonny, his face and torso are in the foreground. He is a captive. His hands are at his back. Sonny has been handcuffed. The camera is stationary and the close-up is shot with a telephoto lens which compresses space. This makes the three policemen to Sonny's rear seem immediately behind his shoulders—but also on another visual plane. This is a wonderful image with which to end the film, for it speaks visually to the nature of Sonny's place in the world—surrounded by people, yet fettered and alone.

NETWORK (1976)

Just as Lumet was finishing *Serpico,* he received a telephone call from Paddy Chayefsky. Chayefsky was considering writing something about the television industry. It was not going to simply be a diatribe against television as a cultural wasteland. That was too easy, and besides, television reflected modern American life; when you satirized television, you satirized this country. He was considering something along the lines of his earlier screenplay *Hospital,* but more broad, that would use dark humor to explore what America was becoming—a madhouse, a loony bin. Some 14 months later the script that would later become *Network* arrived on Sidney Lumet's desk.

Lumet and Chayefsky went back a long way. Although both had become major figures in the world of American cinema, they first

worked together in television, in the "good old early years" as Chayefsky would refer to them bitingly in his screenplay. One of Lumet's
earliest successes in television was a Chayefsky adaptation of a Nelson
Algren short story. Lumet and Chayefsky were old friends who respected one another's abilities, and politically they were kindred spir-
its. They were more or less the same age; they came from similar
ethnic backgrounds. They had weathered World War II and the
McCarthy period and had emerged from such experiences with similar hopes and fears about America. They had watched the political
pendulum swing from the right to the left and back again. Vietnam,
Watergate, and the like seemed to call for a response, a statement.
Network promised to be a vehicle that could make such a statement.

Network also offered Lumet a chance to demonstrate the range of
styles at his disposal, and how much "look to a frame" he could provide when he wanted. More directly than in the past, Lumet had begun to address charges that his films lacked an identifiable directorial
style. "I'm dissatisfied with the middle ground I'm in now," he said
to one interviewer. "But it's ridiculous to say I lack style because I
don't have any identifiable look to my frames. Some dopes can only
recognize cinematic technique if it's focused on a mountain or the sky.
They keep confusing cinema with scenery." *Murder on the Orient Express* had proved how effectively Lumet could adapt a period piece to
the screen; *Serpico* had established his skill with a hard-hitting action
film; *Dog Day Afternoon* had earned him praise for the sense of immediacy he achieved through his "camera verité" approach. Few com-
mercially successful films had achieved the sense of realism of *Dog
Day Afternoon,* and now *Network* promised Lumet a chance to go to
the other extreme. Working with cinematographer Owen Roizman,
production designer Philip Rosenberg, and editor Alan Heim, Lumet
would have a chance to explore the artificial, to compose and contrive
his images in ways that visually suggested the script's themes.

This is true of the film's lighting, and Lumet's use of interiors and
exteriors. The lighting in *Network* is among the most subtle and effective Lumet has ever achieved. The film is increasingly shot in interior spaces to the exclusion of natural settings, and the manner in
which Lumet lights his scenes emphasizes the degree to which interior
space gradually supplants the natural world as the plot develops. As
interiors replace exteriors, the lighting becomes increasingly controlled and more consciously manipulated, until finally the film looks
as if the world inhabited by its characters is lit exclusively by lighting

technicians, as if all the colors of the world must be approved by set designers before they can be displayed. In the daytime scenes during the film's second half, interior colors become television colors, all easy on the eye—blues, grays, tans, well-modulated earth tones. For scenes shot at night, Lumet achieves an extraordinary track lighting effect, giving us nondescript blues, and assorted dark colors against which faces and bodies are highlighted.

The lighting in the film's second half gradually takes on the ambience we have come to associate with polished television commercials selling "big ticket" items. This is television's America—a world without flaws, idiosyncracies, or other bothersome intrusions—and to emphasize this point, the film is often punctuated by sequences that first show us the action as it is happening in the television studio, then allow us to see the continuation of that action on the screen of a television monitor in the control room or on the set. This division between the "artificial" and the "real" is explored throughout the film in other ways as well. Much of the film's second half is photographed in ways that make it seem as though life is being recomposed to fit onto a television screen. Natural light is excluded entirely as the film approaches its climax; interiors, which have dominated the beginning of the film, are later used exclusively, and this transition from outside to inside and from real to artificial happens so gradually that we are virtually unaware of it.

In fact, it is only upon careful viewing that we become fully aware of what has taken place. Exteriors, natural light, and a compositional style that employs far and middle distances gradually become identified with the first half of the film, with Max Schumacher (William Holden), Howard Beale (Peter Finch), and their brethren, a generation of television executives who are being replaced by Frank Hackett (Robert Duvall) and Diana Christensen (Faye Dunaway). The film's second half invites us not only into the world of Hackett and Christensen, but also into their sensibility. Theirs is a world of artifice and surfaces. They are indifferent to suffering; they can feel pleasure but not joy, lust but not passion. They live by no code of ethics, no driving motive beyond personal interest. They have lost all sense of right and wrong, of true and false. They are without meaningful ethical bearings, and hence they cannot appreciate such values in others. Nor can they distinguish between the comic, the tragic, and the simply absurd. Their sense of the world is very close to madness; and Lumet and Chayefsky make that point by inviting us to share this vision with them. Before we realize it, a kind of emotional and dramatic blunting begins to take place—not only for them, but for us as well. What at first seems an absurd idea, for instance, perhaps even a mad idea, later becomes funny. Once it takes place before our eyes, it seems commonplace, even predictable. We no longer laugh, but then neither are we shocked.

The second half of the film invites us to ignore all visual distinctions—between reality and artifice, natural and artificial light, the actual event and its formal presentations in the media. Like the television we watch daily, *Network* invites us to accept all of the images as one, then warns us that to do so is to put ourselves at risk. Late in the film, Max Schumacher says to Diana Christensen, the young executive who has risen at the network as his own career has fallen, that she is "television incarnate," that emotionally and intellectually she reduces all of life's experiences "to the common rubble of banality." The film's beginning and ending mirror one another in this regard, for the film means to take everything we see and gradually reduce it to the level of beer commercials, and then remind us of what it has done.

In the last moments of *Network,* we see anchorman Howard Beale assassinated by a hired gunman on the studio set. Then we see television coverage of this same assassination on three screens of a four-screen monitor bank. Within seconds the assassination becomes indistinguishable in volume, tone, and visual composition from what is to be found on the remaining monitor screens, a series of television commercials—one, ironically, encouraging us to choose "Life," a brand of breakfast cereal. Affectively, life has become equivalent to cornflakes; and a murder has become a television show, then a television commercial. By the time of his assassination Howard Beale has become a pawn of CCA, Communications Company of America; Max Schumacher, Edward George Ruddy (William Prince), and others from the earlier generation of network executives are dead or have left the business. Dramatically and visually, we are very far from the film's beginning. The film begins with two scenes—the first, an exterior, the second an interior. In both, Howard and Max are together. In the first, Howard knows his days are numbered as a network anchorman; a voice-over (Lee Richardson) tells us that Beale's ratings have slipped too far for his position at the network to be viable. Max and Howard are drunk. It is night, on the streets of midtown Manhattan. Max has had the unpleasant duty of telling Howard that Howard is washed up. When we first encounter the two men, they have just come drunkenly out of a bar. The film begins once the firing has occurred. The first action we see takes place on Fifty-seventh Street. The film begins with a mention of suicide, first Max's apparent suicide attempt when he was young, then, once they are inside yet another bar, the possibility of Howard taking his own life. In both cases, the humor is dark and drunken—it is gallows humor, and we are to understand that the "human comedy" is at issue for these two old friends.

Sitting at the bar in the second scene, Howard says drunkenly that he will kill himself on the air in the middle of the seven o'clock news. Howard is not serious. He is simply depressed and he has been drinking. Max has fired him for failing to attract a big enough audience. What more fitting place for his suicide? Max, also drunk, plays along. He says, "You'll get a hell of a rating. I'll guarantee you that. Fifty share easy. Sure. We could make a series out of it. Suicide of the Week. What the hell, why limit ourselves: Execution of the Week."

"Terrorist of the Week," injects Howard. Max continues, sarcasm dripping from his voice. "I love it, suicides, assassinations, mad bombers, mafia hit men, our own vehicle smash-ups: The Death Hour. . . . Great Sunday night show—for the whole family. Wipe that fucking Disney right off the air." Much of what is mentioned here in the spirit of gallows humor will eventually come to pass as Diana Christensen, Frank Hackett, and others of their generation rise to power at the network. There will indeed be a Terrorist of the Week ("The Mao Tse-tung Hour," it will be called) replete with mad bombers, suicides, hit men and the like; Howard Beale will indeed be shot on the air.

The cinematography, editing, and lighting we find in these two initial scenes have the slightly rough, gritty texture we have come to expect from the New York School of filmmaking. The camera range and camera angles are predictable. Director of Photography Owen Reizman relies primarily on a 55mm lens for the opening, and on available fluorescent light, artificially filling in just enough luminescence to give us the sense of "realistic" cinematography. The camera moves freely, but only when it must in order to follow the action. There is nothing particularly stylish about such cinematography, certainly. The cinematography seems straightforward, as does the editing rhythm. The cutting feels slightly unpolished; the scene itself feels unrehearsed, in fact, perhaps even unscripted. In the first scene, the two characters, weaving drunkenly along the New York City side-

Peter Finch stars in *Network*. The Museum of Modern Art/Film Stills Archive.

walk, occasionally threaten to get beyond the horizontal range of the camera. Even the lighting appears naturalistic. There are street sounds and the glare of headlights in the first scene. The second scene—that is, the conversation at the bar—seems conventional as well. It alternates between one-shots and two-shots. It is "cut on dialogue"—one person speaks, the camera cuts to the next person, that person speaks, and the camera cuts away for the response. The camera only shows us what we could see if we were in the bar with Howard and Max, and largely from a human perspective. It moves no more than the space of such an interior might logically allow.

The disparity between the film's beginning and end in this regard suggests the breadth of Lumet's vision. *Network* takes us from one sense of time, space, and the world in general, to another, from absurd humor to human life reduced to the mad and the absurd. The first major step in this direction comes shortly after the drunken scenes between Howard and Max. After a production meeting in which most of the stories to be aired on the nightly news deal with murder, mayhem, assassinations, and terrorism, we follow Howard out of the makeup room onto the air. From a brief scene in the makeup room, we have learned that Howard has been drinking, swigging from a glass of scotch. Nevertheless, he appears serious, intent, dignified, anchormanlike. To all appearances, he is in complete control of his faculties. However, he begins the nightly news broadcast, not with the lead story, but with a promise to commit suicide on the air in an attempt to increase his diminishing ratings. Echoing Max's earlier sarcastic comments, Howard ends his declaration with a forecast of ratings to come. "Ladies and Gentlemen, I would like at this moment to announce that I will be retiring from this program in two weeks time, due to poor ratings. Since this show was the only thing I had going for me in my life, I have decided to kill myself. I'm going to blow my brains out right on this program. A week from today. So tune in next Tuesday—that should give the Public Relations people a week to promote the show. Ought to get a hell of a rating out of that. A 50 share. Easy."

The film shifts to Frank Hackett, an executive from CCA. CCA is majority shareholder in the network, United Broadcasting Systems (UBS). Hackett has recently come to UBS with the assignment of financially straightening out the network. CCA has decided it cannot be affiliated with any commercial enterprise that has finished up in the red so consistently. As we enter the meeting, plans are being hurriedly made to replace Howard Beale with an affiliate anchorman, and how to handle the episode in terms of public relations has been discussed. The next day, Max screens footage of terrorist Laureen Hobbes (Marlene Warfield) and the Ecumenical Liberation Army. The footage is being pitched by an outside producer, Bill Herron (Darryl Hickman). He has footage of the ELA and kidnapped heiress Mary Ann Gifford (Walter Cronkite's daughter, Kathy) holding up a bank in Flagstaff, Arizona. They have filmed the robbery themselves. Max is head of the news division. The footage is the stuff of tabloid journalism and Max seems bored, and unimpressed by it. Diana Christensen, a young executive from programming whom he barely recognizes, has asked to attend. Max is distracted, still contending with the previous night's debacle with Howard Beale. Frank Hackett, who has tried to take charge after the disastrous airing at last night's news, is clearly Max's enemy, and Hackett probably means to use this opportunity to challenge Max's power—the nightly news broadcast is one of the network's greatest money losers. During the screening, all this is complicated by a call from Howard Beale, who asks Max for a chance to go back on the air with a public apology. Howard does not want to retire from the profession by making a clown of himself; he wants to go out with some dignity. Reluctantly, Max agrees to give Howard this chance.

While Max and Howard prepare the evening news, Diana has returned to her office and called a staff meeting. She has an idea. The footage of the Ecumenical Liberation Army holding up a bank has given Diana an idea for a series, which one of her subordinates (Conchata Ferrell) laughingly terms "The Mao Tse-tung Hour." Diana says,

> Look, I sent you a concept analysis report yesterday. Did any of you read it? Well, in a nutshell it said the American people are turning sullen. They've been clobbered on all sides by Vietnam, Watergate, the inflation, the Depression—they've turned off, shot up, and fucked themselves limp and nothing helps. So this concept analysis report concludes that the American people want someone to articulate their rage for them. I've been telling you people since I took this job six months ago that I want angry shows. I don't want conventional programming on this network. I want counterculture, anti-establishment.

Diana approaches Max. The workday is over. Most of the offices are dark. She wants to use Howard's dubious notoriety to advantage, and work with Max. She wants to "program" the nightly news broadcast as if it were any other entertainment offering. Max laughs her out of his office, but not before he accepts her advances. She is attracted to him; Max is attracted to her. And that evening, after dinner, they begin an affair. The film turns to a stockholders' meeting, apparently occurring the next day. Without warning Max, Frank Hackett announces to the stockholders that the news division is soon to be restructured, and that in his judgment this is long overdue. Max Schumacher's news division has functioned in the red for too long. Max turns to network president Ruddy for assistance, and is casually rebuffed. In a huff, Max returns to the studio to put on the nightly news. The timing of Max's semi-public humiliation is unfortunate. He is in no frame of mind to handle what is about to happen. When Howard goes on the air that evening, it is not to deliver the promised apology, but rather with an invective: the world is mad, life is "bullshit." Max, still in a pique over being fired before the stockholders, allows Howard to proceed full steam ahead, profanity and all.

If Howard's promise to commit suicide failed to make him the laughingstock of the television industry, certainly this diatribe will. Max has acted irresponsibly in allowing the broadcast to air. He is promptly fired for allowing Howard to make a spectacle of himself on national television. As for Howard himself, the initial reaction of Frank Hackett (now effectively in charge of the network) is to remove him as well. But Diana has looked at the overnight ratings. Thanks to Howard Beale, UBS is being covered by the more respectable networks, and the audience of the nightly news show has increased diametrically. She approaches Frank Hackett with the idea of leaving him on the air. She admits that the idea sounds absurd; but ratings never lie. Here is UBS's first chance at solid ratings—or rather, "solid advertising dollars." She seems to enter Hackett's office with only the vaguest idea of the pitch she is going to make. The idea of Howard Beale as a "messianic prophet" seems like pure inspiration. She is arguing for a show that has proven appeal to the American public—its content is irrelevant to her. Frank asks if she can be serious. Is she really suggesting that he put an insane man yelling "bullshit" back on the air?

After some hesitation, Frank capitulates. When Howard next appears on television, he is hardly the "magnificent, messianic figure" that Diana has promised. Howard is late for the broadcast, and we can see that he has spent the day wandering the streets of Manhattan in his raincoat and pajamas. But his distressed appearance and manic energy combine with a speech that touches a chord in his viewers. Says Beale,

> I don't have to tell you things are bad; everybody knows things are bad. It's a depression. Everybody's out of work or scared of losing their job. The dollar buys a nickel's worth; banks are going bust; shopkeepers keep a gun under the counter; punks are running wild in the street; and there's nobody anywhere who seems to know what to do. And there's no end to it. We know the air is unfit to breathe, and our food is unfit to eat. We sit watching our TVs while some local newscaster tells us that today we had fifteen homicides and sixty-three violent crimes as if that's the way it's suppose to be. We know things are bad, worse than bad. They're crazy. It's like everything everywhere is going crazy. So we don't go out anymore. We sit in the house, and slowly the world we're living in is getting smaller. And all we say is "Please, at least leave us alone in our living rooms. Let me have my toaster and my TV and my steel belted radials, and I won't say anything. Just leave us alone." Well I'm not going

to leave you alone. I want you to get mad. I don't want you to protest. I don't want you to riot. I don't want you to write to your congressman, because I wouldn't know what to tell you to write. I don't know what to do about the depression and the inflation and the Russians and the crime in the streets. All I know is that first you've got to get mad. You've got to say, "I'm a human being. Goddammit, my life has value. . . ." Things have got to change. But first you've got to get mad, first you've got to get mad as hell. . . . Then we'll figure out what to do about the depression and inflation and the oil crisis.

Howard's plea to "get mad as hell and declare their worth as human beings" works. Soon television viewers all over America are going to their windows, as Howard has directed them. Like Howard, his viewers know that the country is out of control, that their lives are bordering on madness, that nothing is as it should be. Diana's instincts appear to have been right: America's television audience has been waiting for someone to articulate their rage.

Diana uses the impact of Beale's broadcast to begin reprogramming the network's nightly lineups. A voice-over tells us that Howard Beale's ratings proved to be phenomenal. When we next see Diana, she has flown to Los Angeles to meet with Laureen Hobbes. Diana pitches her idea of a "Mao Tse-tung Hour" to Hobbes, who promptly takes it back to the ELA. The idea that we assumed was part tongue-in-cheek—a band of revolutionaries filming themselves as they try to overthrow America—is becoming a reality. Diana offers Hobbes a show created around the ELA, which begins with footage of terrorist acts shot by the terrorists themselves, then turns into an hour-long docudrama. Diana brings this same sensibility to the nightly news program. Howard Beale is billed as "The Mad Prophet of the Airways." The network's nightly news show becomes a tabloid variety hour now known as the "Howard Beale Show." But Diana's nearly meteoric success in changing the direction of the network begins to lose its momentum. Howard announces that UBS has been completely absorbed by a holding company, a conglomerate known as CCA (Communication Company of America), and urges his viewers to turn off their television sets. Howard urges America to be wary of the way a huge conglomerate can use television programming to persuade and deceive the public, and how such a conglomerate can win the hearts and minds of the American people in an attempt to further its own interests. Howard Beale admonishes his audience for turning to him or any other television personality; if they want "truth" he urges them to turn to themselves, to recognize that television is an illusion, that slowly but surely they are all turning into humanoids— that is, losing what makes them vital and worthwhile as human beings.

This line of thought only serves to confuse Howard's viewers; and, predictably, it raises eyebrows around the conference table at CCA. Diana's intentions of single-handedly taking over the network's programming start to stall. Some four months have passed when we next see Max and Diana together. They run into each other on a midtown Manhattan street. Max has come from a funeral parlor after attending services for a friend. He seems to be at loose ends. Without a job to occupy his time and attention, Max appears to have lost direction in his life; and with the problems at UBS caused by Howard Beale, Diana appears even more harried than normal. Max's wife (Beatrice Straight) is out of town visiting their daughter in Washington. Diana has only more fruitless meetings on her afternoon schedule. On impulse, they resume their affair, driving to the beach at the Hamptons for a romantic weekend. This meeting, and the beach scene which follows, are the film's last use of exterior scene and natural light, both of which Lumet has identified with Max; and in some sense they are transitional scenes in the story line, for despite the lighting and settings, the momentum of the scenes belongs to Diana. Her presence dominates, certainly. Whatever passion she may feel for Max is formulated in terms of her work at the network. From the moment they start toward the beach in a car, Diana speaks in a nonstop, manic monologue about the problems she faces with "The Howard Beale Show," with her plans for a lesbian soap opera, "The Dykes," and so on, and this monologue continues over dinner and into bed.

The staccatolike pace of her monologue stands in marked contrast to the scene which follows, when Max confesses the affair to his wife and moves out of his home. The confession's slower tempo and Lumet's use of one-shots and two-shots serve to remind us of the difference between this and the scene we have just witnessed. This scene is structured around dialogue rather than one prolonged speech. It focuses on the reaction of each partner to the actions and words of the other. It explores the bonds and understanding that exist between Max and his wife of long-standing, allegiances which are almost tangible.

In the previous scene, Diana seems to be completely absorbed by her own thoughts and the sound of her own voice. She has little or no sense of Max. Occasionally, it is unclear if she cares whether or not Max is listening; she might just as easily be talking to herself. Is Max so smitten with her that he fails to see how troubled she is? In the scene with Louise, his wife, Max turns out to be fully conscious of this. When his wife asks Max if Diana loves him, Max answers,

> I'm not sure she's capable of any real feelings. She's television generation. She learned life from Bugs Bunny. The only reality she knows comes to her over the TV set. She's very carefully devised a number of scenarios for all of us to play. Like 'Movie of the Week.' My God, look at us, Louise. Here we are going through the obligatory middle of Act 2: Scorned Wife Throws Peccant Husband Out Scene. Don't worry. I'll come back to you in the end. All of her plot outlines have me leaving her and coming back to you because the audience won't buy a rejection of the happy American family. She does have one script in which I kill myself, an adapted-for-television version of *Anna Karenina* in which she's Count Vronsky and I'm Anna.

Diana is honored at a West Coast Affiliates banquet hosted by Frank Hackett. She is credited with making UBS a major force, and she promises the affiliates in the audience still better results in the coming year. But while Diana Christensen is giving her speech, Frank Hackett receives a phone call from New York concerning a different kind of performance. Howard Beale has announced on the air that evening that a consortium calling itself the Western World Funding Corporation, a front for Arab interests, has been buying up a controlling interest in the Communications Company of America, and doing so in violation of Security and Exchange Commission regulations. Howard urges the American public to flood the White House with telegrams in protest.

Hackett is to fly back to New York City and personally escort Howard Beale to a meeting the next morning with the head of CCA, Mr. Jensen (Ned Beatty). Jensen's financial interests, as well as those of CCA, turn out to be directly connected to those of the Arabs. Beale has protested more than a business deal, as Jensen explains. He has tempered with the new world order—one in which human beings have value only insofar as they serve the corporate state. Jensen demands that Beale go forth and preach this evangel.

A voice-over tells us that as Howard begins to preach the new gospel of business according to CCA his ratings slip further. It is a message no one wants to hear, the demise of the individual, the preeminence of the international cartel. No one wants to hear that becoming a humanoid is inevitable. As Howard's ratings fade, so do Diana's powers at UBS. Her fears and frustrations at the network affect her relationship with Max. The gulf between their sensibilities soon grows too wide to bridge. Max says to her,

> After living with you for six months, I'm turning into one of your scripts. This is not a script, Diana. There's some real, actual life going on here. I went to visit my wife today because she's in a state of depression. She's so depressed that my daughter flew all the way from Seattle to be with her, and I feel lousy about that. I feel lousy about the pain I've caused my wife and kids. I feel guilty and conscience-stricken and all those things you think sentimental, but which my generation calls simple human decency. And I miss my home. Because I'm beginning to get scared shitless. Because all of a sudden it's closer to the end than it is to the beginning and death is a perceptible thing to me with definable features. You're dealing with a man that has primal doubts, Diana, and you've got to cope with it. I'm not some guy discussing male menopause on 'The Barbara Walters Show.' I'm the man that you presumably love. I'm part of your life. I live here. I'm real. You can't switch to another station.
>
> "Well what exactly is it that you want me to do?" [Diana asks].
>
> [Max responds,] "I just want you to love me. I just want you to love me primal doubts and all."
>
> "I don't know how to do that" [Diana answers].

A by now familiar voice-over tells us that Howard's show has sunk in the ratings and we watch as Diana sits in a screening room futilely trying to select his replacement. Diana tells Frank Hackett that Howard needs to be fired. Frank's hands are tied. Mr. Jensen is not about to allow Howard to be removed, not when Howard Beale is the voice of Jensen's corporate philosophy. Frank calls a meeting for late that night in which alternatives to dismissing Beale will be examined.

We come home with Diana that evening. She goes upstairs and begins packing Max's bags.

> "I don't like the way this script of ours is turning out," [she tells him]. "It's turning into a seedy little drama, middle-aged man leaves wife and family for young heartless woman and goes to pot. *The Blue Angel* with Marlene Dietrich and Emil Jannings. I don't like it."
>
> "So you're going to cancel the show" [Max answers]. "Don't worry about me. . . . I'm more concerned about you. I figure a year, maybe

two before you crack up, jump out of your fourteenth floor office window. . . . You need me. You need me badly, because I'm your last contact with human reality. I love you and that painful decaying love is the only thing between you and the shrieking nothingness you live the rest of the day."

"Then don't leave me," [says Diana].

"It's too late, Diana. There's nothing left in you I can live with. You're one of Howard's humanoids. If I stay with you I'll be destroyed. Like Howard Beale was destroyed. Like Laureen Hobbes was destroyed. Like everything you and the institution of television touch is destroyed. You're television incarnate, Diana. Indifferent to suffering; insensitive to joy. All of life is reduced to the common rubble of banality. War Murder Death, it's all the same to you as bottles of beer. And the daily business of life is a corrupt comedy. You even shatter sensations of time and space into split seconds, instant replays. You're madness, Diana. Virile madness. Everything you touch dies with you. But not me. Not as long as I can feel pleasure. And pain. And love. And it's a happy ending. Wayward husband comes to his senses, returns to his wife with whom he's established a long and sustaining love. Heartless young woman left alone in her arctic desolation. Music up with a swell. Final commercial. And here are a few scenes from next week's show."

With Max out of her life, Diana returns to the studio that night for her meeting with Frank, key network administrators, and executives from advertising sales. Frank begins the discussion on what we assume is a darkly humorous note, saying if it is not within their power to fire Howard Beale they will have no choice but to kill him. Frank turns to Diana for her suggestions. Diana appears to be playing along with the joke when she says she might be able to get the ELA to assassinate Beale on the air, but the longer she talks, the more serious she seems to be. Soon Diana is discussing the possibility of using the assassination on the first show of the new season in order to drum up viewer interest. One by one the others join in, considering the financial ramifications of an on-the-air murder, its syndication possibilities, and so on.

As they speak, we see the show under discussion—an audience files into the studio and takes their seats, and an announcer kicks off the production. Two gunmen rise at Beale's entry onto the soundstage and murder him in cold blood. We then see a bank of four television monitors, two carrying taped footage of the assassination, one carrying a news broadcast recounting the event, and one promoting a carbonated beverage. The images on the monitors are composed in much the same way. More commercials appear. The four soundtracks are intermixed so that everything runs together. Although the sound continues, three of the monitors go blank. We are left with a still image of Howard Beale's dead body, lit by an overhead spot. Screen credits begin to appear. The credits pass. Finally the screen goes black. The last sound we hear is the ticking of a newsroom wire service.

PRINCE OF THE CITY (1981)

Prince of the City, Lumet's finest film to date, brings the concerns of *Serpico, Dog Day Afternoon,* and *Network* together in one *tour de force.* The protagonist is Danny Ciello (Treat Williams), a character much like Frank Serpico, a beleaguered narcotics cop who seeks the moral high ground by exposing the payoffs that are a daily fact of life on the street in the police force. Like Serpico, he must inform on his friends in order to do this; and the film follows Ciello as he gradually becomes isolated, first from his brother policemen, then from the authorities he has approached with information, from his wife, family, home, and in the end, from the profession he loves.

Like Frank Serpico, Ciello has faith in the authorities at the outset—he, too, comes forward on his own, thinking that with their help he can do good in the face of evil. Finally, like Serpico, Ciello believes he can take control of the situation. In this case, he agrees to work with government investigators Capallino (Norman Parker) and Paige (Paul Roebling) only if he will not have to inform on his partners in the Special Investigation Unit—he will not say one word to the authorities until they give him that guarantee. After this meeting, Danny assures his wife that he will be in control. "I'm not going to implicate anyone close to us," he tells his wife. "I'm going to call the shots. Babe, this is my action. My set up."

But unlike Serpico, Ciello is on the take himself. He steals money and heroin from the perpetrators he pursues. His wife Carla (Lindsay Crouse) knows how his mind works. She says that she knows he feels guilty about the money he accepts, and the drugs with which he supplies his informants in return for their help. Carla knows that he wanted to be a cop so that he could be one of the good guys. She knows what it means for him to live a life on the streets, not unlike the criminals he pursues and arrests. She knows that none of this corresponds to the image he tries to maintain of himself. Sure he feels guilty, Carla explains. Everyone feels guilty—guilty feelings come with being an adult. But what he is about to do, she warns her husband, will not bring Danny the absolution he seeks. Her husband is like a Catholic schoolboy eager for confession, ready for a penance. She warns that what he is about to do will only serve to turn him against—and isolate him from—the most important family he has, his partners. Carla turns out to be right on all counts. We are reminded of one of the first things Danny says to the authorities: "I sleep with my wife but I live with my partners."

The film is based on another true story, a 1978 book by Robert Daley, about a highly effective New York City police detective, Robert Leuci, who came forward on his own to government officials and worked with them to expose corruption in one of the city's drug enforcement operations. Daley's book chronicles in copious detail the intrigues of undercover work, as well as the ramifications of Leuci's decision to step forward, including the catastrophic effect the decision had on him and those around him. Of some 70 men who were his colleagues and friends, 52 were indicted, one went mad, two committed suicide. The book was reportedly sold to Orion Pictures for more than half a million dollars, and then the project stumbled as John Travolta, Robert De Niro, and Al Pacino each accepted the starring role only to decline it before a formal signing. The project might have been shelved entirely if Warner Brothers had not entered the deal as coproducer. It was during this time that Jay Presson Allen and Lumet were approached by Erik Pleskow, then president of Orion. They were finishing *Just Tell Me What You Want*. Within 24 hours, the deal was signed. Lumet made only two stipulations—first, that the starring role be given to a relative unknown. Lumet was attracted to the protagonist's ambiguities and he did not want a star who automatically elicited the sympathies of the audience. Lumet also stipulated that the film be allowed to run for three hours, or perhaps even longer. Lumet wanted enough time to explore these ambiguities in depth.

Lumet put aside several screen adaptations, including versions by playwright David Rabe and Brian De Palma, to come up with a version of his own with longtime associate Jay Presson Allen. They wrote a 240 page screenplay in 30 days, which focused more narrowly on Leuci himself, carefully condensing peripheral characters and events; Brooks Paige, for instance, though he most resembles Mark Schorr is a compilation of several figures in Daley's book. It is Lumet's largest production to date; the film runs almost three hours, with nearly 300 scenes, more than 100 speaking parts and locations. Lumet anticipated reluctance on the part of the police and city officials to cooperate in the film's making, and he knew that location shooting would have to be coordinated more carefully than for any of his previous films. He shot at 131 different sites, from a Mulberry Street pizzeria, to courtrooms, to a tract house in Great Neck. And he coordinated these locations so that each exterior site was located near an interior, just in case of bad weather. He also paid particular attention to casting. He had 126 speaking parts to fill. To do this he considered some 5,000 people, many of them nonprofessionals.

Lumet completed film production 21 days under the allotted production period (in 59 out of 80 days), and under budget, spending 8.6 million of the 10.4 million dollars at his disposal, a remarkable accomplishment. Lumet said, "It's about a guy who thinks he can control the circumstances, and the circumstances wind up controlling him."[3] Despite its apparent oversimplicity, Lumet's summation is perhaps the most intelligent yet. It leads us to consider the relationship of *Prince of the City* to *Dog Day Afternoon*, another film about a protagonist controlled by his circumstances. Here, compromise and capitulation are at issue. The pattern of the Jay Presson Allen/Lumet screenplay is to put Ciello in situations in which he repeatedly does exactly what he has promised himself he will not do, as unforeseen circumstances present themselves. Virtually every compromise Ciello tells himself he will refuse, he makes. Virtually everything Ciello promises himself he will not do, he does. Once he takes the first step, by going to the government and agreeing to cooperate, Ciello becomes caught in a current of events that sweeps him out to sea. Ciello is drowning before he realizes he can no longer touch bottom. At a running time of two hours and 48 minutes, the film, rather than seeming too long, is almost too short; for Lumet means to show us this drowning process in all of its small, insidious increments.

Like *Network, Prince of the City* offers a complex world where simple virtues no longer apply, fundamental human decency is out of place, and right and wrong, good and bad, no longer lend themselves to simple definition. It mixes poetic justice with tragic irony, and asks us to distinguish between them. At what point does Ciello's story become tragic? At what point absurd or even darkly comic? One is reminded of the network executives sitting around their track-lit table late at night talking about the syndication possibilities offered by murdering Howard Beale on television. What line did they cross, and where and when, that allowed that conversation to happen? How much did we have to listen to before we were shocked by what we were hearing? Lumet has said, "The difficulty in separating villains and heroes intrigued me. . . . Whether Leuci was a rat or a hero was one of the things I had to work through for myself while making the film. When you grow up poor, there is this thing about cops. As somebody on the political left, I was brought up on this idea about an informer being a rat. I went into the movie feeling great ambivalence."[4] Lumet shows us a complicated web of loyalties in *Prince of the City*. Everyone we meet betrays someone. That they often do so for at least nominally good, and in some cases, clearly altruistic reasons, also poses problems. Of all of Danny's partners, only Gus Levy (Jerry Orbach), a relatively minor character, remains true to the code of the street and resists the authorities. In a scene that takes the audience by force after so much knuckling under by so many figures, Levy refuses to cooperate. But are we meant to applaud that? What are we embracing if we do? Badge or no badge, Levy is a crook. He is a danger to us all. It is a scene that is meant to make us question what we are feeling and why, as Lumet himself suggested in the 6 June 1982 *New York Times Magazine*. In "Lumet: The City Is His Sound Stage," he told John Lombardi, "The reason people applaud when Jerry goes in and knocks over the prosecutor's desk is that they're thrilled to see one guy holding 'true,' not reversing himself. But those are the easy emotions. I'm more interested in the motives that aren't so easy." *Serpico, Dog Day Afternoon, Network,* and *Prince of the City* all share the same vision of America, a country where the acceptance of corruption in our personal lives has the cumulative effect of a cancer spreading through the national character. Yet it is Danny Ciello who is sure to concern us most in *Prince of the City*—his motives, his naïveté, his victimization, the need he feels to be absolved of guilt—for in many ways *Prince of the City* is a study of one man and the realizations he comes to about himself and his predicament.

The film begins with Ciello and his partners in the Special Investigation Unit rousting a narcotics ring, booking them, and taking them to court. The bust is done with theatrical flare. Ciello and his partners in the SIU seem to model themselves on the rogue cops in a Clint Eastwood film. The film then shifts to the nondescript office of U.S.

Attorney for the Southern District of New York, Richard Capallino, a member of the Chase Commission investigating police corruption. Ciello is one of the elite. Capallino is a foot soldier in the war against crime. Ciello brushes him off, with a hint of disdain. The film then shifts to a barbecue at Ciello's house. His partners and their wives are present. A uniformed policeman arrives with Danny's ne'er-do-well brother Ronnie (Matthew Laurance), who is a petty criminal and junkie. Ronnie is in trouble again. The patrolman who has apprehended Ronnie, Ciello's neighbor Ernie Fallacci (Carmine Forresta), has brought Ronnie to Danny's house rather than book him. Danny takes Ronnie aside. Ronnie tells Danny that he has no right to condemn him, that Danny and his partners are criminals themselves. The brothers' father (Tony Turco) is present in the house and overhears their exchange. There is disappointment in the elder Ciello's voice and his face. Ronnie is right, he tells Danny. Look at how lavishly Danny lives, at what he owns. His is not the life of an honest policeman. Danny has failed Ronnie, his family, himself.

The real action of the film begins with this family squabble. Subsequently, Danny calls Capallino and asks to meet with him at Capallino's home. Ciello is considering cooperating in the investigation, but he is not ready to commit himself. We next see Ciello working the streets, maintaining a network of informants at any price, including supplying them with heroin. Unlike the first time we saw Ciello in action, he is on edge, not fully in control of himself or the situation. This theme is picked up when he next approaches Capallino. Brooks Paige has been asked to join them. Ciello asks why he should trust either one of them. The corruption they claim to be investigating extends up and down the line; why are they investigating the police, he wants to know? Why should he talk to them? Danny has close friends and family in the mafia (Nick Napoli, played by Ron Maccone, and Rocky Gazzo, played by Tony Munafo); all his life Ciello has been aware of the need for family loyalty, and he has brought this awareness to his work as a policeman: "The first thing a cop learns is that he can't trust anyone but his partners. . . . Nobody cares about me but my partners!" But the pressures to come forward and wipe the slate clean are evident. He cannot quite reconcile the man he is becoming with his image of himself as a policeman. Ciello wants to reclaim his innocence. Ciello agrees to work with Capallino and Paige in a third meeting, even though his wife Carla has warned him that he will not be able to control events, once set in motion. Try as he will to protect

Detective Danny Ciello is interrogated in *Prince of the City*. The Museum of Modern Art/Film Stills Archive.

his partners, Danny will have to turn against them. With her words in mind, perhaps, Ciello makes it clear that he is only cooperating because the SIU is being disbanded. He will never betray the policeman with whom he has worked closely. He will never tape-record his conversations with them. He will never compromise his partners in the SIU in any way. Capallino offers his hand. "Dan, we'll never force you to do something you can't live with," he says, "I promise you."

Danny will shake the hands of many government officials in the film ahead, and many of these men will go on to betray him. The extension of Capallino's hand is an important moment in the film. Ciello refuses it. Later on, he will not be able to. We see him shake Capallino's hand only once he has provided undercover information against another policeman. Ciello is not giving up his place in one brotherhood to take his place in another, though that is what he will try to convince himself of in the episodes ahead. Subsequently, Ciello says to his wife that Paige and Capallino care about what happens to him. "No one loves you but your [SIU] partners and me," she tells him. Initially, Ciello means to limit his exposure to the authorities. He begins by confessing only three incidents of his own corruption. As the state's star witness, Ciello is promised immunity. But he is also put on notice that he will have to come forward with more than what he has confessed to thus far. They know—and he knows—that Danny Ciello is far more guilty than this admission acknowledged. Danny cannot go on the witness stand without subjecting himself to charges of perjury.

Ciello begins working undercover for the government investigators by "wearing a wire" against Edelman (E. D. Smith), a crooked cop who offers to sell to Rocky Gazzo the report of an ongoing district attorney's investigation that focuses on Gazzo. The undercover work goes smoothly. Gazzo is Ciello's friend, but Edelman is the prosecutors' prime target, hence the conflict Danny feels is minimal. But there are hints of problems to come. The federal agents who are Ciello's backup protection are unfamiliar with the city; later the batteries of the tape recorder Ciello wears leak and badly burn his skin. Such problems escalate as Ciello becomes involved in the case of an underworld bail bondsman, Dave Benedetto (Ron Karabotsos). Ciello is looking into Benedetto's connections with policeman Carl Allegretti (Tony Debenedetto) and famous trial attorney Michael Blomberg (Michael Beckett). Neither Benedetto nor Allegretti are as trusting as Gazzo and Edelman have been. Street rumours are circulating that a cop is turning information over to officials from the Chase Commission. In the course of his investigation, Benedetto decides that Ciello must be this informant, and plans to kill him. The backup team that should be present to protect Ciello loses track of him; and in order to save his own life, Danny has to take Benedetto to Danny's mafioso cousin Nick to vouch for him.

Clearly the federal prosecutors are not nearly as good at protecting their own as are the city police or the mafia. Ciello demands that in the future, New York City police as well as federal agents serve as his backup. While the agents are concerned with completing the investigation, the police, Ciello says, will be concerned about him. Danny is badly shaken by the incident. Assuming that his wife and children are also at risk, Ciello wants protection sent to his house. Realizing that federal agents are unreliable, Danny thinks immediately of his neighbor Ernie Fallacci. Next, he calls Edelman, the first policeman upon whom he has informed. Edelman promises to have a car at Danny's house in 12 minutes. The irony is not lost on Danny: the people he is helping send to jail are more concerned with his welfare than the investigators with whom he is working. Earlier, Danny had equated his undercover work against the police with his work against narcotics dealers. To him, it is all a game, he says, one he can play with the best of them. But Ciello begins to see that this is not the same kind of game at all. He starts to take stock of how isolated he is. No longer one of the cops, he is not really one of the investigators either.

Gino Moscone (Carmine Caridi) is the first of the police closest to Danny to suffer for what Danny has done. Moscone becomes ensnared in Danny's pursuit of Marcel Sardino (Cosmo Allegretti), an international drug dealer. The ongoing federal investigation takes Ciello above the level of Capallino and Paige. He is flown to Washington where he goes to work for Attorney General Sandrocino (Bob Balaban), Sandrocino puts Ciello in a position to turn state's evidence on Moscone, one of Danny's oldest friends on the police force. Danny protests. His agreement with the government was that he would not "rat" on his partners. Sandrocino will not be deterred: Moscone may be a dear friend, but he is not technically one of Ciello's partners from the SIU.

To avoid involving Moscone, Danny goes to Benedetto. He arranges a trade. If Benedetto will put Ciello in contact with Sardino, Ciello will supply Benedetto with some incriminating tape recordings worth 50,000 dollars to Michael Blomberg. The box of tape recordings comes through Capallino's office. No one has checked them. Inside Benedetto finds a slip of memo paper linking Ciello with the federal investigation. This confirms his earlier suspicions. Ciello is the rat after all. Benedetto decides to kill him.

Danny is saved, not by the federal agents who should be supporting him, but rather by Ernie, the policeman from his neighborhood. To make matters worse, Danny learns that Sardino has already been apprehended. Sardino has made a deal for himself with the government in exchange for turning in others. In effect, Ciello has been set up by the attorney general's office. Ciello has been put on Sardino's trail to make it appear to Sardino's accomplices as though Sardino is still to be trusted. Ironically, what Danny has done in an attempt to protect Moscone has only made his arrest more certain. Now that Sardino is confessing to government officials and implicating his associates, Moscone's will surely be among the names he gives them. Danny's attempt to alert Moscone to this fails. Moscone is caught. When the investigators try to coerce him into indicting other policemen involved, Moscone kills himself instead. Danny begins to realize the dimensions of his entrapment. Capallino says, "How did we get into this Danny?" Ciello responds with tears in his eyes, "I don't know. You did it." It is the first time in the film that Danny has acknowledged that he is not in control of the events underway.

Danny's cousin Nick, and not the federal agents, first saved him from death at the hands of Benedetto, and it is the mafia, not the government investigators, who come to Ciello's aid after Moscone's suicide. Danny meets with Rocky, the first mafioso we have encountered in the film. Rocky realizes now that Danny has used him earlier, that Danny is informing on both his friends in organized crime and the police. Rocky has vouched for Danny earlier, as has Danny's cousin Nick. What Danny is doing will put both Nick and Rocky in peril. Rocky assumes that Danny has been caught by the investigators, that Danny has cooperated with them in an attempt to save himself. Ciello tries to explain what motivated him to become an informant: "Nobody caught me. No one came down on me. I looked at Carla and the kids and I remembered why I wanted to be a cop. I wanted to do something to show that I was a good guy not a bad guy." Rocky offers to provide Ciello with the money to leave the country and begin a new life. Rocky explains to Danny that he is not simply betraying those around him, but also betraying himself. Danny is making a mistake he will regret for the rest of his life, says Rocky. He will never be able to live with himself. Ciello has to get out of the country before it is too late. It is an impassioned and moving speech. Rocky is one of the less articulate and intelligent characters in the film. Yet everything he predicts will prove true as the film progresses.

More moving than Rocky's speech is Ciello's reply. "Where am I gonna go?" Danny asks. Danny knows by this point that he is trapped, but the trap's full dimensions only begin to be clear once news of Danny's role in the investigation is leaked to the press. His life is in danger, as are the lives of his family. With two years of testimony awaiting Ciello, the prosecutors will have no choice but to put him into a witness protection program. Immediately, his family loses their home. They are moved to their cabin in the Catskills where some 18 guards serve as sentries. Danny will later say that he went to jail before anyone he informed on, and that his internment began at this point. Agents providing round-the-clock protection (primarily, Tug McGraw, played by Lane Smith and Ned Chippy, played by Eddie Jones) are to keep out intruders, and to keep his wife and children inside. They are also dividing the family, government officials explain. While Ciello testifies during the week, he will be staying in a military barracks on Governor's Island.

As Danny comes to realize the degree of his entrapment, he must also come to grips with his isolation. The Blomberg trial is the first to reach the courts for adjudication, and it forces Ciello to confront some of the problems he will be facing in the 24 months ahead. As the first trial gets underway, Capallino is promoted to a cabinet level post, and shortly thereafter Paige Brooks is also promoted. Both are moving on, leaving Danny to fend for himself. Those he has helped to indict can be out on bail within hours, while Ciello will be jailed. Ciello will be testifying for two years, and after those two years, then what? Will he and his family ever be safe again? Once again, it is an underworld figure rather than a federal investigator who tries to protect Danny's interests. Ciello's cousin Nick informs him that the mafia has put out a contract on Danny's life. Nick has come to give his cousin fair warning. That the mafia should have a keener sense of honor than the federal government is an irony Danny is too confused to appreciate.

Ciello's greatest long-term problem, however, proves to be the ever-present danger of self-incrimination. If Ciello does not testify truthfully about the corruption in which he has participated, he can go to jail for the rest of his life. If he speaks truthfully, however, sooner or later he will implicate his partners from SIU. Danny decides to risk perjuring himself rather than inform upon his friends. "I'm going to be spending the rest of my life lying," he acknowledges, and this is brought home to him during the trial. In effect, Ciello rather than Blomberg is the defendant. This scene signals the approach to be taken by defense attorneys in the proceedings to come. Defense attorneys will do their best to discredit Ciello by impugning his claim to only three acts of misconduct in a career spanning some 11 years. Ciello is most vulnerable with regard to the drugs he has given his informants, a common practice in the SIU. Under the law, distributing narcotics in this way is tantamount to selling them on the street. This comes to a head when "The King" (Robert Christian), a drug trafficker, submits a deposition to the attorney general accusing Ciello of exchanging heroin for automobiles. If any of this can be proven, the government's pending cases will collectively fall to pieces. "The King" fails a lie detector test, but only after raising serious doubts in the minds of the federal prosecutors about Ciello's credibility. Earlier, Brooks Paige has told Danny, "You're one of us," meaning one of the "good guys," one of the "feds." But Ciello is not—not really. He is caught in no-man's-land. A witness, rather than a law enforcement officer, Ciello's former moral authority is now denied him.

When Ciello's cousin Nick is murdered in a mafia slaying, Danny and his family are moved to Virginia. Flying back from New York one Friday night, Danny talks with prosecutor Mario Vincente (Steve Inwood). Ciello has begun to see that he no longer has any partners. Not only is he isolated, he is apt to be victimized by those with whom he is working. Everything is turning out to be so much more confused and confusing than Ciello had anticipated. Earlier in the film he has confessed, "I'm not sure of anything anymore," and speaking now with Vincente he elaborates. A polygraph is unreliable. Its ability to tell the truth from a lie is minimal, at best. If the reading on "The King" had been different, even marginally different, Ciello would be facing prosecution himself. He says, "I feel like I'm lying even when I'm telling the truth. It's been so long since I didn't have to think about my answer. Man, I was on the streets and undercover for 10 years. I don't know what the truth is anymore. There's only thing I know for sure: Sandrocino, Polito, all those guys, they are not my friends. No sir, they are not my friends."

While the federal government prepares its cases, in New York City an investigation is underway headed by prosecutors Polito (James Tolkan) and Kantor (Bobby Alto). Polito and Kantor are under pressure to prosecute "the French Connection Case," in which 120 pounds of heroin disappeared from police possession. Their superiors are putting pressure on them to indict any policeman who might be even slightly connected to the theft. Theirs is a shotgun approach, one intended to coerce the innocent into providing information about the guilty. Gino Moscone's partner Ralph Alvarez (Tony Page) is one of the first to cooperate. He offers evidence against Ciello's old SIU partner, Gus Levy. When Ciello learns this, he goes directly to Levy, who is working undercover in New York City's garment district. This is as close as the investigation has gotten to indicting Ciello's partners since Moscone's suicide, but Danny can see that he will soon be put to another test. Will he be able to resist the prosecutors as they gather evidence against his beloved SIU? Levy assures Danny that he will never confess, that Levy will not turn in their old partners in return for favorable treatment. Polito anticipates a different scenario. Policemen always cooperate. It is in their blood to want to expiate their guilt. Polito tells Ciello, "Nearly all of them [the SIU] will cooperate. They're cops. In their hearts they want to admit their guilt. That's the way cops are. That's how you got here. Don't you understand that?"

Polito intends to indict Danny. By this point Ciello is drinking constantly, taking valium and other prescription drugs. Having lost control first of the investigation, then later the prosecution, Ciello is now losing control of his life. Even control of his body seems to desert him at times, for he twitches uncontrollably, complains of bleeding gums. Vincente has offered Ciello his friendship, and confides that the attorney general's office has thrown Ciello to the wolves. If he hopes to save himself Ciello has no choice but to trust in Polito and testify. "I won't give up my partners," Ciello responds. "I will not cross that line, ever." But that is exactly what Ciello does. Ciello is encouraged by the prosecutors to confess to them, then to bring his partners in to make confessions of their own. Ostensibly this is in his own best interest; in fact, it is in the interest of the prosecutors. Ciello is no longer quick-witted enough to withstand cross-examination in a trial. If it can be proved that Ciello has perjured himself, all of the prosecutors' work will be for naught.

Dom Bando (Kenny Marino) is the first of the SIU to be implicated by Danny. Vincente urges Danny to encourage his partners to turn themselves in before his confession is made part of the public record. Vincente supposes that each of Ciello's old partners will follow his example, that one will encourage the next, in a chain reaction. But Vincente's plan gets off to a rocky start. Bando is the most timid of the SIU, perhaps the most mentally unstable—his partners have protected and insulated him whenever possible. Technically, Dom Bando is among the least guilty of any in the unit. But fear of imprisonment has caused Dom to panic. Hysterical, perhaps mad, he rejects Danny's plea to speak with the prosecutors. Joe Marinaro (Richard Foronjy) is the next SIU agent approached, then Bill Mayo (Don Billett). A family man and soon to retire, Marinaro is reluctant to come forward. Mayo commits suicide. Learning of this, Danny races to an elevated train platform and leans forward over the rail, apparently contemplating a suicide of his own.

Danny approaches each of his partners with a confession of his actions. When he calls Mayo, the crucifix he wears around his neck is visible, as though Ciello has been toying with it before dialing the number. But there is no absolution in these confessions. Danny is no longer stable. He appears to be in shock, perhaps having a breakdown. When he negotiates an interview on the street with Gus Levy without bringing his guards for protection, Danny may well be hoping Levy will kill him on the spot. With Vincente's coaxing, Danny's initial admission to three deeds of misconduct has grown into an 84-page confession. This becomes a matter of judicial record, as Blomberg's attorney sues for a retrial and puts Ciello on the stand again to demonstrate the breadth of his perjury. Ciello has admitted to some 40 counts of perjury. The federal prosecutors must decide whether or not to indict Ciello. Their meeting takes place in Washington, D.C. in the office of the head federal prosecutor, Charles Deluth (Peter Michael Goetz). Capallino, Paige, and others argue on Ciello's behalf, citing his contribution to their ongoing investigation, and the web of circumstances that have influenced his fate. Polito counters with the depth of Ciello's corruption. The two scenes are intercut so that we see the federal prosecutors trying Ciello at the same time as Blomberg's attorney is cross-examining him, in effect trying Ciello as well. In both cases, the issue is the extent of corruption. Can Blomberg be found guilty on the word of a man as corrupt as Ciello? Can the federal prosecutors honorably indict Ciello given their complicity in using a witness and investigator whom they knew to be guilty of much more than he admitted? Ciello's perjury may have cost them their indictments, but he has also been their victim. Who is the guilty party here, who the most evil? Implicitly, the prosecutors encouraged Ciello to perjure himself in order to win the cases. As one attorney says, "He was never made to understand how formidable, how inexorable the forces against him were. . . . This man was acting out of fear and guilt and remorse. He was attempting to carve out some area of penance for himself in his life. And we used him."

In effect, Ciello wins both cases. Blomberg's conviction is upheld; the federal prosecutors decide to let Ciello go free. But the final sequence has Ciello about to lecture a fledgling class of detectives. Once he is recognized, the members of the class rise and walk out. The final shot is reminiscent of the last shot of *Serpico*. We last see Ciello in a one-shot, photographed against a plain blue background. The scene is edited by John J. Fitzstephens so that Danny seems to occupy one side of the screen and the class of police seem to occupy the other. The last thing we hear is apparently the sound of Danny's heart. This brings to mind the opening shot of the film as Danny and his wife are in bed in the middle of the night. A sound has awakened Danny out of a dead sleep—apparently the sound of his own heart.

Andrzej Bartkowiak's photography and Tony Walton's set design are admirable, as are the work of film editor John J. Fitzstephens and sound editor Peter C. Frank. Their work reminds us of the various stages of Ciello's isolation and entrapment. As Danny begins to cooperate with Paige and Capallino, he meets them in a deserted post office building. Ciello is to begin his cooperation by confessing his own transgressions. Before his admissions get under way, Danny says, "Well, it's been five years since I've been to confession, but . . ." Ciello is making a joke, but nevertheless, it is an appropriate way to begin. Danny has indeed come to the prosecutors looking for expiation. Later in the film Ciello will tell his wife that in high school he was always the one who got to carry the flag during school assemblies. Ciello seeks a return to that state of innocence. He is seeking to reclaim his place on the moral high ground. This Catholic sensibility is developed throughout the drama. Midway through the film, Danny, Gino Moscone's partner Ralph Alvarez, and his old partners from the SIU are seen together at a family barbecue. Moscone is dead by this point. Word has gotten out that Ciello is an informant, but none of his partners knows how forthcoming Ciello has been or who among them might be touched. Danny is feeling the weight of Gino's suicide and his partners do their best to comfort him. They take him into a cloistered room. There Danny makes a full confession of everything he has done to that point. "I want absolution," Danny explains tearfully. "Guys like us take the sacraments with what we do. I wasn't going to go against cops. None of you guys were involved, I swear to God. . . . I didn't want it to happen but it happened." All of his partners say they forgive him, then ask how they can help. Suspecting that Ciello is suicidal, they ask for his gun.

Danny's inclination toward self-destruction and his need for confession parallel each other. When we first see Danny with his younger brother, Danny is asked if he has given Ronnie any drugs. Danny replies that the day he gives his brother heroin is the day he puts his gun to their heads and kills them both. Early in the film Paige and Capallino note that Ciello has stopped wearing a sidearm during his undercover work for them. They hypothesize that Ciello is so ambivalent psychologically about what he is doing to his brother policemen that he has decided not to resist if his life is threatened. The psychological need to return to some state of innocence, through expiation and penance—and when that fails, through self-destruction—is a central concern of Lumet's character study. Danny is naive to believe that he can so easily reclaim what he has lost. The world is not that simple. When federal prosecutors finally meet to determine Danny's fate, Sandrocino wants to throw him to the wolves. But Capallino says that Ciello cooperated with the government "because he was trying to get back [to the right side of the law, to a state of innocence]. Look, I think to most of us corruption creeps up almost imperceptibly. But getting back is something that can only be done in one great big dangerous leap. He leaps and he risks everything." Capallino is surely on the right track, but he is arguing a position here, not explicating Ciello's motives, and his version is an oversimplification of what we have seen for the previous two hours and 30 minutes. Danny Ciello cannot make that leap for himself without betraying those who are nearest to him. When he confesses to only three violations of the law, he is not thinking of self-preservation, he chooses to confess incidents that will not implicate his partners.

Much of the camera work builds upon Lumet's earlier films. Here, too, Lumet favors a moving camera that recomposes as we watch, a camera sitting in judgment, redefining what we see as we observe it. Late in the film, Ralph Alvarez has come forward to speak with Polito, Kantor, and their associates. Alvarez sits at the head of a long, rectangular conference table. Nearest to Alvarez sits Polito (screen-right) and Kantor (screen-left). Alvarez is in the far distance, Polito and Kantor are in the middle distance. Their associates sit closer to us at the table. Each of the prosecutors sits with his hands and forearms on the table, a configuration suggesting that the crooked cop is finally coming to face the "long arm of the law." The camera is at the end of the table opposite Alvarez, who is speaking as the scene begins. Then the focal length increases as we seem to approach him.

Such camera work recalls E. G. Marshall's recapitulation of the evidence in *Twelve Angry Men*. Here, too, the other characters are taken out of the frame as the focal length increases, and we are offered a persuasive rendition of the circumstances at hand. As the camera comes in, Alvarez explains that whatever crimes he may have committed against narcotics kingpins have been committed to fight evil, not to endorse it. Our judicial system does not work, Alvarez maintains. He has taken money from the drug lords he has apprehended, and stolen their heroin, in an attempt to put them out of business, something the courts refuse to do. Unless you take their money, argues Alvarez, the drug lords buy their way out of indictments, bribing lawyers and judges, and using the legal system to their own nefarious advantage. If Alvarez has used illegal wiretaps, he has done so because the legal system is too slow in granting formal permission. Perjury is commonplace. "I don't know why you people don't understand the system. You want a conviction but you've got these stupid Search and Seizure laws. . . . Case One never got made without an illegal wiretap. And you're never gonna get a conviction if a cop don't commit perjury. . . . You're a bunch of fucking hypocrites." Alvarez maintains that, like his fellow policemen, he has been tasked with enforcing laws that cannot be enforced without circumventing formal procedures and breaking written rules. We notice Alvarez's arms and hands throughout this pronouncement. His confession of guilt is actually an indictment of us all. Soon Alvarez seems to be coming toward us, and this person, who stands between us and forces with which we do not care to deal, is soon almost on top of us. It is a powerful image, a reminder that this is the man in whose hands real law enforcement has been placed.

Lumet employs the vertical plane of his camera much as we have seen him do before. The camera tends to view Danny Ciello from above eye level early in the film, then gradually descends. Photographing Ciello in series of low-angle shots puts ceilings, walls, joists, and the like in our field of vision, reminding us that Danny is trapped by his circumstances. The first time the interior of Ciello's home is shown in extreme low-angle shots, is in a scene in which Danny must tell his wife that their phone is bugged. This altered perspective also reminds us of the distortion before us, particularly later in the film. Nothing is as it should be. Despite Danny's attempts to put things right, nothing seems properly balanced. Lumet's use of lenses also recalls his earlier work, such as *Long Day's Journey*. Lumet isolated Katharine Hepburn's character as the play progressed by photographing her in longer lenses, while photographing the Tyrone men in progressively shorter focal lengths. There is a similar pattern of cinematic isolation in *Prince of the City*. Danny Ciello grows wiser about himself and the weight of human commitments as the film evolves, and Lumet underscores this through his choice of lenses for subjective shots. Subjective shots are normally photographed with lenses in the 35 to 45 millimeter range, those lenses which most closely approximate normal vision. Lumet chose his lenses with this in mind. He stays above or below this range for much of the film and moves within it only once Ciello can see clearly, once he can recognize what has happened to him.

In an attempt to rid himself of guilt, Ciello gradually severs relationships with everyone who is dear to him until, by the end of the film, he is completely isolated, from his city, his family, his peers. Lumet underscores this through his lighting scheme and his manipulation of depth of field. In the first third of the film, the backgrounds are generally more distinctly lit than the character. Visually, Danny seems overwhelmed by the underworld in which he works. Danny's first action in the film is dealing with an informant. They meet at the counter of a coffee shop. Danny puts his money down on the counter for the waitress, tucks a packet of heroin, perhaps wrapped in money, in his informant's pocket, then leaves. The informant turns on the stool, drinks from Danny's cup, then palms the money on the counter. Our initial encounter with Danny's world serves as an entrée into a world of betrayal; this culminates in the film's first section, as we spend a night with Danny on the streets of the barrio dealing with his junkies. The night becomes a series of interrelated incidents in which one person betrays another. The film becomes progressively darker during this period, the depth of field increasingly shallow. The night ends with one of Ciello's junkies beating his lover while Danny sits all alone in another room of their tenement staring helplessly at us. Only a tiny spotlight illuminates Ciello's face at the sequence's conclusion. He is surrounded by darkness. Behind him, through a window, we see rain coming down on the street. But the visual space is compressed thanks to Lumet's choice of lenses. We have little sense of a street in the distance or a wall at Danny's back, or of Danny sitting in the foreground. Everything seems to have been reduced to one visual plane, one rainy city darkness.

Ciello takes this darkness with him into his second and third meetings with Capallino. Both meetings occur in Capallino's apartment on New York City's fashionable Central Park West. In the first meeting, we can see the family portraits on Capallino's walls more distinctly than Danny's expressions, for he continually moves toward areas of darkness in the room, particularly corners with shadows. By the time of the second meeting, the blue-black tones of Danny's barrio almost eclipse the room itself. Except for a few points of light, darkness defines Ciello's presence. The scene begins with Danny at Capallino's window looking out over Central Park. He tells Capallino that the day he graduated from the police academy was the proudest day of his family's life. During these initial reminiscences, Ciello is momentarily lit by natural light. There is a disparity between a rookie's vision of police work and what he encounters on the street. Correspondingly, the light fades as Danny confides to Capallino and later to Brooks Paige what life is like on the street.

> You bastards, it's you guys who run the whole fucking thing . . . starting with Assistant D.A.'s who plea-bargain murder one down to a mis-

demeanor or lawyers wearing 400 dollar suits who come up to cops in hallways and say Listen pal this case doesn't mean shit, here's 50 dollars, 100 dollars, 500 dollars, FIFTEEN THOUSAND DOLLARS. . . . We know how you guys become judges: You pay 50 thousand and zap, you're wearing robes. . . . You guys live in Westport or here on Central Park West while we're up in El Barrio on 125th street. . . . You want us to keep everyone on the inside so you can stay on the outside. . . . You guys are winning in the end anyway. We're out there selling ourselves and our families. These people we take from [the drug dealers] own us. I know what you guys think of us, but we're the only thing between you and the jungle. You don't understand. We're on the inside!

It is as if Danny has been "inside" the jungle so long that it is threatening to consume his identity.

Lumet begins to reverse this lighting scheme as Danny makes his initial formal confession and goes to work for Paige and Capallino. Incrementally, Lumet balances the light between Danny and his background, so that as we approach the film's midpoint the light is more or less equally distributed between Ciello and what we see behind him. Dramatically, however this is not all for the best. Following his brush with death at the hands of Benedetto, Danny returns to Capallino's Central Park West apartment. This time it is midday. The light is natural. Lumet puts Danny in the foreground and Capallino and Paige in the background. Thanks to a striking bit of deep-focus photography, we can see both visual planes distinctly. We can also see that Danny is separate from the others, a point that is driven home by the action. Ciello has to call Edelman, the policeman he is helping to put in jail, in order to protect Ciello's wife and children. The film becomes progressively darker as it moves toward its conclusion. Far, middle, and near distances become progressively compressed. Visually, there is much to suggest that Danny's attempt to escape one jungle has only landed him in a worse one. Whereas the lighting pattern eclipsed Ciello in the film's beginning, here it tends to isolate him, to set him apart. As Ciello provides Vincente with a full confession, indicting his SIU partners, the establishing shot is composed of a tape recorder in the foreground, a chair, end table, and lamp in the background, and a window in the far distance. None of these objects is distinctly in focus. Vincente himself is little more than a shadow. Danny alone is sharply focused; all available light seems to point toward him. By the final moments of *Prince of the City,* all the light is on Ciello, and the background is so dark as to be almost indistinguishable. Our last image of Ciello comes as his isolation is complete. Ciello has been reduced to a talking head against a nondescript blue wall completely void of detail.

As mentioned earlier, such an ending is reminiscent of the last image of Frank Serpico, and other similarities between the two exist. As in *Serpico,* Lumet uses expansive, naturally lit exteriors very sparingly in *Prince of the City,* and often ironically. It is aboard the ferry to Governor's Island that Nick tells Danny that his life is in danger. Behind them we see nothing but water, and in the far distance, an urban skyline. Following Bill Mayo's suicide, Danny sits all by himself at a bench in a grassy park, which is inexplicably deserted. Near the film's midpoint we see the Ciello family at the beach. Following Benedetto's threat to his life, Danny has been given a few days vacation by the prosecutors. It is a beautiful day, and the sequence at the beach is a series of radiant, windswept images. But such beauty is ironic: this is also the scene in which Danny futilely tries to convince Carla that Brooks and Capallino have his interests at heart. This sequence is followed by a scene in which Ciello approaches Gino Moscone in the yard of Moscone's spacious suburban home. Moscone is seen with his wife and horse. The backyard extends to the outer reaches of a horse track and the image is somewhat bucolic. But the warm reunion is undercut by our knowledge that Sandrocino is coercing Danny into betraying his old friend. Natural light predominates in a natural setting once again when Danny meets Rocky, who offers him cash in order to make his escape. Periodically, the Statue of Liberty can be seen in the background. Ironically, it is in this scene that Danny first articulates the fact that he has no place left to go.

Far more of the film is shot in interiors or on the streets of New York City than in natural, open settings; Ciello is lit more often by artificial light than he is seen basking in the sun. The skies are overcast more often than not in *Prince of the City.* Lumet's use of rain is interesting in this regard. The turning point in Ciello's career is the night he spends with his junkie informants (Jose Santana, Lionel Pina, Cynthia Nixon), all in need of a fix and willing to do anything to anyone to get it. This nighttime scene is shot entirely in rain, perhaps the most menacing downpour in recent American film. The scene lasts almost eight minutes, taking Danny from the warmth of his suburban bed into the bowels of the barrio. Emotionally, it takes him from the level of a dedicated narcotics detective working the streets, to that of a hoodlum; like his junkies, Ciello descends to a level where he is willing to do anything to get what he wants. The eight-minute sequence distills Danny's spiritual descent during a career of 11 years into a few meaningful scenes, ending with a haunting image of Ciello's face as he comes to this recognition. Initially, the rain is identified with the ghetto, where betrayal is the rule and honor the exception, a world Ciello wants desperately to escape before it drags him down. But Lumet will use rain to mark key points in Danny's odyssey of self-realization, in a way that reminds us of how far this corruption has spread. The first time Ciello goes undercover for the federal prosecutors is the night he introduces Edelman to Rocky Gazzo. They meet in a diner, then drive through the wet streets. Rocky is almost a caricature of a mafioso thug in the scene; the diner itself is a parody of a mafioso meeting place.

The next time we see Danny in the rain he is being taken by Benedetto to see his cousin Nick, another key moment in his self-realization. When Benedetto later tries to kill Ciello, they meet in a neighborhood Italian restaurant. Again, Danny's backup surveillance has failed him; their vision has been obscured by a downpour. Shortly thereafter, Ciello discovers that Sandrocino has betrayed him, has risked Danny's life for nothing. We have moved up from the streets of the ghetto, but rain is still identified with hoodlums and lowlifes. This is modified as Danny and his family are driven to the Catskills by federal agents after a rainstorm. We are reminded that a leak from the prosecutors' office to the press has put the Ciello family in jeopardy. This betrayal is paralleled in a subsequent scene in which Brooks Paige, accompanying Danny on the ferry from Governor's Island to Manhattan, announces his departure. Once again the streets are wet and the sky is overcast. But we are dealing now with government officials who are setting Danny Ciello adrift, not junkies and thugs ready to stab him in the back; we are dealing with men who live on Central Park West, not on 125th Street. In front of a federal building, between rain-soaked classical columns, Vincente urges Danny to betray his partners in SIU, and lets slip that Gus Levy will soon be indicted by Alvarez anyway. Finally there are puddles on the steps of this same building, when we discover Danny and Vincente in extreme long shot, the most elongated space between camera and character in the film. They are going inside where Danny will begin his 84-page confession, implicating his partners from the SIU.

This is a world of corruption and betrayal, extending from the lowest ghetto streets to the highest reaches of our government. Visually, the film takes us from New York City locations as diverse as burned-out tenements in the South Bronx, to the Plaza Hotel, from Manhattan shooting galleries to the inner sanctum of the U.S. Attorney General in Washington, D.C. But *Prince of the City* takes us most of all on a personal odyssey, one with ramifications for our society as a whole. *Prince of the City* calls to mind Dostoyevsky's *Crime and Punishment*, rewritten to speak to the 1980s. "It's a picture about morality not being what it seems," Lumet comments to the *Los Angeles Times* on 7 June 1981. "They all have to be questioned, all of the moralities. Everyone is involved in it, that's why it's a long movie. Everybody's motives go from the basest to the most noble. [Ciello] starts off saying there are certain lines he won't cross. His terms are accepted. Finally, he is pushed, pushed so hard he crosses those lines. I personally think he's a hero."

Ciello's situation has its parallels in Lumet's past. Lumet was working at CBS during the McCarthy hearings. CBS's Edward R. Murrow had been particularly critical of the House Un-American Activities Committee, and CBS was feeling the heat. During this period Lumet was the director of the "You Are There," a series with ties to the network's news division. The week Murrow broadcast the first of his McCarthy shows, Lumet directed "The First Salem Witch Trial." Melvin Block, an executive of Lumet's sponsor, the Amident Toothpaste Company, later told Lumet that Lumet had been named as an American Communist Party member by Harvey Matusow, a friendly government witness. Lumet made little of this at first, but soon he was asked to meet with Matusow and Victor Riesel, a McCarthy crony and the labor columnist of William Randolph Hearst's tabloid, the *New York Daily Mirror*. Recalls Lumet,

> I thought about it and for two weeks went through holy hell. If I agreed, I might be asked to tell what I knew about the organized left in order to save myself. I didn't want to be put in that position, but I also wanted to keep working. I agreed to the meeting. . . . The door opened and I saw these two, Riesel and Matusow, sitting across the room. I started toward them, cursing and screaming. Riesel was still in his seat, but Matusow had risen and he said to me: "Don't get in an uproar," and to them, "He's not the one." . . . I wasn't the guy he'd seen in whatever meeting he was talking about.

Lumet has said that he has never forgotten that meeting. It taught him a lesson about himself, and others. Until summoned by the McCarthy forces, Lumet had been quick to condemn those who cooperated. The meeting with Matusow and Riesel demonstrated to Lumet that none of us can be sure of how we will react in situations in which we have so much at stake. We can never be sure of what we will do until the time comes to act. But it also demonstrated the degree to which we are defined by the choices we make. "I promise you I didn't know *what* I was going to do that night. Finally, what's left any of us is our actions. It taught me a lot about *Prince of the City*. It's my most grownup piece of work."[5] That we pay the price as individuals for the positions we take is an idea to be found in Lumet's work as early as *Twelve Angry Men*. Certainly it is not unique to *Prince of the City*. But in Lumet's more recent work, he has tended to examine this concern in a slightly different context. During the last decade he seems to have been drawn to films that examine the price we pay as children for the decisions of our parents. Sometimes, as in *Garbo Talks*, Lumet has attempted to treat this comically; sometimes, as in *Family Business*, in seriocomic fashion. But in *Daniel, Running on Empty,* and *Q & A*, where the individual's relationship to guilt and innocence in a complex world is at issue, Lumet has explored this theme most thoroughly.

CHAPTER THREE

Lumet's Later Work:
Daniel, Running on Empty, Q & A,
and *A Stranger among Us*

DANIEL (1983)

Lumet may well have as much invested in *Daniel* as any film he has made to date. In addition to the time and effort he spent in trying to interest a studio in the project, he apparently felt ties to the story which were rooted in his own background. "A lot of things came together for me in *Daniel*," he has said. "The background was very close to my own. Not one moment of research had to be spent on it." It is no wonder that Lumet found parallels between his life and that of the novel's protagonist. The son of a famous father, a highly driven man deeply involved in his work on the stage, Lumet was the product of a politically committed, Depression-era New York Jewish upbringing. When Lumet first read E. L. Doctorow's *Book of Daniel* in 1971, he knew he wanted to make a movie of it. Presented with Doctorow's adaptation for the screen two years later, Lumet became virtually obsessed with the project. For 10 years he submitted the screenplay, and had it rejected by studios large and small. He collected 44 rejection slips, but never stopped trying. On the forty-fifth try, he managed to put together the minimum necessary financing. The screenplay required period work in two generations, called for scenes involving thousands of people, and necessitated a considerable amount of location shooting in New York City (the final movie made use of the streets of Harlem, Astoria, Soho, Union Square, the garment district, and the Astor Place subway station, not to mention churches, office buildings, and apartment houses up and down Manhattan's West Side). *Daniel* promised to require a budget of at least 20 million dollars. Nothing even approaching such an amount ever became available. For years Lumet had dickered with the studios, offering to do a film they proposed if they would let him make *Daniel* in return. The means to finance the film were finally found when he entertained the proposal of a made-for-television movie about television evangelists, "Kingdom." Lumet signed the completion bond on *Daniel* himself, and associate John Heyman did the rest, scraping together enough financing to get the project off the ground. The deal Lumet finally worked out allowed him slightly more than eight million dollars to complete the film in less than nine weeks, with most of the set work to be done at Astoria Studios in Queens.

Lumet and Doctorow, as well as most of the cast, crew, and production staff, worked for a fraction of what they might have earned on another project, many taking only the minimum set by their unions. Timothy Hutton became so enamoured of the part that he turned down a one million dollar offer on another picture to work on "Daniel" for 30,000 dollars. Even so, Hutton had to pursue Lumet to give him the starring role. Lumet identified Timothy Hutton with his Academy Award-winning role in *Ordinary People,* the clean-cut, sensitive boy from the frozen tundra of Waspish suburbia. This was not how Lumet had envisioned the title character. Hutton literally arrived on Lumet's doorstep one day unannounced, bearded, and with long hair, eager for a chance at the role. Lumet skimped as much as possible, on what was spent "above the line" (for stars, key production personnel, etc.) in order to make funds available for daily shooting. But Lumet does not think this finally shortchanged the movie he made.

The story begins in a Boston suburb in the house of Robert and Lisa Lewin (John Rubinstein, Maria Tucci) on a Thanksgiving day in the late 1960s. For the last dozen years, the Lewins have been the legal guardians of Susan and Daniel Isaacson (Amanda Plummer, Timothy Hutton), the children of Paul and Rochelle Isaacson (Mandy Patinkin, Lindsay Crouse), a couple found guilty of supplying the Russians with plans for atomic weapons in the early 1950s and subsequently put to death in the electric chair. At that time, money that had been collected in a defense fund was put in trust for the two children by the Isaacsons' attorney, Jacob Ascher (Edward Asner). That trust, to be divided equally between brother and sister, is about to vest. Susan is 20 years old and a university student as the film begins. Daniel, several years older, is a married graduate student in New York City. At his side is his pregnant wife (Ellen Barkin).

The family has reunited at Lewin's house for the holiday. Susan initiates a discussion with Daniel at the Thanksgiving table about how the money is to be spent, a discussion that soon grows heated. Susan is a campus radical, proud of the fresh bruises on her arms left by police at a political demonstration; as further proof of her commitment, she suggests they pool their money to establish the Isaacson Foundation for Revolutionary Study. She professes to believe in her parents' innocence. They were falsely indicted, she says, then murdered by the American government for their unpopular political beliefs. Their executions were meant to serve as an example to others on the political left. Linking their name to the foundation will help to give meaning to lives cut short so tragically. Daniel is uninvolved in campus politics. He is less convinced than Susan of his parents' martyrdom. Paul and Rochelle Isaacson have become names linked by the left to political repression, to an America gone wrong. Were his parents in fact simply a working-class Jewish couple from immigrant stock who were wrongly executed for their political beliefs? Were they victims of the American government's attempt to divert attention from foreign policy failures? Were they instead what the political right still maintained, conspirators who aided the Russians in achieving nuclear parity with this country? Or, were they somewhere in between? Susan is as eager to link her life to the Isaacson name as Daniel is to shun it. He questions whether she is really as politically involved as she claims. Is this perhaps the latest in her series of attempts to come to terms with the scars she bears as the Isaacsons' child? Is this really different from her earlier attempts to find answers to her problems in religion, drugs, sex? What if her supposed political involvement is really one more means of escaping from questions to which she cannot find answers?

Within the year, the group is together again, this time at a Holiday Inn on the Massachusetts Turnpike where Susan has attempted to take her own life. Present as well is Daniel's newborn son, and Susan's psychiatrist (David Marguiles). Daniel blames himself for Susan's slitting her wrists with a razor blade. As they grew up, they grew so far apart that now they barely communicate at all. Susan had not even bothered to leave Daniel a suicide note, he recognizes. She assumed he would want her car. On the dash she has left an opened package of blades; on the front seat, a poster with her parents' photographs from a political rally she and Daniel attended as children. Daniel goes to the mental hospital where Susan has been sent to recover. Daniel sees his own plight in Susan's sorry state. Both of their lives have been darkened by their parents' shadow. Both the Thanksgiving scene and this meeting deal with legacies—one that can be calculated in dollars and cents, the other that is more difficult to measure. In hope of clarifying these issues for his sister and himself, Daniel sets out on a quest to discover the truth about their parents.

He goes first to a *New York Times* reporter (Lee Richardson) who covered the Isaacsons' arrest, trial, and execution. Daniel is looking for a way to announce the formation of the Isaacson Foundation. To please his sister, Daniel intends to put his share of the legacy with hers. But this meeting soon leads to a discussion of the Isaacsons' trial. The reporter says that it was widely believed that the government framed the Isaacsons. The government withheld valuable evidence that might have exonerated the couple, classifying it top secret so it could not be used in court. Common sense alone proved Paul Isaacson's innocence. How could a minimally trained radio repairman copy highly sophisticated and detailed plans for nuclear weapons and then reduce them to a size that would fit on dental x-ray film? It was impossible! But even if the Isaacsons were innocent of conspiracy to commit treason, they were not necessarily entirely innocent. The FBI would not have selected them at random. They were well-known members of the American Communist party, and they may well have been guilty of much. Not enough to justify their executions, to be sure; but guilty nevertheless.

Daniel goes next to the widow of Jacob Ascher (Carmen Matthews). He wants Ascher's papers from the trial—perhaps something there will lead him to the answers he seeks. But the papers have all been given to Lewin. Lewin's father was Ascher's partner; Lewin himself was a lawyer with the firm for a short time. Ascher's widow Fanny is less certain than the reporter that the Isaacsons were innocent of spying. But even if they were, she tells Daniel, they allowed themselves to be used by both the Communist party (as martyrs), and the American government (as treasonous Reds). She holds the Isaacsons responsible for hastening her husband's death. Despite her husband's urgent pleas, they would not let him call several witnesses whom

Ascher wanted to put on the stand. Daniel, curious about these un-called witnesses, goes to Lewin. Lewin says that what Fanny Ascher has told Daniel is tainted by her own prejudices. Ascher was sick long before he took the case. Despite a formidable career, he has gone down in legal history as the lawyer who bungled the Isaacson trial. As for the uncalled witnesses, their testimony might have been rele-vant, but it is possible as well that they would not have made a dif-ference in the trial's outcome. The Isaacsons may simply have had too much to overcome. Following World War II, American foreign policy had depicted Russia as a backward nation, virtually a feudal state. The policy had been to reassure Americans that this country alone had nuclear capabilities. When the Soviets came forth with atomic bombs of their own, the government had to make it appear as though the plans had been stolen. If not, Lewin explains, it would be clear how severely our foreign policy experts had underestimated Soviet potential.

Lewin then goes over the fatal flaws in Ascher's defense of the Isaac-sons. Just because Ascher made strategic mistakes that led to their convictions does not in and of itself prove the Isaacsons' innocence, he explains. What kept Paul Isaacson from implicating others, if not the desire to save his own and Rochelle's lives? Paul Isaacson was im-plicated by a family friend, Dr. Selig Mindish (Joseph Leon), a fellow member of the Communist party, as well as their friend, neighbor, and family dentist. Lewin speculates that Mindish implicated Paul Isaacson in order to mitigate his own sentence once he recognized the government was intent on punishing him, whether he was guilty or not. Mindish was neither smart nor courageous; perhaps after weeks of grilling he actually began to believe that he was part of a spy ring. What had prevented the Isaacsons from doing the same thing? It was possible that Paul Isaacson was so obsessed with Marxist ideology that he took pleasure in playing the role of the martyr. Perhaps he thought the Communist party would come to their aid in the end. Perhaps he thought that that appeals process would serve them more favorably than it did. Or perhaps he knew all along he was going to be executed, and was so fervent in his beliefs that he was willing to pay that price.

A law professor rather than a practicing attorney, Lewin tries to put the case in a historical context for Daniel, then offers a learned analysis of Ascher's approach, the prosecutor's approach, and the fine points of law raised by both. Lewin is a caring, reasonable man, an appealing figure. But there is bad blood between him and Fanny Ascher—Lewin refused to take over the law firm, preferring an academic career. Too, having reared Daniel and his sister, having served in effect as their father (Daniel, in fact, calls him Dad), Lewin has good reason to question the Isaacsons' refusal to cooperate with the government. Both Daniel and Susan have suffered mightily for the stand their parents took. More than any other adult, perhaps, Lewin has a right to feel that Paul Isaacson's choice was a selfish choice, showing a lack of concern for his little boy and girl. Lewin's supposition that the Isaacsons were arrested only in an attempt to gain information about other party members is given more credence when Daniel subsequently learns that the state never believed Paul Isaacson and his wife were the masterminds of the spy ring. Until the moment of the Isaacsons' deaths, the government was trying to coerce them into giving over the names of their superiors. The only reason for arresting Rochelle, in fact, was to pressure her husband into naming the others. Daniel recalls hushed conversations in the Isaacson household about a couple with children who were working clandestinely on very important matters. He seeks out Mindish's daughter, Linda (Tovah Feldshuh), hoping she can lead him to them. Linda is now a California dentist using an assumed name in conservative Orange County. Her version of events is quite different from those Daniel has heard to this point. She assures Daniel that his parents were indeed the masters of a traitorous conspiracy, that they were guilty of far more than the government's accusations. Of course, Linda has good reason to see things in this light. Her father has gone down in history as a traitor to the political left, and a spy to the political right. It is surely satisfying to envision him as the Isaacsons' victim instead of their betrayer.

Linda leads Daniel not to the couple he has come about, but rather to her father. He alone would have access to the information Daniel seeks; Daniel seems to have found a source of truth at last. But Mindish is a broken man. Daniel finds him in a rest home, little more than a stone. Whatever secrets he once knew will go to the grave with him. Daniel had hoped to save Susan by clarifying their parents' guilt or innocence. He leaves Mindish realizing that "there's such a thing as too much hope," and this is borne out by Susan's death. Susan dies as she has lived, in her parents' shadow. But the film's final moments suggest that Daniel will be more fortunate. If his odyssey into the past has demonstrated the limits of what we can learn about our parents' passions and the actions they inspired, it has also put Daniel in contact with material he can use to free himself, and begin to live his own life.

Lumet has said that in order for Daniel to find himself, he must virtually climb out of his parents' graves, freeing himself as much as
possible from the traumas of the past. This is reflected in the film's
structure, in which the past informs the present, and the present informs the past—though neither can explain the other definitively. The
film alternates between Daniel's quest to help Susan to find meaning
in her life in the 1960s and material from the 1940s and 1950s, the
latter often photographed in muted, warm, sepia hues. Action in the
present, by contrast, is often harshly lit, producing stark images that
are uneasy on the eye. The film begins with such an image, an extreme
close-up of Daniel's face. Virtually all but his eyes and nose are cut off
by the outer reaches of the frame. Daniel faces the audience unblinkingly and begins an encyclopedialike explication of electricity. This is
spoken in faceless, academic prose. As the account turns to the use of
electricity in executions, the film shifts to a death row in a prison some
years in the past. We are in a hallway that ends at an execution chamber. We will hear this account repeated near the film's end, when we
will enter the chamber ourselves and stand witness as Paul Isaacson
and his wife are put in the electric chair and killed. In between, the
film will return periodically to Daniel's account of various forms
of capital punishment as they have been employed throughout the
ages, each associated visually with the execution of his parents. What
seemed initially an analytic essay on electrical power, is in fact a tract
about capital punishment, and the willingness of societies to use it on
the lower classes. It is a political tract, with Marxist overtones, perhaps. It is academic and learned in tone. But it is also personal.

In his interviews about the issues he meant to raise in the film,
Lumet has said that all acts are in some sense political acts; all human
concerns are in some sense political concerns. We cannot understand
who we are if we attempt to divorce ourselves from the politics of our
time. Daniel begins his quest for knowledge as much out of guilt as
personal curiosity. He holds himself responsible for Susan's having
lost her way, so he seeks to find the answers that will shepherd her,
the truth about their parents that will allow them to live their own
lives. Such a quest is naive for a number of reasons. As Daniel quickly
discovers, the truth is neither discrete nor definitive. Daniel approaches the matter as a well-trained graduate student might, assuming dogged research and a keen analytic ability will give him the
answers he seeks, only to discover that the facts are largely lost. What
he uncovers instead are impermanent human truths, each colored by

the speaker who supplies them. Daniel is naive, too, in believing that he can save his sister from herself. There is a history of insanity in the family on Daniel's mother's side. Rochelle's mother lost her mind while Daniel was still a little boy. "She can't stand the pain of her life," Daniel's mother explained to him. At one point Daniel wonders if Susan is beyond his help. Susan's psychiatrist tries to tell Daniel that he and Susan are separate people living separate lives, that it isn't always possible to save someone, even if one tries. This lesson is lost on Daniel until the very end.

The information Daniel uncovers about his father speaks to this point, for Daniel discovers parallels between his father and himself, between his parents' marriage and his own. Paul Isaacson emerges as an ideologue caught up in the passions of his time, a first-generation American who—like many of his class and immigrant background—sought an antidote to the inequities of capitalism in the promises of socialism. The degree to which his ideology led him to fanaticism, and the extent to which he used Marxist beliefs to heal his own psychic sores, are issues only suggested. They become issues to Daniel, however. The first time we see Paul Isaacson he is a politically active student at City College of New York and is demonstrating in favor of unionization before the offices of the *New York Telegram.* Mounted police appear at the end of the block and move to clear the street at a leisurely pace. All the demonstrators but Paul Isaacson scatter. He beams at the sight of the approaching police. He carefully pockets his eyeglasses, steps forward into their path, yells "Cossack" at one mounted policeman in particular, then is summarily knocked to the ground. On leave at home from training as a radio operator during World War II, he is eager to see combat and join the Soviets in a second front. Apparently, he does not consider the risk to his young wife and infant child. Returning from a Paul Robeson concert with his wife, family, and assorted party members later in the film, Isaacson puts himself in jeopardy once again. Their bus is ambushed by a mob of rednecks armed with baseball bats. The driver succeeds in keeping the door closed, and the attackers at bay. While everyone else cowers, Isaacson hurries to the front of the bus, passes along his glasses to Dr. Mindish for safekeeping, and finally succeeds in getting out of the bus and into their hands. His is almost a religious fervor. Virtually everything can be seen as a lesson in socialism. Paul Isaacson instructs his children. A box of Wheaties is used to teach a lesson in social inequality based on racial discrimination. A tiresome ride in heavy traffic to the Coney Island beach is offered as proof that the end is justified, no matter how painful the means. Aside from his fervent socialism, Paul Isaacson is a bespectacled, somewhat stolid radio repairman in a working-class section of New York City. He only becomes animated when he can bring his ideology to bear on the issue at hand. He literally seems to grow in height and stature then, to become physically larger on the screen. This pattern comes to its climax near the end of the film as Paul is awaiting execution in prison. Susan and Daniel are brought to visit him. Their father is maniacal. Paul Isaacson is more like a caged beast than the children's loving father. Perhaps he is going mad. He seems to see himself as a political martyr of worldwide importance, a latter-day peasant whose life, like Joan of Arc's, will inspire the peasant class around the globe. At the beginning of the visit he seems to want to assuage his children's fears. Their father seems partly an ideologue, mouthing the party line, and partly a dutiful parent. But soon his speech is staccato, disjointed. The more he speaks the less aware he becomes of the children.

Early in the film, a young Daniel (Dan W. Mitchell-Smith) tells his mother that his father uses his politics to dominate and hurt her. Daniel seems to have made a similar marriage. Daniel has picked a wife who will be subservient to him, who will accept his point of view as her own, and for much of the film, he is virtually oblivious to his own son. His wife says about Daniel what Daniel said about his father: that he works out his frustrations and fears by mistreating her. Daniel's quest to find the truth about his parents also borders on fanaticism. He, too, grows larger before our eyes, physically dominating more of the situations as the investigation proceeds.

Daniel's relationship with his wife grows warmer near the film's conclusion, suggesting that Daniel now understands the mistakes his father made and is trying his best to keep from repeating them, thus breaking free of the hold of the past. One of the most striking cinematic sequences comes in a flashback to the "FREE THEM" rally mounted on behalf of the Isaacsons after their arrest. Ascher brings young Daniel and his toddler sister (Jena Greco) to the rally to be put on display. They are being used by the organizers to heighten the sympathies of the crowd. Daniel is barely old enough to understand the rally's purpose, and Susan seems to have no idea at all. They see only a threatening mob. The children arrive with Ascher near the back of the crowd. To get them to the speaker's platform at front, they are passed along hand to hand over the heads of the sea of people. Posters of the Isaacsons, marked "FREE THEM" (the same poster Susan will leave in her car for Daniel when she tries to commit suicide) are in the crowd. Daniel and his sister are frightened, helpless. Daniel tries to remain brave. Susan screams out his name repeatedly. As they are passed, a chant begins of "Free Them, Free Them," meaning, of course, the Isaacsons; but the visual effect is to make the words refer to the children. They seem caught in a tide that pulls them forward against their own will. This motif is developed visually in a number of ways, one of which is the curious composition of the extreme close-up that begins the film. Virtually all Daniel's features, except for his eyes, are hidden. This gives one the sense of a mask, perhaps a cowl with only the eyes left exposed. Lumet achieves much this same effect near the film's end. As Paul and Rochelle Isaacson are executed, they are hooded, leaving only their eyes visible. Their executioners finally close their cowls and pull the switch.

A rabbi is present in the execution chamber as Rochelle Isaacson is led to the electric chair. She sends the rabbi away. She says, "Let our deaths be [Daniel's] bar mitzvah." Unfortunately, this proves to be so, for Daniel's coming of age is directly linked to the fate of his parents. Assimilating, understanding, and putting to rest the lives of our parents are central to the film's final moments. Susan's meager funeral is intercut with a flashback of Daniel and Susan as children attending the elaborate service of their parents in the same cemetery. Together the two episodes show us Daniel burying his collective dead, and finally mourning them both, chanting his own form of kaddish, and beginning the process that can help set him free to find his own identity. This culminates in the final few shots of the film. Daniel leaves a university campus as a peace rally is beginning. He telephones his wife. She arrives with their child. After locating Daniel and his family in Central Park, the camera takes us above the crowd, then finally beyond it. The camera tilts upward. The last thing we see is blue sky, a frame of clear, unhampered expansion.

Daniel begins the film by assuming he can find himself independently from the political issues raised by the war in Vietnam, campus activism, racism, and the like. Susan begins with the opposite view, assuming she can only find her own identity through radical causes. The truth is surely somewhere in between. Daniel is not an organizer of the rally, much less a speaker. He has not gone to the barricades and put his safety on the line, as his sister might have done. He is with his wife and child, one young family amid thousands of others, but he is a participant. He is neither blindly carrying on the party line of his parents, nor is he acting out of guilt on his sister's behalf. Rather, he is someone beginning to make free choices about his own possibilities in the world in which he lives, and taking his rightful share of responsibility for the future.

RUNNING ON EMPTY (1988)

Lumet explores similar issues in *Running on Empty*. Here, too, identity is a central concern, and children are asked to carry the burden of their parents' lives. But here the distinction between fact and fiction is ostensibly clearer. As early as *Long Day's Journey* Lumet concerned himself with characters who insulated them from the harsh realities of their past and present, by creating a version of events that is easier to handle. In *Running on Empty* he explores the limits of that method, for Arthur and Annie Pope (Judd Hirsch, Christine Lahti) have created a series of fictive identities for themselves and their two sons, Danny (River Phoenix) and Harry (Jonas Abry), in an attempt to elude capture by the law.

As militant student radicals in the 1960s, intent on ending the war in Vietnam, Arthur and Annie blew up a laboratory where napalm was being manufactured, unaware that a janitor remained inside. Maiming the janitor, and blowing up the building, created a chain reaction that has determined the course of their lives, and the lives of their children. During the past 15 years they have moved from town to town, doing their best to blend in to modest, middle-class life. Supporting themselves primarily through low-visibility, menial work, with the periodic assistance of an underground network, the Popes change identities and homes with the frequency with which the rest of us might wear out our shoes. Life for them has become a series of castings off, of partings and flights. This point is made in the film's opening moments. Danny returns home on his bike from a baseball game. As he approaches his home and gets off the bike, he notices a government car that has driven up behind him. The car passes where Danny lives, moves toward an intersection, pauses, and turns around. A similar car appears across the way. Danny has been on the run since he was two. Clearly he has been through this before. He inspects his tire and chain as though he has only stopped here long enough to see if he has a mechanical problem. He rides away to a field where he disposes of the bike, circles around, and finally rushes through the tall grass toward his house from the rear. He calls the family dog, Jomo. He gives the dog his shoe and tells him to take it inside to Harry, Danny's younger brother. Soon Harry appears. He has Danny's shoe with him, and he is carrying Danny's practice keyboard for the piano as well. Harry takes Jomo. Danny takes the keyboard. They hurry away together to where their mother waits to pick up their father in a van. Arthur is involved in a grassroots effort to keep nuclear waste from being dumped in this Florida community. The two boys wait for their parents around the corner. The parents pick them up. Danny tells them what he has seen. They make no attempt to go back to the house and pick up their possessions. Even Jomo must go—he is put out of the van at the curbside, left to fend for himself.

We met the Popes in Central City, Florida. When we next find them they are in a northern Florida motel. Danny's hair had been dark in the first scenes of the film; here his mother dyes it blond. Danny's dark eyes are suddenly blue. Initially bearded, Arthur will leave the motel clean-shaven. A newspaper that Danny finds reports that the police are hot on the trail of these fugitives. A local television show carries word of their pursuit, as well as old photographs of Arthur and Annie. With the help of an underground network of political radicals, the family makes its way to Watertown, New Jersey. Using new names, the family sets up house. The boys are enrolled in school. Annie gets a job as a medical receptionist. Arthur gets a job as a cook in an Italian restaurant. Everyone gets a new set of clothes—most of which must come from secondhand stores. Too many new clothes on new people in the community might raise unwelcome questions. Chameleons, the Popes survive by blending in with their surroundings. Middle-class anonymity is the camouflage they need if their real identities are to go undetected.

This has served them well for some time, but now their 17-year-old son Danny has begun to separate himself from the family in order to seek his own place in the world. In his new school, for instance, he lets his music teacher Mr. Phillips (Ed Crowley) know that he is a gifted pianist. Phillips takes an immediate interest in Danny, inviting him to use the piano at his house when he learns Danny has none at his own. At the Phillips house, Danny meets his teacher's daughter, Lorna (Martha Plimpton). The two are immediately attracted to one another. A student in the school where her father teaches, she has sought an identity apart from his, casting herself in the role of an outsider. Danny, who has spent his life casting himself in the role of the insider, is a perfect foil. Lorna invites Danny to play at a chamber music recital at her house the coming Saturday. Danny attends the recital over his father's objections. He knows there is truth in what his father has said, that he cannot risk drawing attention to himself and his family, and he avoids playing for the group. But it is not music alone that brought him there, is it also Lorna, and her stable home. She is also curious about Danny. She thinks there is something "phony" about Danny, perhaps even mysterious. One minute he is polite and formal; the next he is a clown, a bully, a maverick. She also notices that he refuses to talk about himself and avoids any topic of conversation that might invite a personal disclosure.

As Danny is taking the first steps toward trying to establish a future of his own, Arthur and Annie are reminded of their pasts. Gus Wynant (L. M. Kit Carson), a member of the radical underground's Liberation Army whom they have not seen in 12 years, arrives at the physician's office where Annie is employed, then follows her home. Gus tries to recruit Annie and Arthur for a bank robbery the Liberation Army is planning. Arthur wants no part of any armed robbery, and Annie wants no part of Gus's weathered ideology.

One critic compared Gus to the Japanese soldier who remained undiscovered in a New Guinea forest for 20 years after the end of World War II. When he was found, he thought the war was still on. That is true of Gus, as Annie tries to tell him. "The war's over," she says. What gives their lives meaning? For Annie, she has her children, certainly, and her marriage, apparently. But Gus? She sees that identity, or its lack, is an issue in both their lives. This is true of Arthur as well. He comes home drunk following the unwelcome arrival of Gus, demanding to be called by his own name, spewing out to anyone who will listen the social security and draft card numbers of Arthur Eli Pope. Most immediately, though, identity is an issue to Danny. In adolescence, when few of us know who we are, Danny's dilemma is particularly troubling. Like his parents, his life is a thin veneer of constantly changing lies. Lorna wants to know more about him, as does her father. Danny is the most gifted music student her father has ever taught, and he urges Danny to seek admission to Julliard. But there is a problem, Phillips discovers. Julliard will not consider applicants whose high school transcripts are not up to date. A check at the high school which Danny supposedly last attended has turned up nothing.

Danny's attempt to strike out on his own escalates when he brings Lorna to Annie's birthday party without warning. The Popes are an enclosed "unit," as Arthur says. They must be. To bring a stranger into their midst flies in the face of all the precautions taken to preserve their anonymity. But Danny's most dangerous act of defiance is confessing his identity, and his parents' identity, to Lorna. He explains that he cannot attend Julliard without putting his whole family in peril. Danny's confession is painful on a number of levels, for he is entrusting her with the most important covenant of life among the Popes. He is putting the Popes' fate in the hands of someone beyond their immediate family. Lorna sees Danny's pain from still another perspective, however. Danny's confession is pained because of what he owes to his family; Lorna asks him to question what his family owes him. Without telling his parents, Danny decides to accept an audition for admission to Julliard arranged by Lorna's father. He is admitted, but provisionally; there is still the matter of his incomplete transcripts. When Danny does nothing to supply them, Phillips meets with Annie and tries to enlist her help. This is the first she has heard of Danny's desire to go to Julliard, and she takes the matter to Arthur. Arthur refuses to hear of it. If Danny were to go to Julliard, they would never be able to see him again. Except for a few clandestine phone calls and momentary meetings in out-of-the-way locations, Danny would be lost to them forever. All the Popes have is each other, Arthur maintains.

Annie recognizes that Arthur is absolutely right, but she also sees another side to this. "Look what we're doing to these kids," she tells her husband. "They've been running their whole lives like criminals, and they didn't do anything. It isn't fair! . . . Danny's all grown up. We have to let him go." Without Arthur's knowledge, Annie arranges a meeting with her father (Steven Hill) in New York City. They have not been in contact with one another for some 14 years. Understandably, it is a strained reunion. About to separate herself from her children, she sees not just her own father but another parent as well, someone who was deeply hurt when his daughter disappeared from his life. Annie asks her father to take Danny into their home. She wants her father and mother to give him a place to live and support him through his musical studies. Annie wants for her son what her father wanted for her, for we learn that she has been Danny's primary music teacher; his talent is hers, and she was once headed toward Julliard. Ironically, Annie is asking her father to provide Danny with a life similar to the one she fled when she became a political revolutionary.

After some hesitation, her father agrees. But Arthur's reaction to the news that night is unyielding. He wants to "break camp" soon and move on. When Danny comes to him and asks to stay behind, Arthur means to stand firm. But his tone betrays him. Made frantic by the thought of losing his son, Arthur says, "I taught you we cannot break rank. A unit is only as good as its weakest link. We're a unit. I taught you all of this, don't you remember that?" Arthur's outburst reveals that his interests are at stake here, rather than Danny's. Arthur is rootless, homeless, forever adrift. Arthur's children are all he has left, for his life has been mitigated so often by so many changes of identity that the only firm sense of self he has is that of father, the leader of the "unit." This is what Danny tries to tell Lorna when the family discovers that it has to leave Watertown sooner than expected. During his visit to Annie's office, Gus stole a credit card from a patient's purse and used it to rent a car involved in a failed bank robbery. Gus escaped, but was later killed while heading back toward Watertown, apparently hoping to hide out with the Popes. The family hurriedly gathers what it can and agrees to meet at a campground near an entry to the New Jersey Turnpike. Danny seeks out Lorna at school in order to say goodbye to her. He explains that he cannot stay behind and go to Julliard, after what he has learned in his confrontation with his father. His father is falling apart, Danny says. Arthur needs his family to prop him up. Without his children, Arthur will not be able to keep up the endless flights and changes of identity that have become the Popes' way of life. Lorna urges Danny to think of himself, even at the expense of his loved ones. "Whole families break up," she sobs. "Why do you have to carry the burden of someone else's life?" Danny answers simply, "He's my father." But when Danny arrives at the campground, Arthur, Annie, and Harry go on without him. If a son owes something to his father, a father also owes something to his son, Arthur realizes. Freedom from parents is as much a birthright as parenting itself.

Danny's relationship to his parents is reflected in two scenes involving Arthur and Annie and their respective parents. Both scenes deal with how their parents have been affected by Arthur and Annie's decisions in life, and the responsibility the couple must bear for this. The scene with Annie comes late in the film as she meets with her father, in order to ask for his help, re-establishing (if only momentarily) ties that have been severed, salving wounds that have grown nearly fatal.

Arthur's scene comes much earlier, and is a key scene dramatically, for it explains why Arthur is so hard on Danny later on, so insistent upon his son's fidelity. Arthur is more vulnerable and lost than he appears to his family. The death of his mother, Sophie, pushes Arthur toward the brink of a life change. Early in the film Arthur stops in a city long enough to make contact with a member of the underground (Lynne Thigpen), who tells him that his mother died of cancer some weeks before. Pope was not told about this sooner because no one could risk contacting him. The meeting is brief, barely long enough for Pope to hand over the keys to the van he has been driving and accept the keys to another truck parked behind it. We watch in extreme long shot as the first vehicle drives away, exposing Pope leaning into the second, his body bent almost double with emotion. Later in bed he tells his wife about the news of his mother's death from cancer. We are now so close to him, and the camera is kept at such curious angles, that Annie's reactions are only partially available to us. Her reactions are important, for earlier in the evening Arthur had inexplicably browbeaten Danny about learning his new name and assuming his new identity convincingly. Arthur's invective had sullied the family's buoyant mood and apparently caused Annie to wonder what had gone wrong. Arthur says his mother died of a cancer a month earlier. "There's nothing left to go back to now," concludes Arthur. "There's only us and the boys. We're all that's left. We must—we have to hang on to each other." The street scene and the scene in bed together amount to less than three minutes of screen time, with less than a dozen camera placements in all. But the way Lumet handles these scenes cinematically is indicative of what bothered some of the film's reviewers.

Reviewing the film in the 19 September 1988 *New Yorker,* for instance, Terrence Rafferty wrote "There's not a moment in the movie that feels authentic, not a scene that isn't marred by some jarring detail of inept camera placement (the director's favorites seem to be extreme long shots and gigantic, pore-enlarging close-ups). . . ." The "inept" camera placements noted by Rafferty and other critics are perhaps most pronounced in those sequences in which the Pope family is photographed together. And while one might argue the camera placements lend an unauthentic quality to what we see, such inauthenticity underscores a central concern of the film. Consider the birthday party. The camera seems to be so close to the characters sitting around the table that it cannot hold them in view as a group. If characters get up from the table and move, they seem about to collide with each other or the furniture. The small dining room looks unnaturally shallow. Our vision of a character may be clumsily obscured by another character, or by some miscellaneous party ornament; characters at the periphery of Lumet's frame are in danger of slipping out of the frame entirely. Nothing appears balanced.

Of course, the party we witness is not what it seems, and Lumet reminds us of this. Lorna is present, and she is the only non-family member we ever see inside the Pope home. They can hardly afford to have anyone in their midst who might get to know them and later expose them. Danny is acting on his own when he invites Lorna without telling his mother and father; he is asserting himself. Danny is seeking a place for Lorna in his life, and to do that, he will have to find some place for her in the lives of his parents. There is no place for her in either case, of course. Danny knows that. So do the others. No one wants to confront that fact immediately, however. Birthdays are special events for the Popes, and no one wants to spoil the mood of the party; so, both literally and metaphorically, a place is made for Lorna at the Popes' table.

That Lorna's place in the lives of the Popes is only temporary is a point Lumet makes cinematically through his overcrowded frames, his apparent inability to find the proper visual balance between the characters sitting around the table. Lorna cannot be aware of this. Nor can we, judging by the action alone. Lorna seems to find her place among them rather well. But the cinematics of the scene tell us otherwise. They remind us of the disparity in the Popes' lives between appearance and reality. Lorna sees a middle-class household. She sees her new boyfriend's parents as a couple more free in spirit than her own mother and father. We see something else. Lorna's world and what it represents to Danny are matters Lumet handles through a different cinematic approach. Lorna's home is stable. She knows who her parents are. They have not changed since she was little. Over her protests, her father continues to walk through the door of her room unannounced—not because he is spying on her, but because to him she is still a child. She says they see in her what they want to see, not who she is. They see only as much as they want to see. Lorna says her parents approach all of the world with the same fixed set of values and judgments, learning only as much about people as suits their expectations.

Danny is as attracted to the stability and order of Lorna's home as he is to her, initially. After knocking and calling out, he lets himself

The Pope family celebrates in *Running on Empty*. The Museum of Modern Art/Film Stills Archive.

in the first time he visits there. Danny goes directly to the drawing room where he sits down at their grand piano. He assumes that the house is empty. For the moment, he makes it his own. He plays Brahms as he has practiced it on his keyboard. He is sitting before a concert-quality Steinway now. There is delight in his face, not the anguished concentration we have previously witnessed when we've seen him at home. Here things have a more proper dimension: strike the right keys and the right sound emerges. One of the first things he notices about the Phillips' house is the display of family photographs. Danny asks Lorna if the little girl in the pink dress is her. It is just the kind of question Danny might logically ask. One would not find such photographs in his own home. With hurried escape always hanging over their heads, the risk that someone might find the photographs is too great.

Danny seeks the same sense of stability and order in music that he seeks through Lorna and her world, and Lumet often photographs scenes that deal with these matters accordingly. The scenes with Danny at the piano (as opposed to his keyboard) are photographed in ways that carefully define spatial planes and organize the elements we see to make use of them. The first of these comes after Danny has distinguished himself in Phillips's music class during his first day at a new school. He has recognized a passage of Beethoven and helped to distinguish rhythmic repetitions in Madonna's popular song, "Lucky Star" from the metrical inconsistencies of Beethoven's work. This is an appropriate distinction to have Danny make. Danny is as familiar with inconsistencies and variations on a theme as the rest of the class is with life's formal patterns. Danny proves to be more than a well-tutored student, however. Later, he comes to Phillips's classroom and is put before the piano. The camera puts us at long shot range to the action. There are two distinct visual planes. Phillips is working at his desk in the distance, while Danny is in the foreground at the piano. As Danny begins to play, the camera cuts to his hands gently touching the keys of the piano. Gradually the camera rises, putting Danny's face and torso in view, then slowly moves back and to the left. Without a cut, Phillips moves into the frame from screen-left. He blocks our view of Danny. The camera then follows Phillips as he moves screen-right toward the chairs where the pupils normally sit. Phillips sits and listens attentively to the music. As the passage Danny is playing nears completion, Phillips rises and heads toward the piano. Danny reenters the center of the frame as Phillips leans against the piano's corner, frame-right. Danny then breaks into a bluesy riff. Danny raises his eyes. He wants to learn how this will be received. Phillips's nodding says it all.

Lumet makes use of similar spatial distinctions when Danny goes to the Phillips house for the first time. In a take that lasts more than a minute, the camera follows Danny into the house then to his left where he enters a drawing room filled with antiques. The Phillips's Steinway is the centerpiece of the room, and Danny goes directly to it. He sits down and begins to play Brahms. The camera remains in the entrance to the room until Danny begins to play, then it comes forward. This seems to be the same pattern of camera work we have seen at school, but the film cuts to Lorna upstairs. Lorna has been listening to rock-and-roll using earphones. Taking them off, she hears the Brahms below. She comes downstairs. The camera returns to the drawing room. Lumet positions it behind her left shoulder. Like her father before her, Lorna enters the frame in response to Danny's playing, then the two characters are seen together. Danny has felt the presence of someone behind him, and he stops playing. Once again, there are two distinct visual planes.

Lumet tends to use such patterns when photographing Danny apart from his family. In these scenes, the moving camera generally works to keep elements balanced in the frame, to compose and recompose as Danny takes his place alongside others. Music is all he has to put his life in proper perspective. Within the script, Lorna will offer permanence amid change, passion amid fear and dread. The camera tends to reflect this, for some of the same camera patterns associated with Danny at the piano appear when Danny and Lorna are together.

There is certainly a sense of inauthenticity to be found in the film, but whether this is due to Lumet's ineptness as a director is subject to debate. Nothing in the Pope household is real. Everything can be cast off at any moment. The Popes call each other by their newly assumed names throughout the film; hardly any discussion of their pasts is allowed. Fearing a mistake outside their home, they often play the roles they have assumed over dinner as they might at work or at school. Danny is not allowed to have his picture taken with the rest of the class. The Popes cannot afford an easily traceable record. "Sam" is the only name they allow themselves to carry from place to place. It is the one thing they can salvage beyond themselves with each move they make, and it is the name that appears on Annie's birthday cake. When she tries to break the news of Danny's application to Julliard to Arthur, he begins the conversation by calling her "Sam" and she braces: "Don't call me that," she snaps. Dramatically, it is the right response, for Annie realizes what their way of life has done to her son, how it may entrap him just as she and her husband find themselves entrapped. Danny does not even have a complete set of school records. Everything has had to be falsified. When Lorna demands to know late in the film who Danny is, his admission is telling. "I'm a liar," he says. "My name isn't Michael. It's Danny. My parents are Arthur and Annie Pope. They're in trouble with the FBI. . . . I've been doing this since I was two. I don't know any other way." Significantly, when Danny's true identity is demanded, he can only confess who he isn't, and who his parents are.

Q & A (1990)

Q & A begins late at night in Upper Manhattan in a Latino ghetto outside the After Hours Social Club. It is a Members Only club, a common strategy to circumvent state liquor laws that require a standard curfew. We watch from overhead as Lt. Mike Brennan (Nick Nolte) leads a slight Hispanic man, Roger Montalvo (Paul Calderon) toward the club's entrance, then pushes him inside. Soon the same man comes out, hurrying away. Brennan has situated himself behind the door. A second man follows, pursuing Montalvo apparently. This is Tony Vasquez (Harry Madsen). Montalvo is gone by the time Vasquez gets out on the sidewalk. As he turns to go back inside, Brennan steps out of the shadows, shoots Vasquez squarely between the eyes, then proceeds to plant a gun on his person, to corral witnesses from the club who have emerged upon hearing the gunfire. Brennan identifies himself as the police.

A young assistant district attorney, Al Reilly (Timothy Hutton) is awakened in the middle of the night by a call from Kevin Quinn (Patrick O'Neal), chief of the Homicide Bureau, Office of the District Attorney, County of New York. This is to be Reilly's first case as a member of the district attorney's office. Formerly a police patrolman working in Harlem, he has gone to Brooklyn College Law School at night and has only recently assumed his post. Quinn says that he has asked for Reilly by name. When he arrives at Quinn's office, we learn more about Reilly, and why he may have been chosen over those with more experience. Reilly is the son of a police force veteran, a hero killed in the line of duty; like Quinn, he is Irish-Catholic. Quinn braces when Reilly recalls his tour in Harlem with a note of sympathy for its residents, and Reilly notices. But for Reilly, Quinn's response is easily dismissed. Quinn apparently is tough but fair. And Quinn is willing to overlook Reilly's sympathies as well. "Your father was everything the police department used to be," Quinn tells him. "He was part of a tradition that had been built by our people [the Irish], a tradition that justified the use of those words 'the finest.' That's why I brought you in here. I want to hold on to those values, and the people who reflect them." The investigation he wants Reilly to conduct follows from the movie's first scene. It is "a classic case of justifiable homicide," Quinn assure Reilly. A drug dealer, Tony Vasquez—"a piece of vermin," Quinn calls him—has been shot in self-defense by Lt. Brennan, an Irish-American like themselves.

We are reminded of the After Hours Club, a means of staying just inside the boundaries of the law. Clearly Quinn is coaching Reilly here, telling him that he wants a thorough and impartial investigation that will find Mike Brennan innocent. The Q & A of the film's title refer to the formal, stenographic transcription of questions and answers that produce an evidentiary record to be sent on to the grand jury. Reilly is intimidated by Quinn, in awe of him. He is quick to do as he is told. He asks Brennan only enough questions to elicit a statement. Brennan says he was investigating the murder of Julio Sierra, an associate of Vasquez in the drug world. Vasquez drew a 45-caliber automatic on Brennan. Brennan defended himself. The weapon turns out to be the same gun used to murder Sierra.

The first note of doubt is introduced into Reilly's case over lunch with Blumenfeld (Lee Richardson), an aging associate on the district attorney's staff. Blumenfeld has known Quinn since Quinn was trying his first cases. Quinn is ambitious, Blumenfeld warns Reilly, and worse, bloodthirsty, a bigot. Touted as an able prosecutor, Quinn's record of convictions is at least partially attributable to the fact he has the heart of a killer. Blumenfeld goes on to discuss the Vasquez case. Vasquez was well known to Blumenfeld. He would never have carried a 45 automatic, Blumenfeld maintains. It had to be a plant. Reilly listens with interest, but he is hardly convinced. The matter of the gun is raised again by another party, however. Two policemen have been assigned to help Reilly, one Puerto Rican, Luis Valentine (Luis Guzman), the other black, Sam "Chappie" Chapman (Charles Dutton). Reilly has left much of the legwork to them, but there are three witnesses who were in the club that night whom he wants to interview personally: Larry Pesch (Dominick Chianese), a well-known mafioso, Bobby Texador (Armand Assante), a Puerto Rican drug lord, and Texador's common-law wife, Nancy Bosch (Jenny Lumet). Pesch is a likely choice, since Vasquez was a drug dealer and the drugs in Spanish Harlem are known to come from the mafia. Texador is less likely. It is Nancy Bosch's name that has caught Reilly's attention. He once planned to marry her.

As Reilly takes their statements, Valentine and Chapman are present as well, and when Valentine and Texador get into a heated confrontation, Texador, in anger, corroborates the statement Blumenfeld made in disgust: Vasquez never carried a 45 automatic in his life; Brennan surely planted it there. As Chapman reminds Reilly, this is not the sort of formal testimony Quinn is apt to welcome. Now part of the official transcript, it is a charge that will have to be explored. Chapman, a longtime colleague of Brennan's, as well as a fellow veteran of the Marines, is angry. Chapman is loyal to Brennan, admires him, and is also in his debt. Brennan once saved Chapman's life. Valentine is not as certain as Chapman that Texador should be ignored. Valentine has known Texador all his life. They grew up together in the Puerto Rican projects. As boys 20 years ago, Texador, Vasquez, and Sierra were all members of the Sinners, a Latino gang. As gang members trying to cut into the criminal activities of the Italian mafia, they first found their place in big-league crime. Valentine says that it does not make sense that Vasquez would have killed Sierra, even though all the evidence seems to prove that. Vasquez and Sierra were too close for too long. Their loyalties to one another were too strong.

The closest they have to an eyewitness is Roger "The Dodger" Montalvo, a small-time informant and junkie. But Montalvo has disappeared. Upon learning of Texador's testimony, both Brennan and Quinn realize Reilly's investigation is not going as planned. Quinn scolds Reilly, telling him it is too late to have the charge expunged. Reilly will simply have to work around it before the grand jury. Less trusting than Quinn, Brennan puts word out on the street that he is looking for Montalvo himself, that he wants to find Montalvo before the investigators do. The reintroduction of Nancy Bosch into his life has given Reilly pause. She walked out on him carrying his baby (which she later aborted) when she saw his reaction to learning of her father's race. Reilly had assumed she was hispanic, but in fact she is the daughter of a Puerto Rican mother and a black father. Brennan is racist, a bigot, perhaps psychotic, but his prejudices are only extensions of those Reilly is encountering at every turn of the case. The assumption among the police is not simply that Brennan is too good a cop to be indicted, but also that the lives of a couple of Puerto Rican drug dealers are of no consequence to anyone. Brennan makes the mistake of confiding in Reilly. He virtually confesses to killing Sierra, then killing Vasquez in a way that would provide evidence enough to close the case. Reilly's father was something of a hero to Brennan, apparently. Brennan assumes that Reilly is of the same stock. He also knows that as a patrolman Reilly was partnered with Moon Mullins, someone widely known to be corrupt. Reilly, he assumes, is also compromised. Reilly will surely understand what life is like on the street.

Convinced after their conversation that he cannot depend on Reilly, Brennan sets off on his own. He seeks out Chapman and asks that Montalvo be turned over to him rather than taken in for questioning. Brennan seeks out Valentine next, first threatening him, then putting a 10,000 dollar bounty on Montalvo's head. When Reilly learns of Brennan's attempt to subvert the investigation, he goes to see Blumenfeld. Clearly desperate, Brennan is turning into a rogue cop, he tells Blumenfeld. Earlier in the film, as Reilly tries to woo Nancy away from Texador, she says, "Whatever he is and whatever he does he's a hell of a lot more honorable than you are. He is what he is, but he has one face not two and he's color-blind." As Reilly's investigation continues, her words take on more meaning, for Reilly discovers in himself the same duplicity he sees in others. But her words are true on a larger scale as well. Despite what Reilly has learned about corruption and crime while a patrolman in Harlem, he has begun his career in the district attorney's office too naive about people like Quinn. There is duplicity and corruption at every level, from the lowest street junkies to the mafia drug lords, from the most meager of patrolmen to the upper echelons of powerful political officials.

Reilly's investigation takes him back to Texador. Having named Brennan in his formal statement, Texador must now protect himself, for Brennan, Texador knows, would not have a second thought about killing him. Texador imports two bodyguards, Armand and Alfonso Segal (Martin E. Brens, Gustavo Brens), two Sephardic Jews from Cuba. Their appearance draws the attention of his mafia drug suppliers, and a mafia delegate (John Capodice) is sent to tell Texador not to harm Brennan. Brennan apparently has mafia ties of his own. Texador is to leave town. Texador does as he has been told. He, his wife, and bodyguards leave for a vacation in San Juan, Puerto Rico, planning to remain there until tensions on the street diminish. But before they leave for San Juan, Texador is contacted by Roger Montalvo's transvestite lover, José Malpica (International Chrysis), who takes him to Montalvo. Montalvo is afraid of Brennan as well. In return for the promise of Texador's protection, Montalvo confesses to his role in the killing of Vasquez, and more. Brennan has used Montalvo in killing two of the three surviving members of the Sinners. Clearly, Texador is to be the third. From Puerto Rico, Texador sends for Reilly, promising information that will not only serve Reilly's case against Brennan, but also tie Quinn directly to the killings. In San Juan, Reilly learns from Texador that as a boy Quinn was sometimes in league with the Sinners. He was well known as a "shooter." Texador and the others saw him gun down a boy some years before; it is Quinn, not Brennan, who has been behind the recent murders. About to run for public office, Quinn is doing his best to eliminate the witnesses that remain. Reilly reasons that Quinn must be blackmailing Brennan to get him to do as Quinn wants.

In the meantime, Brennan has gone to the godfather of the mafia, Nick Petrano (Leonard Cimino). Brennan has served the mafia as well as the police during his career, and he threatens to expose their operations unless Texador is killed before testifying against him. Petrano grants him his wish, instructing Larry Pesch to carry it out. Pesch flies to San Juan with two assassins, but Texador's bodyguards kill them both before an attempt can be made on Texador's life. Texador sends Pesch back to Petrano with word that Texador is on his own now: Bobby Texador wants out of the business. Brennan has come no closer to finding Montalvo in New York City than his lover, José, whom Brennan strangles. Before killing José, Brennan has learned that Montalvo is in Puerto Rico, apparently under Texador's wing. Brennan follows Reilly, Valentine, and a third policeman, Detective Zucker (Maurice Schell)—known as "The Virgin" since he has not had to fire his gun in 18 years as a policeman—to San Juan. Shortly after Reilly learns of Quinn's role in the killings and heads back to New York City, Brennan locates Roger Montalvo aboard a yacht Texador keeps moored at a slip. Brennan uses Montalvo to lure Texador out of his hotel suite, then strangles Montalvo, as he strangled José. When Texador comes aboard with one of his bodyguards to see what Montalvo needs, Brennan sets off an explosion that kills both Texador and his protector.

The most senior members of the district attorney's staff have been called into the case by the time Brennan returns to New York City. The police are waiting for Brennan at the airport, prepared to apprehend him. Members of the district attorney's staff think they have uncovered what Quinn has been using to blackmail Brennan. It was the first case Quinn tried. Brennan killed a 16-year-old in Harlem. The "Q & A" that might have convicted Brennan conveniently disappeared. Brennan manages to elude the police at the airport and goes directly to Al Reilly's office. Brennan is so severely deranged by this point that he is practically a wild animal. But this is not a film about one rogue cop, as Lumet reminds us in Brennan's climactic speech. Brennan is only the personification of deeper evils all around us.

> "You're not the man your father was, Al," [he says to Reilly]. "You sidin' with the shoo-flies and the rats. You don't love cops right."
> "I love my father, Mike," [Reilly answers].
> "Right. You just love the idea of your father. Your father was dirty. Your father was dirty as they come. Nothin' big, just penny-ante stuff.

You know, free meals, a place to go. For a while he was a bag man. . . . He took home 100, 150 a week, that's all. But Al, what a cop! I mean, like me, he was the first through the door, the window, the skylight. I mean he knew there was animals out there. He knew there was a line that the niggers, the spicks, the junkies, the faggots had to cross to get into people's fronts. He was that line. *I* am that line. Your fuckin' judges and Jew lawyers, the alderman, the guinea D. A.'s are rakin' it in now. And we take a fuckin' hamburger and it's goodbye badge, gun, and pension. And all the time it's our life that's on the line, and our widows and our orphans."

Reilly's life is saved by Chapman, who intercedes. Brennan shoots Chapman, perhaps fatally, and then dies in a shootout, killed, ironically, by "The Virgin."

At the film's conclusion, Reilly returns to Quinn's office, then Blumenfeld's. After all that he has learned, Reilly assumes he has the upper hand in the interview with Quinn. Quinn knows better. Texador, the last remaining Sinner, is dead. Brennan is dead as well. There is nothing that immediately links Quinn to anything illegal. Reilly assumes this is only bravado on Quinn's part. Later, Blumenfeld assures Reilly it is not. Early in the film Blumenfeld has told Reilly that they are fundamentally alike. Both Blumenfeld and Reilly think it is important to make a positive difference in the world. What separates them is experience, says Blumenfeld, and he has reached the point where he doubts that anyone can make a positive difference. The corruption has spread too far in our society. No individual, no single group of individuals, can do anything positive of substance. In their first meeting in the film, Blumenfeld tells Reilly that he hopes "they [Quinn and other political officials] don't break your heart." In their last meeting, Reilly goes over the evidence they have against Quinn with Blumenfeld. Blumenfeld assures him that the evidence against Quinn will be buried, including any "Q & A" that might be of use. That is the way power works. "You're breakin' my heart, Blumy," says Reilly. "It's a dirty job," answers Blumenfeld, "but somebody's got to do it."

The denouement of the film finds Reilly traveling to a Caribbean island in the hope of being reunited with Nancy Bosch. Reilly is smarter about himself than he was when the case began, and many times smarter about himself than when he let her walk out of his life six years earlier. "I know I have to fight back," he has said earlier. "I just don't know how to start." "Maybe," he says in the film's closing line, "I just got to start with myself."

The final shot of the film finds Reilly sitting beside Nancy on an empty beach looking out toward the ocean, his life apparently about to take a sea change. Water is one of the ongoing motifs of the movie. The film begins on the murky, green, rain-soaked streets of upper Park Avenue, and ends with images of the azure blues of the Caribbean Ocean. For miles, there is nothing to impede Reilly's vision, nothing to distract him. Here, Reilly can see clearly, we are to understand. This is in contrast to earlier work in Q & A. The opening credits do not appear until Reilly has taken the call from Quinn, dressed, and entered the backseat of the squad car Quinn has sent for him. The credits are superimposed on images of the car ride that takes Reilly to Quinn's office. In a well-edited sequence by Richard Cirincione, we travel with Reilly through the wet streets, seeing them from Reilly's point of view. From the backseat of the car we look through the splattered windshield as its wipers struggle against the downpour to clear a field of vision. Reilly's vision, like our own, is periodically blurred, a foreshadowing of what we will find as he begins his first case for Quinn.

Following Brennan's death, Quinn places a late night phone call to Reilly, demanding to see Reilly in his office within the hour. The sequence is meant to parallel the film's opening. The camera is positioned in the same place beside Reilly's bed as he picks up the phone; the dialogue is similar. Again, Reilly rides in the back of a squad car late at night through the streets of New York City in the rain, and we see what he sees, nearly empty streets in a downpour as windshield wipers struggle to clear a field of vision. Again, it is an appropriate image. Reilly is bruised and battered, no longer the fresh-faced boy he was. But he is still naive. Quinn knows how power works in this world, that he will get off scot-free, even if Reilly believes otherwise. It is only after Reilly's subsequent interview with Blumenfeld that he finally understands where he must begin if he intends to change the world around him, an interview that will lead him to a beach in the Caribbean.

Many of the camera patterns Lumet employs in Q & A are variations on his earlier work: the moving camera that recomposes within the frame; a tracking camera that leaves one character to follow another as he or she comes into frame; the use of the camera's vertical plane to put walls, ceilings, and other impediments in our field of vision, as the protagonist becomes entangled in a web of conflicting circumstances; and changing the focal length of the lenses to expand and compress space in ways that serve the story line. One of the most interesting patterns to be found in Lumet's lensplot in *Q & A* harkens back to *Twelve Angry Men*. As E. G. Marshall set out his case against the defendant, the camera gradually increased its focal length, eliminating other characters from the frame, a compositional technique to be found in many of Lumet's films since. Lumet uses a variation of this technique in *Q & A*. The first time we see it is during Brennan's initial statement to Reilly as a "Q & A" begins. Brennan sits sprawled in a chair; Reilly is standing across from him. This will be one of the few times in the film when Reilly seems to be looking down at Brennan—normally the opposite is true. But Brennan is not intimidated by Reilly or his questions. He has been through this sort of thing before. He is well rehearsed. He can see Quinn stretched out on a couch behind Reilly. He assumes everything is in order. As Brennan tells of investigating Sierra's murder and his fatal confrontation with Tony Vasquez, the focal length gradually increases. Reilly is sitting on the edge of a table. Two policemen sit at the table between Brennan and Reilly. The camera begins behind Reilly's shoulder and to the left. Gradually we are brought closer to Brennan as he speaks. We have seen the crime committed in the film's opening moments. We know that he is lying, that his account does not square with what we have seen. As peripheral characters are eliminated from the frame, we are left with Brennan. The sequence takes roughly two minutes. It is punctuated by three brief cutaway shots, the longest two seconds in length. These cutaways take us to Valentine, who looks suspicious; to Quinn, who smiles at the bravado with which Brennan is performing; and to Chapman, who has to avert his eyes to keep from smirking at such a show of gall. This pattern is not used again until the penultimate minutes of the film when Reilly goes to Blumenfeld's office following his interview with Quinn. Blumenfeld is positioned screen-left in a chair behind his desk; Reilly is sitting on a couch screen-right. The camera is centered between them and will take us from long-range to close-up. As Blumenfeld explains to Reilly that without Texador, Montalvo, and Brennan he has no case against Quinn, the film cuts between two slow zooms, one approaching Blumenfeld's face, the other approaching Reilly's. As we approach Blumenfeld, he tells Reilly that the evidence against Quinn will be burned or buried, and that he will take part in that process. He explains that nothing is to be gained by doing otherwise. The compositional pattern associates Blumenfeld's position with Brennan's earlier testimony, for the camera seems to be assigning guilt in both instances. Of course, the camera is also singling out Reilly, whose expressions suggest his shock at Blumenfeld's being part of a cover-up. But Reilly is more like his mentor here than he seems to acknowledge. Neither he nor Blumenfeld is able to see that justice is done. He is no more willing to risk himself than Blumenfeld is willing to rock the boat unnecessarily. For both, it would be pointless and accomplish very little.

In *Q & A,* Lumet was working once again with cinematographer Andrzej Bartkowiak. He had worked with him regularly throughout the previous decade on such films as *The Verdict, Daniel, Power, Garbo Talks,* and *Family Business.* Bartkowiak is a color specialist, a cinematographer with a growing reputation for color effects. The muted reds, browns, and yellows in the Paul and Rochelle Isaacson section of *Daniel* are one example. The color effects achieved in this film are also of interest. Whites, off-whites, eggshells, ambers, grays, tans, and browns dominate the film. Here the colors might be called noncolors, for the grays, tans, and browns blend together. Primary colors (bright reds and greens, for example) predominate only when the action takes place in the Latino club at Broadway and Ninety-second Street, the "San Juan Hill" section of Upper Manhattan where Valentine lives, the gay bars and transvestite clubs. The opening sequence of the film is shot late at night in the rain. We are high above the After Hours Club, apparently across the street from it, looking down on Mike Brennan taking Roger Montalvo by the arm. A traffic light is in our line of vision. Its green glow casts a green patina across the wet street that extends to the buildings. Since it is night and natural light is absent, the green is thick and dark. Algaelike, it reminds us perhaps of pond scum, or the fauna found at the edge of swamps. Only when the doors of the club are thrown open in response to gunfire, do red and orange hues come on-screen, and then only momentarily. The camera cuts to a close-up of the badge that Brennan has pulled from his pocket. Inexplicably, we seem to see it from a perspective that puts that same traffic light in our line of vision. But now the light has turned red.

Reilly's apartment is new to him, still largely unfurnished. Beside his bed sits a lone white light. His home is virtually without color. We move from his world to the office of Kevin Quinn. There, save a red book he has open before him, the only true colors are the red, white, and blue of the flag behind his desk. This is true once again as Reilly prepares to take Brennan's initial statement. The only color is the blue of an occasional police uniform, but thanks to Bartkowiak's photography, the blues lose their hue. The initial effect of this, both here and throughout, is to make us think that Lumet is painting from a dull palette, but the net effect gives one the impression of a color-blindness, which counterpoints what we hear.

No one is color-blind in a figural sense. The color of skin, religion, parentage, all affect how one is perceived. "Jesus Christ," Brennan says with his dying breaths, "taken out by a virgin hebe." The line is symptomatic of what Reilly encounters in the course of his investigation. A Jew is a "hebe," "a matzah eater," a "hymie"; an Italian is a "wop," a "guinea cocksucker"; a Puerto Rican is a "spick," a "p.r.," a "nigger with straight hair," a "rice-and-beaner"; a black is a "watermelon-eating jungle bunny," a "coon," a "nigger," a "night fighter"; an Oriental is a "chink"; homosexuals are "faggots," "fags," "cocksuckers"; a Caucasian is "white-bread," a "honky." Such prejudice is present among the junkies, the police, the members of the district attorney's office, and the mafia. One minute we are sitting with Quinn and his political cronies in the stately Montauk Club as he plans his campaign for attorney general. An extensive demographic analysis of voters has shown that a ticket with a Jew, an Italian, and an Irishman stands the best chance of getting into office, that ethnic loyalties, though perhaps no longer acceptable to speak of in public, inform the voters' choices. In the hands of a good demographer, all of New York State can be understood through its ethnic divisions. In the hands of a good politician, racial prejudices are easily tapped. Despite a difference in tone, this is not far removed from what we find in the underworld. Ushering Brennan out of his palatial home after agreeing to have Texador killed, mafia don Nick Petrano says, "It's not like the old days. Now we got spicks and niggers mixed up with everything. With us. With the police force. Detectives. Inspectors. It's gotten so when you get to the crime scene you don't know who to shoot. . . . You see what happens when you go outside your own?"

Thus, Lumet connects personal to institutional failings, individual responsibility to the culture we have created. The street thugs in Harlem are "fucking animals," Brennan tells Reilly. "It's all coming apart, Al. I want it the way it use to be. . . . You lose fucking control in this jungle and you're finished." But coming from Brennan's mouth, this seems less a statement about crime in Upper Manhattan than a metaphor for what is happening to Brennan psychologically; Brennan, too, is coming apart. He, too, is losing control.

Al Reilly is like so many of Lumet's characters: for at least the first half of the film, he puts too much faith in the system, in simple divisions between innocence and guilt, crime and commensurate punishment. Brennan nicknames Reilly "the choir boy." Nancy reminds him of his strict Catholic upbringing. He is investigating the deaths of two Sinners. All of this fits his character. Reilly is reminiscent of Danny Ciello since he, too, trusts the magic of a darkened confessional too much. But Reilly gets further than many of Lumet's earlier protagonists, as his revelations about himself and the harsh realities of the world around lead to a positive—if only personal—step toward restitution. Reilly is not broken like Ciello, nor is he a fugitive seeking asylum like Serpico. He is not simply isolated from the group at large, like so many of Lumet's earlier protagonists; nor is he simply struggling to find the right penance. Like Emily Eden in Lumet's next film, *A Stranger among Us,* and like Daniel Isaacson and Danny Pope before him, Reilly can identify (if only tentatively) a point from which to begin to gain control of his life.

A STRANGER AMONG US (1992)

Like *Q & A, A Stranger among Us* is a police film shot on location in New York City, primarily the Diamond District on West Forty-seventh Street and the Ridgewood section of Queens, with special attention paid to the Eldridge Street Synagogue on the Lower East Side of Manhattan and the Park Slope Jewish Center. Again, the protagonist is a young Irish-American, a second-generation police officer. Emily Eden (Melanie Griffith) is a New York City police detective who enters the closed and cloistered world of the city's Hasidic community, when she responds to a missing persons report that soon leads her to a murder investigation.

The opening montage of the film reminds us that Manhattan is an island unto itself, and the same is true for Eden. Although still a young woman, Eden seems weathered. To survive in New York City as a police officer, she has had to insulate herself emotionally from the corruption and human tragedy she witnesses daily. Since graduation from the police academy, she has been partnered with Nick (Jamey

Sheridan), who is periodically her sexual partner (although not precisely her lover), as well as her comrade-in-arms. Eden has shut herself off from the possibilities of love. She feels close to no one. She is known as a "rogue cop," a "cowboy." None of the other police officers is eager to work with her, for Eden is known to be a danger to herself and to others. Nick has found his place in her world by letting her lead the way. ("You made the rules," he tells her later as the two prepare to part. "You called the plays.") She takes orders reluctantly. She puts her full trust in no one, not even Nick. This independence is epitomized by her unwillingness to call for backup help during the first arrest we watch her make. After waiting outside a movie theater late at night, Nick and Emily move in to apprehend two suspects about to hold up the cashier behind the ticket window. As the arrest is made, one of the suspects stabs Nick with a knife. The fleeing suspect gets only a few feet away before Emily guns him down. Emily's superior, Lt. Oliver (David Marguiles), later asks Emily why she did not call for backup protection. She says she thought she and Nick could handle the situation alone. Oliver has worked with her too long to accept that. He says, "No, you thought *you* could handle it by *your*self. We've got 27,300 police officers in this city. Isn't there anybody you trust? What are you trying to prove?"

Emily feels responsible for what happened to Nick, and she's partially right. From his hospital bed, the severely wounded Nick calls Emily a cowboy, and she says, "Yeah, Calamity Jane." She is not far wrong. Her life is approaching the point where it will indeed become calamitous. The daughter of a retired police officer (Burtt Harris), a cold, embittered, angry man, incapable of love or any normal human ties, Emily has become a police officer in an attempt to gain her father's love. She has adopted his swagger, his bearing, even his salutation; repeatedly she greets people with his favorite line, "So what's new and exciting?" Emily's drive to be as rugged as any man in the police force is really an attempt to be a lovable daughter; and as the film begins, she is paying the price. Her independent stance is really a way of explaining away her loneliness; her aggressive police work is little more than a way of venting her furies. Unconsciously, perhaps semiconsciously, she has begun to look for law enforcement situations in which she will have reason to draw her weapon. She may even be seeking situations in which her own life is at risk. When Lt. Oliver offers Eden some time off, she asks to work instead. Later in the film, while Nick is recuperating, she is partnered with Levine, played by

John Pankow. Levine knows her. In order to persuade Eden to sleep with him, Levine argues not that he is sexually attractive, but rather that he is an efficient police officer, "an insanely great cop," as he puts it. Such responses to Eden are apropos. Emily's life is her work. Her relationship with Nick, someone she can embrace sexually but also keep at arm's length, is the closest thing she has to a meaningful relationship with a man.

The only case Oliver has available is that of Yaakov Klausman (Jake Weber), the son of a Hasidic diamond merchant who has been missing from his parents' home for 48 hours. We have met Yaakov Klausman earlier, if only incidentally. The film's opening sequences alternate between scenes of Emily and Nick on their stakeout and scenes of the Hasidic community—Ariel (Eric Thal) instructing children in Hebrew at a heder, religious services led by Ariel and his stepfather, the Rebbe (Lee Richardson), religious study during which Ariel is approached by his best friend Yaakov Klausman and asked for advice. Ariel is wise beyond his years and Yaakov wants to know if Ariel thinks he should marry Mara (Tracy Pollan), a troubled young woman with whom Yaakov has fallen in love. We follow Yaakov from this meeting in which Ariel has given his blessing to the union. We watch him take the elevated train into Manhattan, and finally watch as he walks to the Klausman's offices in the Diamond District on West Forty-seventh Street late at night. There we see Yaakov working at his trade, cutting diamonds. The action returns to Emily and Nick just as Yaakov responds to the buzzer at the shop's front door.

While Eden's journey into the Hasidic community takes her only a few miles from her precinct headquarters in Brooklyn, emotionally and spiritually it is a journey of extraordinary length. Eden's investigation takes her into a world where order and structure are indigenous to the culture. The Hasidim constitute a rarified, isolated group, clinging to traditions, practices, and a sense of moral order that extend immediately into eighteenth-century Poland, but ultimately back to a time before Christ. Here family, custom, and respect for the past are as much a part of daily experiences as bloodshed and mayhem are to Eden's experiences of life on the street. This point is first explored when she goes to the house of the Rebbe, the Hasidic leader, to meet with the Klausmans. Eden thinks she is coming to interrogate the missing person's family—that is, his mother and father. But the Hasidic sense of family is far-reaching. Yaakov's father (David Rosenbaum) has asked to meet her not at his own home but at the Rebbe's because the Hasidic community is itself a familial unit; Mr. Klausman may be Yaakov's father by blood, but the Rebbe is his father in a higher sense. This is one of the first things Emily notices: "You're *all* like a family," she says. "In a manner of speaking," answers Klausman. When Emily learns that nearly a million dollars in diamonds is missing, she assumes that this is not a missing persons case at all, but in fact a crime of grand larceny. She assumes that all families are failed, like her own. "Maybe your son ripped you off," she says to Klausman. "I've seen it a hundred times." The Rebbe answers rather than Yaakov's father. "In your world perhaps," says the Rebbe, "not in ours." Later Emily will press this point: "I got experience. I know human nature," she says. Again, it is the Rebbe who responds: "You will pardon me, but you do not know our nature."

Subsequently, Eden meets with Ariel, the Rebbe, Klausman, and his wife (Ruth Vool) at the Klausman's shop. Hundreds of thousands of dollars in diamonds are exchanged daily among the Hasidic jewelers, all without written contracts. Deals are made with a handshake. Honor and trust are the foundations of both business and human conduct. All of this is foreign to her. Eden still supposes that Yaakov has pocketed the diamonds, altered his identity, and fled. Everyone is corrupt, she assumes. Eden, ironically named, is the voice of a post-lapsarian world: innocence is out of the question.

> "Inside every honest man," she assures the Rebbe, "there is a thief trying to get out."
> "You're positive?" he asks.
> "When you've seen what I've seen in this life, okay?" answers Eden.

While in the Klausman's place of business, however, Emily finds Yaakov's mutilated body. She notes that Yaakov must have turned off the alarm before answering the door, suggesting that he knew his assailants; and since he would not have trusted anyone beyond the Hasidic community, it follows that his killers were Hasidim. This line of logic leads her to approach the Rebbe with an offer to enter his house as his guest and work undercover. It was in an earlier conversation with Ariel that the idea of working undercover has first come to Eden, apparently. Ariel tells her that Yaakov made it a practice to befriend strangers, "people who felt lost in the world, overwhelmed." This catches her attention for two reasons. First, Yaakov's killer would have necessarily inspired his trust and compassion. His killers had to be close enough to Yaakov for him to confide that he would be returning to work after evening prayers. If not one of the Hasidim, then it had to be someone in whom Yaakov might feel comfortable confiding.

More personally, Eden has begun to feel lost and overwhelmed herself. She is seeking a refuge, and while the Hasidic community certainly seems an unlikely one, she is intrigued by Ariel's sense of self-possession, his faith, his good mind and reason. Everything in his world seems to make sense to him. A Talmudic scholar, he lives according to the 613 rules of Orthodox Jewish faith: 365 negative, 248 positive. Answers not found in the Talmud, Ariel seeks in the Cabala, which looks beyond reason to find eternal, divine truths in the spiritual realm. Ariel is the stepson of the Hasidic community's leader, its Rebbe, and will someday become the Rebbe himself. Ariel is worlds apart from any young man Eden has ever met before. True to Hasidic tradition, as an unmarried man he has had little contact with women, and certainly no intimate, physical contact. This amuses Emily at first, and it gives her a power over him, for she can see that he is attracted to her. But she is also attracted to him, she finds.

Emily is a rule breaker. She refuses to follow established police procedure. When we see her waiting at the hospital for Nick to come out of surgery, she is smoking a cigarette with her back to a "No Smoking" sign. Upon moving into the Rebbe's house, Emily makes a point of telling Ariel's sister Leah (Mia Sara) that she is "an independent woman" who feels free to fly in the face of established conventions. Emily does what she wants, when she wants, she explains to Leah, and she brings this sensibility to life among the Hasidim. Initially, she enjoys flaunting Hasidic notions of proper behavior between the sexes. Ariel is as determined to follow the rules of his world as she is to break the rules of hers. Ariel finds meaning in his life, not by setting himself apart from convention, but by finding his place within it. Ariel achieves his identity not by asserting his independence, but rather by finding his place in a timeless, traditional sequence of practices and events. What to Emily is freedom, to Ariel is alienation; what Emily calls repression, Ariel thinks of as propriety and order.

Midway through the film, Emily goes to visit Nick as he is recovering in the hospital. To pass the time, they play the card game "War." It would seem to be the perfect game for her. Emily seems to be confrontational and aggressive by nature. Here, however, Emily has to struggle to maintain her interest. She is losing her taste for the game, she says. This concern extends throughout the film. Later, Leah calls Emily a "warrior"; both Levine and Oliver tell her she needs "some R and R," a military phrase meaning rest and relaxation. Emily is a modern day warrior, an urban cowboy, but she is also weary of those roles, and her remark about the cards—"I'm getting really sick of this game"—seems to be true as well about the way she lives her life. She is less the biblical warrior Leah refers to than a "guard dog," Emily says. She has not become an independent woman at all, she later confides; she is not free of the gender stereotypes that she says entrap young women like Leah. Instead, Emily has become a police officer like her father. Trying to become a daughter he will love, she has become her own worst enemy, adopting the most ridiculous masculine conceits as proof of her liberation.

As the film begins, Emily thinks she is liberated sexually and professionally. Gradually, she comes to doubt this. Levine, her only immediate police support in the investigation, says they are destined for one another: "We deserve one another. No commitment, no romantic hassles, no illusions, tell me I'm wrong." Levine promises her orgasms without any emotional entanglement. Earlier, she has called him "a cold-blooded bastard." What if Levine is right? What if her attempt to be as good a cop as any man on the force has simply made her as loathsome as Levine? What if Levine is the only sort of man for whom Eden is fit? Ariel sees more good in Eden than she perceives in herself. Early in their relationship, Ariel speculates that women police detectives must have an advantage. The Cabala teaches that women are on a higher spiritual plane than men, more attuned to their world, more sensitive and intuitive. This proves to be true as the undercover investigation gets under way. Not long after Yaakov's murder, two small-time mafiosos, Tony and Chris Baldessari (James Gandolfini, Chris Collins) try to sell protection to Ariel and Leah. They enter the store one day and promise to prevent any further killings in return for a monthly fee. Both Emily and Mara overhear them. Mara charges Chris, flailing at him with her fists, accusing him of Yaakov's murder. She finally has to be restrained. It appears that these two minor hoodlums from the Bay Side section of Queens have attempted to expand their operation into midtown Manhattan by killing Yaakov, then selling protection after scaring the Hasidim. Levine is posted nearby, watching the scene down the block through a surveillance camera installed in the shop. Like Mara, Levine assumes the Baldessari brothers are Yaakov's murderers and he proceeds to mount a case to that effect. Mara later reports she was assaulted by two men driving a car like the Baldessaris's; the brothers had extensive dealings with Yaakov; Yaakov's murder was the sort of crime of which they were capable, particularly if they wanted to extort money from other Hasidic diamond merchants in return for protection. All evidence seems to point in the Baldessaris's direction. But Emily remains unconvinced: they are clearly extortionists, but she remains certain that the murder was an inside job, even if Levine can mount significant evidence to the contrary.

The Baldessari brothers give Ariel and Leah one week to make their first payment. During that week, Emily becomes more integrated into the customs and worldviews of the Hasidim, and progressively more attracted to Ariel. A marriage has been arranged for Ariel to the daughter of a famous Parisian rebbe, however. The French Rebbe Singer (Ira Rubin) and his daughter Shayna (Francoise Granville) are coming to America so the wedding can take place, which brings matters to a head between Emily and Ariel. Although attracted to her, indeed in love with her, Ariel cannot jeopardize his place in the Hasidic community by breaking the covenant the Rebbe has made with the Singers. Ariel must subjugate his own desires to the needs of the community. Each of us, he says, is destined to play a role ordained by God. Ariel is soon to become a rebbe. Ariel was an *illui,* a child prodigy of Talmudic study ("He is to Jewish learning what Mozart was to music," Leah tells Emily); Ariel is destined to play a central role in the community's future, and its future is more important than his alone.

Eden and Levine apparently solve the murder case when the Baldessari brothers reappear within a week. While arresting them for extortion, Eden finds evidence in one of the brother's possession that places them at the scene of Yaakov's murder. The two are killed as they attempt to flee, but with his last words, Tony Baldessari protests their innocence. The Rebbe is an Auschwitz survivor. In the death camps, he lost his wife and children. He has been on "intimate terms with evil," he tells Emily. It has informed his soul. If Ariel is to be a fit successor, he surely needs to know evil more intimately than he does at the film's beginning. Impressive as a scholar, Ariel nevertheless lacks the wisdom necessary to be a great leader of his people. The first counsel we see him give is to Yaakov. Ariel encourages him to marry Mara. "She's a fine girl. You'll be very happy," Ariel assures Yaakov. Within a few hours, Yaakov will be murdered at her hand.

Although she has no evidence to this effect, Emily suspects Mara from their first meeting, perhaps because she senses in Mara some of her own capacity for evil. Mara was one of the lost souls to whom Yaakov was attracted, a stranger who was given a place in the Hasidic community by Yaakov and the Rebbe. "The Rebbe saved me. I almost died. I treated my body like trash," she confesses to Emily. "I slept with men I didn't love. I took drugs. A little over a year ago, I was walking down the street. I think I was drunk or stoned—actually I don't remember. I looked up and there [Yaakov] was." Mara is a *Baal Teshuvah,* one who has returned to the fold, someone whose sins are believed to be forgiven even if repentance comes late. This is the same identity given to Eden. To explain her presence in the Rebbe's house, she is presented to the Hasidic community as a *Baal Teshuvah.* Emily has partially revised her initial estimate of the human condition by the last third of the film. She no longer thinks there is a thief in each Hasid waiting to get out. She knows, however, that there is darkness in the human heart. Of those nearest to Yaakov—the Rebbe, Ariel, Leah, and Mara—Mara is the most worldly. It follows that her heart is surely the darkest.

Throughout the film, Emily taunts Ariel about his virginity. Ariel acknowledges that her sexual experience is far greater than his own, but he is more impressed with the violence she has known. He wants to know what it feels like to shoot a gun, to kill a man, to confront evil, to look it in the eye. These two concerns come together after the Baldessaris have been put to rest and the case has been officially closed. On his way home to meet his arriving fiancée, Ariel stops at Emily's apartment. She tries to seduce him, and nearly succeeds. But his sexual virginity is of less consequence to the greater good than his inexperience with evil. Ariel has come to see Emily on Yaakov's behalf, as much as on his own. Intuitively, neither he nor Emily can accept that the Baldessari brothers killed his friend. Together they determine that Mara was responsible.

They drive to the Rebbe's house. While Ariel has been with Emily, Leah has accidentally uncovered evidence that links Mara to Yaakov's killing. Amid the confusion of the Singers' arrival, Mara takes Leah at gunpoint out of the house and into the night. They are intercepted within a block of the house by Emily and Ariel. Emily calls for backup, then gives Ariel her spare gun. She intends to deflect Mara's attention. Mara is sure to want to search Emily, but, Emily reasons, Mara would have no reason to suspect that Ariel would be armed. Emily's plan works. It prevents Mara's escape, but it also puts Ariel in the position of having to kill Mara in order to save his sister. The film ends with both Ariel and Emily beginning their lives anew. Each in their own way are in virginal states. Previously Ariel has been seen solely in dark clothes; white cloth prevails in the wedding scene. We watch as Ariel is wed to Shayna, then as Emily arrives at police head-quarters. Eden runs into Levine. He offers her a two-week trip to the islands, promising her an erotic experience sure to make a new woman of her. She assures him she is no longer interested in casual affairs. As for the trip's promise of renewal, she is already a new woman, she tells him.

This renewal is underscored by cinematic means that we have seen Lumet use previously. Rain and bodies of water are often identified with the relationship between the values of Ariel's world and those of Emily's. The final scene between Levine and Emily takes place in the rain outside their police precinct on Knickerbocker Avenue in Brook-lyn. Emily is carrying an umbrella. She extends it to Levine, momen-tarily putting him under her protection. It is an inclusive gesture on Emily's part, something of which she would not have been capable when we first met her. The rain in this scene has its parallel in the shooting of Mara. With Mara lying dead, Ariel comes out onto the rain-soaked streets. The Rebbe has been drawn out of his house by the sounds of gunfire. He joins Ariel, and for once, Ariel is the dom-inant figure. This is appropriate, since Ariel has just advanced his knowledge of evil, and is now better prepared to take the Rebbe's place.

Nick proposes to Emily late in the film in the physical therapy unit of the hospital. They have their backs to a window that looks out onto the East River and the bridges that span it. Emily's values have changed since we first saw them. She can neither marry Nick now, nor continue sleeping with him.

Earlier we have seen Emily crossing one of these bridges on a bus as she rides with the Hasidim to the Diamond District. She has begun to blend into their community by this point in the film. Physically, she appears much different than when we first met her. Her hair is dark. Her clothes are modest. Her skirt is long; her stockings are opaque; she wears tan buck oxfords instead of pumps. The opening montage of the film was shot from an aircraft. We skim the water, ascending over the bridges that link one borough of New York City to another, then finally descend into the world of the Hasidim. The water reflects the light, and though it is nearing dusk, the visual im-ages of Manhattan are bright. This is in contrast to the lighting of the heder, where we first encounter Ariel instructing the children in Hebrew, and it establishes a contrast that extends throughout the film.

As in *Daniel* and *Q & A,* Lumet and his cinematographer Bartkowiak employ lighting patterns that distinguish between environments. The world of the Hasidim is photographed in somber, sepia tones that seem to radiate warmth. These sequences are often dominated by vibrant, radiant light, often sunlight, even in interior scenes. Artificial light seems only sparingly supplied in the world of the Hasidim, most often by candles or incandescent bulbs surrounded by glowing arcs. The scenes are generally shot using soft focus, often lighting the characters from behind or from the side. Most often, the natural light employed to illuminate interior scenes comes from screen-left, often filtering into a room through stained glass windows.

Emily returns to her police headquarters and to Nick's hospital room once she has changed her appearance and begun to work undercover in the Hasidic community. When Nick sees her, he says that she looks "radiant." This is paralleled by the reaction of her fellow police officers at her Brooklyn headquarters, who fail to recognize her at first. One says she looks like a lady. Even Levine, who lusts after her, suggests that she looks virginal. In all of these cases, the response is anticipated by the way Lumet lights Emily within the Rebbe's house. When Emily first comes under his roof, she waits momentarily in an anteroom while Leah announces her arrival. Hasidim crowded around the room's edges, Emily stands in the middle of the room, obviously feeling out of place. Lumet lights her from screen-left with natural light that seems to spotlight her, making her discomfort all the more palpable. But placing her in filtered, natural light also gives Emily a radiant quality, and this is increased when she enters the Rebbe's inner sanctum. Leah ushers Emily to a chair before the Rebbe's desk. Natural light filtered through stained glass on her left illuminates Emily's hair and face. She is more softly focused than she has been up to this point in the film. Lumet does much to remind us that Emily is still out of place; but the lighting gives her a dimension that is less abrasive than in our previous encounters with her, and it forecasts changes ahead.

Similarly, Lumet uses different compositional patterns when photographing Emily in the Rebbe's house, and outside of it. Many of the shots in the Rebbe's house have a formal compositional quality. Lumet distinguishes visually between screen-left, screen-center, and screen-right, then balances what we see in each, using focal planes and lighting to bring the elements into visual harmony. In Emily's first interview with the Rebbe, Lumet puts her in the center of the frame, with Leah behind her and to her right. The Rebbe sits before her and Ariel stands behind the Rebbe's right shoulder. Then Lumet composes shots lighting each spatial plane (near, mid, and far distance) so that they balance and complement one another. Upon entering the world of the Hasidim, Emily asks Leah if the Rebbe is a rabbi. Leah says the Rebbe is much more. He is a spiritual leader, a presence in all their lives. Lumet develops this idea photographically. In the Rebbe's house, Emily is generally photographed at or above eye level. The Rebbe, by contrast, is photographed in low camera angles, putting him in a dominant position. His image often extends into the frame's upper quadrants, even when he is not central to the action. Lumet employs interesting variations on this motif, the few times we see the Rebbe beyond his own house. When Emily meets with the Klausmans in their place of business, for instance, and tells them there is a thief inside every honest man, the Rebbe is completely out of frame. Emily is all alone as she speaks, but his shadow is visible behind her, extending toward the ceiling.

When we first encounter Emily, she is photographed in low angles. This will be true at key moments, as Emily takes charge of situations on the streets of New York. This is her world, and here she is dominant. As she draws her revolver and shoots the escaping Baldessari brothers late in the film, the camera is so low that her image appears grotesquely large. This complements the film's beginning. We meet Emily late at night as she and Nick wait for the holdup of a movie theater to occur. They are both on the curb, leaning against a parked car. The camera angle is so drastically low that spatially it skews what we see. Visually, it puts the movie marquee directly over their heads. The marquee's red and white neon casts an eerie glow across their faces. The lighting and the camera angle suggest a world of artificial qualities and general disarray. We follow the ambulance carrying Nick to the hospital. Hovering over his body, Emily is photographed in low angles. Cutaways to the speeding ambulance as it moves through the New York City streets, reveal its revolving emergency light, which casts arcs of light against the pavement. Such images remain identified with Emily's world until the very end of the film. A similar ambulance appears on the streets of the Hasidic community once Ariel has killed Mara. As arcs of blue and red light punctuate the night, it is as if Emily's world has come to theirs.

Everything about Lumet's camera work in the Hasidic community suggests repetition and order. Lumet uses some 20 dissolves in *A Stranger among Us*. He uses these with the Hasidim, to gradually blend one scene into another. It is unusual for Lumet to use dissolves so consistently, yet they provide a very appropriate transitional device here, reminding us of the continuities that are so much a part of the Hasidic worldview. In addition, Lumet establishes several camera patterns when photographing the Hasidim, lending the scenes a sense of continuity and formal repetition. One of these is done with a crane. The camera begins high overhead, focuses on a single image, gradually descends, then pauses or withdraws. As the focal length shortens, the frame is filled with Hasidim. The initial image is often iconographic, most often a Star of David. We enter the interior world of the Hasidim, for instance, with a Star of David cut in stained glass, then move downward to find Ariel instructing his pupils. The scene of Yaakov's funeral begins with the image of a wrought iron Star of David filling the frame. When the camera moves down and pauses, we see that the image has come from the top of a wrought iron fence that marks a Jewish cemetery. The camera withdraws and the screen fills with mourners as the kaddish begins. Similarly, a circling camera will generally move clockwise in the Hasidic community. This is true throughout much of the extended Sabbath celebration near the film's midpoint, from the first time the camera circles the table to show us the number of people present, through the lovely dance sequences which mark the celebration's emotional high point.

Emily's usual salutation, "What's new and exciting?", seems to come from a different era than the Hasidim, for among them there is little that is new. The formal balance of the lighting and composition, and the moving camera work suggest formality and repetition. The major exception to this has to do with Mara. Mara's presence alone disrupts the balance of lighting and composition, otherwise associated with the Hasidic community. Occasionally we are too close or too far from her to see her clearly. Sometimes we hear her voice without being able to see her—on the bus ride into New York City, at the Sabbath table, and when she pretends to have been attacked by the Baldessari brothers. In the latter case, the others are inside preparing food for the Sabbath celebration, when Mara's screams draw them outside. She is discovered in an alleyway. Claiming to have been beaten, she is taken inside, where her skinned knee and cut cheek are bandaged. Emily calls Lt. Oliver and demands that additional squad cars be sent to patrol the neighborhood, then moves into the frame with Mara. They talk, and Mara confesses her past to Emily. Throughout this sequence, Lumet violates the formal compositional patterns that have marked the Hasidic way of life. Generally, there is only one source of natural light; here there seem to be two. One is to Mara's side. The other enters the frame from a different part of the room, near the phone where Emily places her call. Generally, Lumet puts the central character in the center of the frame, who is balanced by others to either side. The central character is generally in sharpest focus. But that is not always true in this sequence. Elements we might look for on either side to balance Mara's image tend to be missing. Mara is gradually made the center of attention to the exclusion of everything else.

Late in the film, Ariel arrives at Emily's apartment as she is watching *Carefree* on television, one of the finer Ginger Rogers-Fred Astaire films. (Emily is a fan, apparently: the only artwork we see on her walls is an Astaire-Rogers poster.) Specifically, Ariel arrives just as the "Change Partners and Dance" number is airing. Any fan of Astaire and Rogers will recognize it as a classic moment in their work together, and a classic example of choreography. Predictably dressed in black-and-white formal wear, Astaire and Rogers move together and apart in harmony as the space between their bodies is extended, then reduced. The choreography reflects their feelings for one another, a mutual attraction that invariably moves Astaire's and Rogers's characters to overcome the obstacles between them. Since Hasidim neither watch television nor go to movies, Ariel has never seen the duo before. He can tell at a glance, though, that what they are doing is "magical." The choreography that so impresses Ariel (and leads him to accept Emily's seductive offer to dance) has its counterpart in *A Stranger among Us*. Unlike Mara, Emily can generally find a balanced place in the frame. But when she and Ariel are alone, Emily cannot maintain this balance. The pattern Lumet generally employs in this regard is to put them at opposite edges of the frame, bring them together gradually; then, once their attraction to one another is pronounced, put space between them visually and end the scene with one character leaving the frame.

Perhaps the best example of this occurs late at night after the Rebbe's announcement of Ariel's pending marriage to Shayna. The sound of backfire from a passing car draws Emily down to a courtyard behind the house. There she finds Ariel sitting alone at a table, considering his marriage. The scene begins in long shot range. Initially, one-shots predominate. In the distance, we see Emily descending the steps that lead from the back door of the kitchen, then, at equal distance, Ariel sitting at a metal table. Gradually the camera moves closer, and two-shots begin to prevail. After accepting Ariel's coat for warmth, Emily discovers his copy of the Cabala in an inside pocket. She asks him to translate for her. They sit together at the table as he translates what he has been reading about romance and marriage. They are physically close to one another at this point in the scene, and emotionally close as well. Clearly, they have fallen in love. But as Emily begins to broach that point, Ariel rises from the table and moves away from her toward the steps. We are reminded of the distance between their ways of life by the physical distance that separates them on the screen. Emily does not understand how he could consider marrying Shayna Singer, a girl he has never met, when he is obviously attracted to Emily, and she to him. Emily enters the space he occupies near the steps, then starts to move past him, intending to return to the house. Earlier in the sequence, Lumet has carefully balanced the light between the characters and the physical setting. Gradually the lighting changes so that the illumination emphasizes the characters at the expense of the setting. Emily sits next to Ariel on the steps as he tries to explain the duty he feels to the Rebbe and to his community, and the necessity of subjugating his personal interests to a greater good. Here, Emily and Ariel are closer together in the frame than they have been up to this point. Yet, ironically, the gulf that separates them as lovers is vast.

Lumet uses a variation on this pattern when Emily and Leah are together. While working undercover, Emily shares Leah's bedroom. As she unpacks, the camera is placed in the center of the room. The two women talk, trying to find some common ground of understanding. Their instinctual warmth for one another, as well as the differences in experience which separate them, are visualized through Lumet's use of the screen space. The camera picks up Emily in the middle of the room, then lets her walk out of frame to the right as she hangs up her clothes. It then cuts to Leah, who moves out of frame in the opposite direction, screen-left. The camera then returns to Emily, then goes back to Leah, and so on. Although the two occupy the same bedroom throughout the film, Lumet generally keeps them in two different visual planes. Emily's bed is next to a window; Leah's is flush against an adjoining wall. It is only when they are closest spiritually that they can maintain the same spatial plane in the bedroom for the duration of a conversation. After leaving Ariel in the courtyard, Emily returns to the bedroom. Leah has eavesdropped on their conversation from her bedroom window on the second floor. She joins Emily on Emily's bed. She confesses that Emily is the first non-Hasidic friend she has ever had. Emily confesses in turn that Leah is the first female friend Emily has had since the third grade. Leah then tries to make Emily understand that Ariel must marry Shayna, no matter how much he loves Emily.

This spatial pattern is also used in scenes set beyond the Hasidic community, as when Emily returns to her father's house. There are only a few pages of dialogue in the scene, and virtually no action. In all, the scene takes less than five minutes. Yet it is pivotal to understanding Emily's character, and the spiritual crisis that she experiences. Earlier, after Levine propositioned Emily, telling her they are two of a kind, Emily called him a "cold-blooded bastard." In the following scene, Emily parks in front of her father's small house. It is shabby, perhaps vacant. We watch as she walks toward the front door in the dark. An edit takes us inside. The camera is located at the far end of the small living room, perhaps slightly beyond it in a dining area. We watch as she lets herself in. She looks around tentatively, unsure of whether she is welcome or not. Everything in the house speaks of disorder. Photos are tacked onto a bulletin board in no particular sequence. Worn and dirty, the furniture is arranged haphazardly. Whereas in the world of the Hasidim, everything looks aged, here everything simply looks old. The lighting in the Rebbe's house seems to soften the images. Here, an overhead lighting fixture near the kitchen produces a harsh glow from a number of bulbs. One of the bulbs has burned out. No one has gotten around to replacing it.

We do not know initially that Emily is returning to her home. We will not know this until she calls out "Pop? Pop?" Emily comes forward, walking past stairs that lead to a second floor. She pauses in the dining area. She turns around just in time to find that her father has come downstairs. Even when her father appears and she acknowledges him, Emily appears to be breaking and entering. She might easily be a stranger here, perhaps sneaking into another person's house. The initial shot of Emily and her father together emphasizes the physical space that separates them, just as the dialogue emphasizes the emotional distance that keeps them apart. Her father greets Emily less like a daughter and more like a neighbor. He is unable to talk about himself. Emily has changed her hair style and color, and the style of her clothes. When she returned to precinct headquarters, her closest colleagues did not recognize her. In fact, she looks completely different from the last time her father saw her, and he is baffled by the change. Something is not right. It must be her clothes, he finally determines. Emily fishes for a compliment. He changes the subject. He opens his arms, apparently offering her an embrace. A cut to a one-shot of Emily reveals her hesitation, or perhaps her surprise, at the offer of affection. When Emily steps toward him, her father doubles up his fists and feigns a jab. This startles Emily, stops her in her tracks. "Still can't keep up with the old man," he laughs. The laugh is forced, betraying his own ambivalence. Any offer of intimacy is balanced by a need to keep Emily at arm's length. She asks him if he would like to go out for something to eat. He says that Emily should have called first; he is on his way to a meeting of Alcoholics Anonymous. After the meeting, she suggests. No, he has plans.

It is clear from his tone that he has no plans. He may be genuinely glad to see her, but he is equally eager for her to leave. The tension between these conflicting desires is visually manifested in the frame. The room is small and shabby. Physically, it demands that they come together. There is not enough room for each individual to have space. Lumet uses the tight physical dimensions ironically. Lumet's lensplot throughout the sequence will be to photograph the two characters primarily in one-shot, to isolate them from each other. This is underscored by the few times he puts them in the frame simultaneously. We do not have the impression that they are together; instead, we are reminded of the distance that separates them. The conversation has barely begun, and already it has reached its conclusion. After an awkward pause, her father greets Emily as though she has just appeared. "What's new and exciting?" he asks her. He means, "What's new at work?" Emily understands this immediately. Police work is their common ground, and she tells him about Nick being stabbed in the course of an arrest. Emily does this in a language he is sure to understand. Police jargon is the only tongue they share. "We were pattin' down [searching] some perps [perpetrators] and one of them stuck him with a blade," she begins. Her father does his best to offer his sympathies, but the offer is perfunctory. He changes the subject to how much easier it is for her generation of police officers than it was for his. Clearly, Emily has heard this before. They are sitting at an angle to one another, her father in his easy chair, Emily on the edge of a couch. But Lumet reminds us through his use of one-shots that, emotionally, they are barely in the same room. They are no closer together than at the beginning of the sequence, when they were at opposite extremes of the frame; if anything, they are farther apart.

Emily is seeking her father's approval. The only time he offers it is when he asks if she killed the suspect who stabbed her partner. When she says she did, he beams. "That's my little girl," he tells her. Shaken by her earlier conversation with Levine, Emily has come to her father hoping to be told that she is loved, but she does not know how to broach this subject with him. Emily uses what he has said about the dangers he faced while serving on the police force. She asks him what he would do if she were killed? The question startles him; anything heartfelt signals trouble ahead. He asks Emily if she has been drinking. Apparently her father cannot imagine that anyone would pose so bluntly intimate a question unless they were drunk. He gets up from the chair and heads for the kitchen, putting as much physical and emotional space between himself and his daughter as he can. He treats the question as though it concerns police procedures. He assures Emily that he would take steps to get her an inspector's funeral, "departmental honors and all. The works!" With tears in her eyes, Emily rises to leave. The scene ends with the camera on Emily's father. "What kind of craziness is this?" he asks. "Are you okay?" He waits for her to leave before he makes any gesture to stop her. When he next speaks, he is speaking to himself. "Hey, you can talk to me," says her father. It is the perfect line with which to end the scene, the perfect one-shot. A lesser director would have needed five scenes and 20 pages of shooting script to convey what Lumet achieves in minutes. It is a high point in an otherwise flawed film, for suddenly we know why Emily is the way she is. We know what she wants, and why she wants it. It is not a watershed moment in the history of American cinema, to be sure. Of the 10 major reviews the film received, not one reviewer mentioned it. But it is a moment when craft and art come together so completely that one is indistinguishable from the other. Even Lumet's flawed films contain many such moments.

CHAPTER FOUR

Sidney Lumet, Consistently Inconsistent

Screenwriter Robert Avrech's remarks on his choice of Lumet to direct *A Stranger among Us* indicate Lumet's reputation in Hollywood today. "I knew I wanted a class Hollywood director. I didn't want one who'd made two films and now gets five million dollars because he knows how to work the room at Spago."[1] Lumet has standing and clout in the industry. In most circles he is considered a consummate professional, and if a studio wants his services, it should expect to pay accordingly. Negotiations with Lumet reportedly begin in the two million dollar range, and he has commanded the final cut of all of his films since *Serpico*. Lumet's current position in cinema scholarship is less assured. He has yet to shed his dubious reputation, established early in his career, as a bankable director with considerable technical skill who is only as good as the material he is handed. He has made a few first-rate films and a few that should not have been made at all, with most of his work falling somewhere in between. He has been making films for almost 40 years in an industry in which such longevity is rare, but his scope only complicates the matter of his reputation. Too inconsistent to be placed among the work of America's great film artists, Lumet's work is nevertheless consistently good enough to demand attention.

Sometimes a New York School "realist," sometimes a highly stylized director, sometimes a maker of message films, and sometimes of fluff, sometimes successful in what he sets out to do, and sometimes not, Lumet has posed a problem to fan and foe alike.

This study also considers the relationship of Lumet's artistry and craftsmanship. Lumet completed the production of *Twelve Angry Men* in 19 days of shooting. More than 20 years later, he was directing

Deathtrap. The shooting script called for the production to be done on one primary location, one physical set representing the house of the protagonist. Lumet had decided before production began to keep the camera moving. He recognized the need to make the film visually interesting, and he also saw in the moving camera a means to produce a menacing, stalking effect, that would reflect the mood of the narrative. When work began, however, Lumet realized that using a moving camera was slowing down production to a point where the actors' concentration was broken, causing delays that were counterproductive to the performance. Every dolly shot meant that tracks first had to be laid across the handsome wood floors, then painted over so that they would not appear at the edges of the frame as the camera moved on. The process was maddening, and in an industry where time is (literally) money, quite costly. Lumet finally came up with an inexpensive solution. He ordered a new floor made in four-by-eight sections. Each section was assigned a number. Together, the pieces fit together like a jigsaw puzzle, each piece easily numbered to insure speedy reassembly. That way, all Lumet had to do was to add or subtract a section to make room for the camera and keep shooting. It was a simple solution, and one that saved a million dollars in production costs.

The walls of the set proved to be problematic as well. They were "wild walls"—that is, built so that they came apart and could be moved about as production continued. They were 25 feet high, and much heavier than most wild walls used in normal production. Lumet anticipated the problems their weight and size would impose, and once again he came up with a simple solution. Lumet had the walls built so that they hinged in the middle when measured from top to bottom. Lumet had hooks put in them so that they could be hung from overhead. When the camera needed to get through a wall, its bottom was raised by its hinges. This allowed the camera to achieve a frightening, circling effect, one Lumet went on to use successfully in the final production. "One way or another," Lumet has said, "when you solve a creative problem, you also solve a technical problem. And when you solve a technical problem, you get a creative plus."[2] It is this sort of logic that helps to explain Lumet's choice of cinematographers for *Network*. Chayefsky's story uses television as a means of exploring the corruption of human experience, and Lumet saw in the script a corresponding opportunity to corrupt the visual image for dramatic intent. Virtually all of the film was shot away from a studio set. Only Max Schumacher's office had a wild wall. All other interiors were photographed in available physical spaces. Only two sets had to be built, the motel room in the Hamptons where Diana and Max have their liaison, and Howard Beale's office. Everything else was done on location. The UBS building we see is actually the MGM building in New York City; the television executives' offices were dressed on one of the building's vacant floors. Diana's speech to the West Coast affiliates was shot in the grand ballroom of the Plaza Hotel. Beale's meeting with Mr. Jensen was shot in a conference room at the New York Public Library. When we first meet Beale and Max crying into their drinks, they are actually sitting at the bar in the Warwick Hotel.

Lumet wanted to work away from soundstages. If he was going to visually corrupt the real, he wanted to work in real locations. He chose Owen Roizman to shoot the film for him. Nominated for three Academy Awards, for his work on *The French Connection, The Exorcist,* and subsequently for *Network,* Roizman is primarily known for two things, his preference for "wide open" shooting—that is, for exposures in low light that lack depth of field and obscure normal spatial planes—and his ability to work with available light, using portable equipment only to fill in what natural light cannot provide. Roizman's skills were well suited to both realistic and stylized photography, and thus fit Lumet's plan for the film. Lumet wanted to take the audience from naturalistic photography in the film's first third—using a moving camera and relying almost entirely on available light—through realistic photography in the second third (there balancing moving and stationary cameras, available and artificial light) and finally end the film primarily with stationary camera work and completely artificial illumination. Working with Norman Leigh, one of the best gaffers in the business, as well as camera operator Freddie Shuler and Roizman's assistant, Tommy Priestly, Roizman and Lumet overcame the inherent limitations of shooting in real sets with decided aplomb.

The scenes shot in Frank Hackett's office are exemplary. Another director might have chosen a soundstage for these scenes, as a matter of convenience. Through Hackett's windows we see the windows and building facings of neighboring skyscrapers. A common way of filming this would be to have Hackett's office dressed on a soundstage, then have an inexpensive skyscraper facade constructed. By using a process called Translight, the facade and the set would have simulated an office in a skyscraper located amid other skyscrapers. But for Lumet, the effect would not be real enough.

Shooting on location, the primary problem Roizman and Lumet faced was balancing interior and exterior light values. That was particularly difficult due to the prevalence of windows in the background buildings, all of which, of course, reflected any natural light. Lumet and Roizman finally resolved this by using a complicated scheme of acrylic neutral density filters that were cut to fit the windows in Hackett's office, and by adjusting the exposure of the cameras accordingly. The problem of balancing exterior and interior light became still more difficult at night. The scene in which Diana comes to Max's office late at night in an attempt to seduce him is an example of Roizman and Lumet's skill in solving problems in a way that serves the drama. The interior of Max's office is dimly lit, suggesting an intimacy and atmosphere conducive to seduction. But its low-level lighting was initially an attempt to compensate for the myriad lights in Manhattan that can be seen through Max's window. If Roizman and Lumet had raised the light in the room, the lights in the distance would have been all but extinguished.

Lumet is famous for his technical knowledge. Perhaps no contemporary director is more knowledgeable about lighting, cinematography, and the craftsmanship of filmmaking. Lumet cannot be judged in this regard by his successes alone. *The Wiz,* for example, was fraught with technical problems, which seem to have stimulated Lumet creatively as much as in *Network,* if to decidedly less rewarding effect. *The Wiz* has been perhaps Lumet's greatest failure to date. A 13-week shooting schedule and a 10 million dollar budget did not prove sufficient. Esteemed for completing his films on time and under budget, in this instance Lumet failed. The film turned out to be a critical failure and a disappointment at the box office. Lumet turned a Broadway musical that won seven Tony Awards into a film that hardly found one word of praise.

Lumet was offered the project by Ned Tannen, then head of Universal. Tannen had negotiated the screenrights with Ken Harper, the Broadway musical's producer. Lumet saw in the property the potential for an urban fable, a contemporary *Pilgrim's Progress* about the search for personal identity. Rather than MGM's classic story of a Kansas farm girl's thrilling visit to a world of dazzling fantasy, Lumet found the material more appropriate to someone the age of Diana Ross, the film's star. An entirely new script was written by Joel Schumacher based on Lumet's conception. For his director of photography, Lumet chose British cinematographer Ossie Morris, with whom he had worked earlier on *The Hill* and—more recently—*Equus*. Morris is internationally renowned for his work with stage and literary properties—among them *Oliver, Scrooge,* and *Fiddler On the Roof*—and for his work with bright, vibrant colors. On *The Wiz* he employed the innovative Lightflex system that allowed more color correction possibility than conventional methods. Color was central to Lumet's vision of the project. For instance, Lumet envisioned the Emerald City as New York City's World Trade Center at night. Both shooting on location, and the vast scale of the World Trade Center, posed a formidable problem for Morris; Lumet increased the difficulty by marking the entry into the Emerald City with musical numbers performed on an illuminated floor, and made *that* still more difficult by wanting the floor to change colors three times, from green to red to gold. To achieve this, a Perspex floor was laid on location, then illuminated from underneath with 27,000 light bulbs, 9,000 in each of the three colors. Lumet used 400 dancers. Since they change costumes three times, that meant 1,200 costumes, down to the smallest detail—jewelry, hats, and shoes. Lumet lit the dancers with 35,000 lamps, and mounted 72 speakers to achieve surely the most complicated musical sequences ever shot on location.

Such fantasy is almost always set amid reality in *The Wiz*. Lumet's yellow brick road consisted of 26 miles of yellow linoleum laid on top of the actual streets of the city. There is graffiti on the subway walls. There are hookers walking the streets. Much of New York City itself appears in the film. The stages of Dorothy's odyssey downtown are signaled by recognizable city landmarks, such as Coney Island, the Public Library, the Chrysler Building, and the Brooklyn Bridge. The first bridge we see is actually the Flushing Bridge in Flushing Meadows (the number was done with a matte constructed by Albert Whitlock). The Scarecrow (Michael Jackson) enters on One-hundred-and-sixth Street. The Lion (Ted Ross) enters at Forty-second Street. The poppies are encountered at the intersection of Eighth Avenue and Forty-fifth Street. The sweatshop sequence is set in the garment district on Thirty-seventh Street. But Dorothy's journey is a fantasy, and in this spirit, virtually everything we see is made to appear surreal, and sometimes supra-real. The change of colors serves this as well. The movie begins in cool colors, grows gradually warmer in tone and hue, then cools off again at the end. Blues (that sometimes border on gray) are used for concrete spaces and public arenas, while reds dominate the sweatshop sequence, dawn as seen from Eighth Avenue. As the characters are liberated from the sweatshop, freed to become themselves, the predominating reds very slowly shift to orange.

Such lighting and color schemes signal a movement from reality to fantasy, and are in keeping with the dramatic structure of the story. The film begins in Harlem where Dorothy lives with her Aunt Em (Theresa Merritt). The first musical number is Aunt Em's. It takes place in their Harlem home at the dinner table. The number is worked into the dialogue, as though it is nothing more than a natural extension of the conversation underway. It sets in motion Dorothy's trip downtown (she is whisked away by a Harlem snowstorm), where all the musical numbers are clearly staged. The trip finally brings us back to where we began. By the end of the film, each of the characters is figuratively prepared for such a return, for the Lion is now a human being, a real person, with the voice, bearing, and physical posture of a man. This is also true of the Tin Man (Nipsey Russell). He no longer rattles, nor does the Scarecrow come apart or stumble. They are each prepared to stand on their own two feet and come home, that is, to come to terms with themselves as individuals. Such considerations— the odyssey that takes the protagonist toward self-knowledge, the need to part with the group—are familiar to anyone who has paid close attention to Lumet's career. The film's structure, and its dramatic symmetry are also familiar. There are a number of circular images in the film—the playground where we encounter the munchkins, the crows that menace and taunt the scarecrow by encircling him, and the circular arena at the World Trade Center, are some examples. The film itself is circular in structure, as might be said of many Lumet films. Often, cinematic patterns we see early in a film are repeated with variations as the film moves toward its climax. *Twelve Angry Men* begins and ends with images of the edifices we build in the name of justice. The beginnings of *Daniel, Serpico,* and *The Pawnbroker* offer us material out of the past that is repeated or complemented by sequences near the films' ends.

As I noted in the preface to this book, critics have tended to divide Lumet's work into his highly stylized films (*Network, Power, The Wiz,* and *Equus,* for instance) at one extreme, and his gritty, realistic films (*The Pawnbroker, Dog Day Afternoon, Serpico,* and *Prince of the City,* for example) at the other. But as earlier chapters demonstrate, most of Lumet's films contain both elements. The jarring, almost surreal quality of the memory sequences in *The Pawnbroker* complement the realistic photography in the rest of the film. Lumet envisioned *Network* as taking us from realist to naturalist to stylized cinematography. "It's great deception," Lumet has said about the lensplot of *Network*. "I love it. It absolutely sucks you in. It begins on a totally naturalistic level, and one-third of the way through it starts moving—in terms of style, visuals, language—until by its end it's totally surrealistic. The last scene in that office when they decide to kill Peter Finch, if you analyze it shot by shot, you'll think you're looking at de Chirico. What we did is corrupt the camera. We started off totally real and honest and wound up like a commercial."[3] The decision to shoot *The Wiz* on location in New York City reflects the same directorial sensibility, playing reality and artificiality off of one another. *Equus* is another example of Lumet's attempt to balance the real with the highly stylized, in this case in both form and content. In "Suddenly, I Knew How to Film the Play," a 24 July 1977 *New York Times* article by Tom Burke, Lumet discussed at some length how he came to accept the project. "For 18 months I refused the *Equus* movie, because the stage production is about as perfect as it could get. There was nothing I could add. . . . Peter Shaffer came to my Easthampton place, we talked endlessly. I still didn't know how a movie could add something." Shaffer persuaded Lumet to start work nonetheless. As he began, Lumet decided that the dearth of physical action could be used to great effect on the screen, if he could find a way to handle it properly. In the 1977 article Lumet continues:

I knew the piece wasn't a psychodrama, and for me, a face can be the ultimate landscape. Then one day, at a meeting, Tony Walton said, "In the boy's hospital set, will you want a ceiling? Because if you have one, you could try that thing where he's lying in bed, and a car passes outside, and the windshield reflects overhead."

And I thought, My God, that's what this movie is about. As a kid, I'd never believe that passing reflection was what I knew it was. I always let it be slightly frightening, mysterious. Suddenly I knew that's how the movie could reinforce something that matters hugely in the play, thematically—the duality of everything. Nothing's quite what you expect it to be. That if "Equus" is about something, it's about duality, Jekyll and Hyde, Apollonian versus Dionysian thought, the double-edged sword we all carry. Creativity and its direct counterpart, our capacity for destruction.

In the film Lumet chose to focus not on the boy (Peter Firth) but rather on the boy's psychiatrist, Dysart (Richard Burton), and to use two distinct cinematic approaches. Dysart's life is mundane, predict-able, and the photography used to record it should reflect these qual-ities, Lumet determined. But Dysart's identification with his patient touches a psychic core in the psychiatrist himself. His darkest Dio-nysian longings are stirred. These scenes Lumet chose to photograph in the most stylized manner possible.

In earlier chapters, I have discussed the recurring cinematic patterns in *Dog Day Afternoon, Prince of the City,* and *Serpico* that belie their apparent spontaneity. They are all stylized films, with stylized visual motifs. *Fail Safe* seems to be shot in accord with patterns we know from other such thrillers, at least until its midsection, when Lumet's use of the vertical plane suddenly turns Expressionistic. In virtually all of Lumet's films, tendencies toward realism and stylization con-stantly tug at one another.

In Lumet's most successful work, craftsmanship and artistry, real-ism and stylization, inform one another to their mutual advantage; this is less true of his lesser work. His critics accuse Lumet of failing to sustain a particular authorial vision, spreading his talents too thin, and accepting to produce popular fare when his talents would be put to better use on loftier material. Lumet has almost acknowledged as much. Describing *Daniel,* Lumet said, "I am, I hope, like every intel-ligent American, a political human being, but I don't make political films. I hope I make films about feelings, about emotions, about fam-ilies, which is basically what *Daniel* is about. But if I don't have a *Daniel* to do, I'll do *The Verdict,* which is a 'very good movie,' or an *Anderson Tapes,* 'a good caper movie,' and while I think, I hope, *Daniel* is a really magnificent, popular movie, it's risky, and if the public doesn't take to it, well, it's always there, and I'll always be enormously proud of it and the people who helped me make it. In the meantime, I'll keep on making movies. Because that's what I do."[4]

This study has argued that there is more consistency to Lumet's thematic concerns as a filmmaker than such statements acknowledge. Lumet's critics have divided his films into those made as pure enter-tainment, and those with a political message, ascribed to Lumet's traditionally liberal, left-leaning views. Most of Lumet's films are political in the broadest sense of the word, at least insofar as we cannot reasonably distinguish between individuals and culture. In the films considered here, self-definition repeatedly comes about as the individ-ual distinguishes himself from the group. But the relationship of in-dividuals to groups at large might be better understood as a dialectic instead of a dualism, for one informs the other. This is true even in *The Wiz;* the trip downtown is taken as a group but Dorothy ends the film alone. "The two [concepts] are not in conflict," Lumet has said. "They amount to the same thing. To me, self-knowledge moves in precisely those steps, the ability to be alone being the requisite for any relationship anyhow. This is why Dorothy's last song was shot with the figures receding into the background, within the lights going out one after the other. And yet, all the time, she's traveling toward home."[5] In *The Wiz,* it is only once the characters can be made aware of both their limitations and capacities that they can be fully free to function as human beings. Indeed, Lumet has said that watching the rough cuts he realized that all of the major sequences were of "liberation, that somebody always starts stuck or immovable and makes progress. This is true about the graffiti children, the Scarecrow, the Lion, the Tinman, even the Wiz [Richard Prior] himself."[6]

It is only once the characters in *The Wiz* can break with their pasts, with their earlier fears, misconceptions, and initial self-images, that they can be free to pursue their lives in the present, and this general concept is to be found in many of Lumet's films. The past and the present do not stand in inherent opposition to one another. The challenge before Lumet's characters is often to learn from their past as they look toward the future, and to do this they must revise the way they have lived up to the point when we first meet them. Similarly, innocence and guilt seem thematic polarities in Lumet's films, but, at least in his later films, the viewer is hard-pressed to discover a truly innocent character. Everyone is guilty of something, just as most of Lumet's guilty parties are also partly innocent. This theme is first clearly articulated in Lumet's *The Offence,* when the child molester Baxter says to Johnson, his police interrogator, that he has done nothing that Johnson himself has not longed to do. *The Offence* was released in 1973. The question of guilt and innocence has been a concern of Lumet's ever since.

Pure innocence is out of the question. It belongs to another time, another place. And even when Lumet can envision something approaching an innocent state, it is apt to be viewed with some reservation. In *A Stranger among Us,* purity and innocence are identified with the otherworldliness of the Hasidim, foreign to the rest of modern America. In films like *Serpico* and *Prince of the City* innocence is identified with ignorance. One recalls Mary Tyrone's entrance into the living room in her white wedding dress in the final moments of *Long*

Day's Journey into Night, where the quest for past innocence is identified with madness. Scholar Tod Gitlin has said that Lumet's "characters are sequestered in cramped physical and moral spaces. A superior
Lumet film doesn't open out, it closes in."[7] This is a fine observation,
for, as we have seen, Lumet's characters tend to find themselves entrapped by the situations they face. For Lumet, there seems to be one
reality above all that is inescapable: the world is simply too corrupt
and too complex to be dealt with by conventional heroes. Lumet's
comments about Danny Ciello in *Prince of the City* come to mind: "It's
a tragic picture. A tragedy in which a person goes in thinking he can
control the circumstances and winds up with the circumstances controlling him. It's a terrific allegory for life just now. After all, we're
all just using each other, aren't we?"

Lumet has grown reluctant to refer to his protagonists as heroes, to
his antagonists as villains, and such reluctance is surely instructive. It
is tempting to try to understand Lumet's protagonists by comparing
their strengths and weaknesses. But often, their strengths are also their
weaknesses. The naïveté that leads Frank Serpico or Danny Ciello into
circumstances they cannot control is simply the underside of the virtue
that motivates them to try to do good. The desperation that drives
Sonny Wortzik to hold up a bank also keeps him going once the robbery is foiled. The emotional blunting that isolates and limits Sol
Nazerman for the first half of *The Pawnbroker* is identified with a survival instinct that keeps him alive while others around him perished.
Perhaps Davis in *Twelve Angry Men* is as close to a genuine hero and
a pure character as Lumet has put before us. *Twelve Angry Men* was
made more than 30 years ago. The world of Lumet's films has grown
increasingly complex and corrupt during the intervening years.
Though he has portrayed that world with an ever-decreasing sense of
individual possibility, Lumet has never relinquished his belief in personal responsibility. Whether or not we like the message, Lumet has
reminded us that we are only as good as the society we create, that its
ills are ours, and that if America is out of control, headed for rack and
ruin, so are we. From *Twelve Angry Men* to *A Stranger among Us,*
Lumet does not simply put good characters in a bad situation and
leave them stranded. That would let them—and the rest of us—off the
hook too easily. In a Lumet film, the individual shares the responsibility for society's ills, even if he or she suffers its injustices.

The tension in a Lumet film between the protagonist pursuing an
individual identity while simultaneously seeking his place in the group

produces a synergism like that between other apparently contradictory alternatives—past and present, corruption and innocence, the protagonists' personal strengths and weaknesses. These dichotomies are not always present in a Lumet film but they do constitute a kind of signature. Certain cinematic patterns are generally present as well. Lumet has said repeatedly that he brings no personal, idiosyncratic cinematic style to a project, that he prefers to serve the material. In an article appearing in the 31 December 1981 *New York Times,* Lumet said:

> I don't consciously deal with trying to get the work into one line, one theme. . . . Obviously, it happens because it passes through one person, so that gets reflected in the work. But there is no preconceived philosophical or moral point of view that I'm initially aware of and therefore select the material accordingly. If it comes out that way, it comes out subconsciously. I respond totally instinctively to a script. . . . I subjugate myself to the material. . . . You find the technique to tell the story. You don't tell the story with your technique.

There is evidence to that effect when Lumet's films are viewed chronologically, but it is also clear that certain cinematic concerns reappear throughout Lumet's career. A few of these have been mentioned already. Some, like Lumet's use of water, are only incidental to the larger concerns of his work. His sense of composition, his use of a moving camera to redefine and recompose what we see before us, his interest in lighting, and his sense of spatial planes, are more central to those larger themes.

Lumet is one of the few directors working today who does his own camera "setups," that is, he personally sets the camera angle. This choice of physical alignment is normally the prerogative of the director of cinematography. Lumet reserves the right for himself to save time (Lumet prefers to have his cinematographer oversee the lighting while he oversees the camera placement), but also as a matter of artistic principle. If the setup is wrong, so is the scene. No doubt this concern goes back to Lumet's training in television, when the monitors allowed him to see what was about to go out over the air. The way Lumet composes shots within the frame may hearken back to this early training as well. Few bankable American directors have more consistently demonstrated an interest in the use of screen space. The "aspect ratio" of the movie screen, that is, the design of a screen proportionately wider than high, provides Lumet with composition possibilities that an early television director was denied. Lumet's composition runs the gamut. At one extreme, in *A Stranger among Us,* one finds formal balance, shots in which elements are arranged symmetrically within the frame. At the other, one finds such Expressionistic motifs as extreme low-angle camera work, a tracking camera that moves in concentric circles, the awkward compositional patterns noted in *Running on Empty,* and other techniques meant to distort and disrupt the viewer's sense of order.

Lumet's work also reveals an interest in moving the camera and recomposing within the frame with a minimum of edits, redefining what we see as we watch. Lumet's use of the moving camera varies from film to film. An extreme use of camera movement may be found in *Dog Day Afternoon.* The action seems to be photographed at normal focal range (about 55 mm), with one camera. (In fact, *Dog Day Afternoon* was photographed with many cameras, and the footage was carefully edited to produce this effect.) The characters threaten to pass out of our frame of vision. Objects seem to block the camera's path. We seem to be there on the spot, watching as the action unfolds and the camera records it with a sense of immediacy and realism. At the other extreme is the careful, conscious, moving camera work of *Twelve Angry Men* or *Long Day's Journey into Night,* where Lumet's moving camera "defines" and "reveals," to use his words. There, Lumet's camera capitalizes on a wider range of visual alternatives than would be possible on the stage, and it achieves an immediacy unavailable in print literature. This is more stylized than the work mentioned above. It puts us in the hands of a filmic presence that carefully manipulates what we see and how we see it, a thirteenth juror in the case of *Twelve Angry Men.*

Much of Lumet's moving camera work falls between such extremes. To appreciate Lumet's camera work, it is perhaps more accurate to think of such extremes as marking one end or the other of a continuum, and to locate each film along it. This is also true of Lumet's use of high-angle and low-angle cinematography, of his use of the height of the frame. Through changes on the vertical plane, the spatial context in which we are to understand the central elements of the shot are altered. In a few films—*Fail Safe,* for instance—the distortions of the low-angle camera work border on Expressionistic technique. More commonly, Lumet's films are less dramatic. One of the ways he underscores the progressive entrapment of his characters in the films I consider in this study is by lowering the camera on its vertical plane, so that walls, joists, and ceilings come into view. The characters' actions become circumscribed by their physical surroundings; as the plot entraps them, so does their environment.

As early as *Twelve Angry Men,* we noted, Lumet was interested in arranging characters within the frame in particular spatial relationships, sometimes isolating a character, and sometimes crowding his characters together. This interest has remained constant throughout his career. Particularly through changes of camera placement, Lumet redefines the frame's contents, and the spatial relationship of his characters to each other, in ways that underscore dramatic tensions and thematic concerns. For the last 15 years, he has emphasized the use of near, mid, and far distances. There tend to be several spatial levels in Lumet's frame at key moments in the drama, each offering a different element of information. This is not an entirely recent phenomenon, of course. *Long Day's Journey* made use of it 30 years ago. But since the early 1980s, Lumet has used such spatial referents with particular care. What we see—or do not see—behind Danny Ciello is often central to understanding Ciello's predicament. The bars and fences in the far distance behind Daniel Isaacson often tell us more about his plight than the dialogue to which we are listening. The corruption of common spatial referents in *Running on Empty* reminds us that few things are as the Popes would have them appear.

Since his collaboration with Andrezj Bartkowiak on *The Verdict,* Lumet's films have become increasingly dependent upon color. There are the blue, red, and orange patternings in *The Wiz,* for instance, the sepia hues of *Daniel,* the coloring in *The Verdict,* in which Lumet determined before filming that everything was to be auburn, yellow, red, and deep green. *Twelve Angry Men,* the work with which Lumet established his reputation as a serious director, was done in black and white, and Lumet has often spoken of the reluctance with which he first attempted color filmmaking, finally accepting *The Appointment* in order to work with color specialist Carlo DiPalma. But Lumet dipped his toe in the waters of color photography several years earlier while making *The Deadly Affair,* a production on which Freddie Young was Lumet's director of photography. The protagonist of the film, Charles Dobbs (James Mason), is one of Le Carre's spies who have been in the cold too long. Dobbs is spiritually depleted, barely alive when we meet him, and Lumet uses color to define him, much as he would to define Paul Newman's role in *The Verdict* some 20 years later. Working together, Young and Lumet found a way to decrease the tonal differences between hues of color, and between one color and the next, a process today known as "prefogging," in which the color value of blank film stock is reduced by exposing it to low-wattage incandescent lighting before loading it in the camera. It was perfect for Dobb's time of life; "colorless color," Lumet has called it, used to define the life of a colorless man. Lumet took what he learned while working on *The Deadly Affair* to his next project, *The Sea Gull*. There, too, he used a form of color reduction. Much of the film has a muted, autumnal quality; its central image is the white gull against a grey sky and blue-grey water, suggesting not only the passage of summer, but a long, cold winter ahead.

Lumet's growing interest in color is surely a logical extension of his use of lighting to achieve tonal differentiations in the frame. Bartkowiak and Lumet spent a full day analyzing the relationship of background to foreground in the paintings of Caravaggio as they were preparing to shoot *The Verdict,* and this is indicative of Lumet's interest in near, middle, and far distances within the frame, as well as his interest in lighting all three. Directing his first film, with Boris Kaufman as cinematographer, Lumet found lighting possibilities that had been denied him on the stage. While Lumet was a neophyte, Kaufman was a filmmaking veteran. He had first gotten worldwide attention for his work with Jean Vigo on *Zéro de conduite* in 1933; prior to working with Lumet on *Twelve Angry Men,* he had won an Academy Award for his cinematography in Elia Kazan's *On the Waterfront*. Kaufman was a master of the grey scale of black-and-white photography, able to achieve gradations of tones as well as any cinematographer of his generation, or better. Lumet has said that Kaufman could produce a hundred tonal variations, while a "marvelous" cinematographer would be defined as one who could produce up to 10. Lumet has suggested that anyone who doubts Kaufman's abilities has only to put two stills of Ralph Richardson in *Long Day's Journey into Night* side by side, from early and late in the film. Thanks to Kaufman's lighting, they appear to be two different characters.

The range of Lumet's editing is similarly broad. At one extreme are the lengthy takes in the middle of *Fail Safe,* one running almost five minutes, while at the other extreme are the flash frames in *The Pawnbroker,* in which shots appear for less than one-quarter of a second. One recalls the montage work in *Fail Safe* as New York City is being bombed, the opening minutes of *Dog Day Afternoon* and montages that begin films as widely varied as *Murder on the Orient Express, Bye,*

Bye Braverman, and *The Group*. Not surprisingly, perhaps, Lumet's editing is most impressive in films like *Dog Day Afternoon* (where he worked with Dede Allen), or *The Pawnbroker,* (where he worked with Ralph Rosenblum), that is, when working with his most gifted editors. This is not meant to detract from Lumet; on the contrary. About learning to work with color, Lumet has said, "That's one of the basic things I've learned about color—it begins with the art director and that's who you have to do your heaviest work with. Why leave it all to the camera? Let the camera augment it."[8] Lumet brings a similar sensibility to his work with all the key personnel on his crew. They compare judgments, then he makes the final decision. Ossie Morris has described what it was like to work with Lumet on *The Wiz*. "He feels, as a director, that he has the right to get the setups and this I will defend all the time. . . . On the other hand, he respected the fact that I had a right to comment on a particular setup if I was not happy . . . if anything [this method] saves time, because while he is getting the setup with the [camera] operator, I can be getting the lights roughed in."[9] Similarly, Lumet lets the editor edit whenever possible. Recalling their collaboration on *The Pawnbroker,* Ralph Rosenblum has said, "despite his mastery of editorial technique, Lumet was respectful of the editor's point of view and contribution; he never rejected something of value simply because he didn't originate it. Under Lumet I rarely had the opportunity to work out long stretches of film on my own, and I would have found working with him in recent years unsatisfying for that reason; but we operated as a team, and I always felt well used."[10]

In addition to his camera work, lighting, and editing, Lumet's work is marked by a few recurring motifs. His use of rain has been mentioned as one example. Rain is often associated in Lumet's films with baptism, initiation, or some other central change in his protagonist's life. When legendary Japanese movie director Akiro Kurosawa first saw *Prince of the City* he was impressed by the camera work and lighting. But what impressed him most of all was the rain. (One has only to watch the twenty-minute battle scene in the last reel of *Seven Samurai* to see why Kurosawa might have an appreciation of such things.) Shooting in natural rain produces visual images that are hardly rainlike, and Kurosawa was impressed not only by the verisimilar quality of rain in the film, but too, given the production problems it must have raised, by how many scenes employed it. Lumet's secret in creating rain had to do with the equipment he used and the weather in which he worked. He selected both carefully. He used four-hundred-foot "cherry pickers" equipped with hoses and pipes which extended nearly fifty feet above their uppermost reach. He waited for the wind, and then, after crossing the pipes and adjusting their spinning nozzles, he let the natural wind carry it. Tens of thousands of gallons of water were used in the process. Moving the cherry pickers about and positioning them outside the range of cameras required the patience of a monk and the forethought of a commanding general. The technical expertise required for this was developed over a period of some 20 years, but most immediately it came from Lumet's work with Owen Roizman on *Network*. Beale's growing messianic complex is marked by his "I'm mad as hell" speech which brings America to its feet. Beale's speech was intercut with the aftermath of a New York City thunderstorm, complete with biblical bolts of lighting. The decision to include the rain was made after primary production had ended. It was intended to be only a few hours work, but it turned into more. Owen Roizman has described how the scene was shot using fire hoses and cherry pickers.

> "We did a sort of second unit thing and it was supposed to be a lot of intercuts for the sequence in which Peter Finch yells . . . 'I'm mad as hell and I'm not going to take it anymore!' We [Lumet, Roizman] decided to give it a little extra visual punch by having it take place just after a rain, with lightning still in the distant sky. Well, that became the biggest shooting of the picture. We went out and did the whole thing in two or three nights and ended up by having fire trucks with water hoses to wet down all the buildings, so that we could get a little sheen from the water dripping off the windowsills. There were huge cherry pickers with lightning machines on them and we used one lightning machine to light each building. . . . We would shoot a section and then jump to another area and maybe do two or three a night."[11]

Of course, this scene had its precedent in the opening moments of *Serpico,* when the ambulance carrying Frank Serpico to the hospital rushes through the rain-soaked streets of New York, just as some 15 years later a squad car would rush young Al Reilly through the streets of New York in the rain in *Q & A*. About Lumet's sense of cinematography, Owen Roizman has said, "Sidney likes to work with a lot of cuts, but he will put in definite moves—and very important moves—when they're dramatically called for. But he's not a believer in moving the camera just to move it."[12] This is perhaps the key to understanding Lumet's sense of camera work: the best camera work does not immediately draw attention to itself at the expense of the story. Perhaps that is a key to understanding Lumet's overall cinematic technique.

Lumet has been periodically criticized for giving his screen adaptations of theatrical properties the sense of working within a proscenium arch, something he learned on the stage. A more profitable way to understand his working method might distinguish between our view from a chair in a Broadway theater, and what we can see through the eye of Lumet's camera. Certainly this is a distinction that Lumet has made. He has said,

> I was attacked for years about photographing stage plays—*Long Day's Journey into Night* and *The Sea Gull*—which is nonsense. Most critics are constantly confusing cinema with scenery. I say it's a movie if the camera can define it and reveal it as no other medium can. The decision about the degree of text to be kept, opening up or not, is predicated on one question: Can I get what I want out of it this way, or do I have to change the text as well? In both *Long Day's Journey* and *The Sea Gull*, I didn't need another in. That particular interpretation of *The Sea Gull*, I have never seen anywhere, and I don't think it can be gotten on the stage. I don't think that particular interpretation of *Long Day's Journey* can be gotten on the stage. [13]

Lumet has protested repeatedly that he is not an auteur, and this is true. He does not have a directorial signature in the sense of someone like Ingmar Bergman, nor such singularity of vision. Directing is an interpretative art for Lumet; his filmmaking is above all a collaborative effort, not a personal statement on the part of the director. Yet no matter how diverse and uneven it might seen at a glance, there are consistencies to be discovered in Lumet's work, in both form and content. Lumet is neither "the Second Coming," as he has put it, nor, again to use Lumet's own words, is he "just a good worker." Instead he is a gifted, intelligent director whose best films far outweigh the bad, a working director who surely deserves to be defined by his successes at least as much as his failures. Says Lumet,

> People keep saying: "What are you? You do a melodrama, then a drama, then a comedy, then a satire, a musical." . . . I don't understand all that. I know that our talents are our limitations. It's the narrowness of our understanding which forces us to go deeper, and then spread out down

there. The limitations make us good. But the form, the way of telling a story—I don't think any kind of work is superior. Bergman is the only real genius we've got as a director—and what Ingmar does, none of us can learn from. There's nothing to be learned from a genius. The root of the word even implies genetic difference.

For those of us who are simply good workers, all the rules are idiotic. It's just what Lena Horne sings in *The Wiz:* "Believe In Yourself." Whatever my limitations are—intellectually and emotionally—if I'm any good, they'll turn out to be my strengths."[14]

NOTES AND REFERENCES

Chapter One

1. Quoted in Anon., "Sidney Lumet," *Current Biography* 28 (September, 1967), 28. Appeared originally in the 21 May, 1962 Washington *Post*.
2. Frank Cunningham, *Sidney Lumet: Film and Literary Vision* (Lexington: University of Kentucky Press, 1991), 125.
3. Cunningham, 135.
4. Ralph Rosenblum and Robert Karen, *When the Shooting Stops . . . the Cutting Begins* (New York: Viking, 1979), 141–42. I am indebted to the authors throughout this section.
5. Rosenblum, 153.
6. Rosenblum, 162–63.

Chapter Two

1. Gwyn Robyns, *The Mystery of Agatha Christie* (New York: Doubleday, 1978), 175–76.
2. Peter Benchly, "The Direct Approach," *American Way* (November, 1983), 185.
3. William Wolf, "Director with a Conscience," *New York* (August, 1981), 54.
4. Wolf, 55.
5. W. Wolf, "Director with a Conscience," *New York,* 55. Lumet has told this story often, with slight variations. See, for instance, John Lombardi, "Lumet: the City Is His Soundstage," *New York Times Sunday Magazine* (June 6, 1982), 36.

Chapter Four

1. Anon., "Murder on 47th Street," *Premiere* (August, 1992), 36.
2. Dan Yakir, "Whiz Kid," *Film Comment* (November-December, 1978), 51.
3. Yakir, 54.
4. Benchly, "The Direct Approach," *American Way,* 185.
5. Yakir, "Wiz Kid," *Film Comment,* 51.
6. Yakir, 51.

7. Todd Gitlin, "The Blunder Years," *American Film* (September, 1988), 50.

8. Yakir, "Wiz Kid," *Film Comment*, 51.

9. Anon., "Photographing *The Wiz*," *American Cinematographer* (November, 1978), 1136–37.

10. Rosenblum and Karen, *When the Cutting Stops*, 152.

11. Anon., "*Network* and How It Was Photographed," *American Cinematographer* (April, 1977), 402.

12. "Network," 402.

13. Yakir, "Wiz Kid," *Film Comment*, 54.

14. Yakir, 54.

SELECTED BIBLIOGRAPHY

A. F. "Lumet, Sidney." *Film Ideal* 107 (11 January 1962): 626. Professional entry, one solid paragraph; suggests that Lumet was becoming identified with "serious" films and adaptations of stage material.

Appelbaum, Ralph. "Color and Concepts." *Films and Filming* 24 (May 1978): 13–16. Lumet had just done some of his best work; with that in mind, this article is just good enough to make one want it to be much better.

Bean, Robin. "The Insider: Sidney Lumet Talks to Robin Bean about His Work in Films." *Films and Filming* 11 (June 1966): 9–13. Sometimes cited—mistakenly—as Lumet's first in-depth interview (Bogdanovich's interview, cited below, preceded it chronologically, and is better); Bean is interested in Lumet as someone like Schaffner, Frankenheimer, and Penn, part of a new generation of film directors with a background in television.

"Behind the Scenes of *The Wiz*." *American Cinematographer* 11 (November 1978): 1068, 1104, 1120. General background on the making of *The Wiz*.

Bell, Arthur. "Prints of the City: A Talk with Sidney Lumet." *Vogue* August 5–11, 1981, 38. Lumet as a big city film maker.

Benchly, Peter. "Group Embalmed." *Holiday* 39 (May 1966): 155. Probably most interesting to someone about to read Pauline Kael's "The Making of *The Group*," cited below.

Bogdanovich, Peter. "An Interview With Sidney Lumet." *Film Quarterly* 14 (Winter 1960): 18–23. Although still a neophyte as a film director, in this interview Lumet is keenly aware of bringing to cinema what he has learned on the stage and in television.

Bosworth, Patricia. "Grouptalk—Groupthink." *New York Herald Tribune,* August 22, 1965, 12–18. Like Benchly's shorter article (above), this is best read in conjunction with Pauline Kael's "The Making of *The Group*" cited below.

Bowles, Stephen E. *Sidney Lumet: A Guide to References and Resources.* Boston: G.K. Hall, 1979. For more than a decade the only book-length work on Lumet; essentially a fine annotated filmography (with casts and plot summaries), a fine—if limited—bibliography, and more.

Brooks, Dick. "Sidney Lumet: Director with A Taste for Realism." *Motion Picture Herald* November 11, 1964, 16. Written as Lumet was making *The Hill;* the piece shows, in retrospect, that Lumet was on the brink of being touted as one of the gritty New York "realists."

Buckley, Peter. "The Direct Approach." *American Way*, November 1983, 182–85. What it took to bring E.L. Doctorow's *The Book of Daniel* to the screen.

Burke, Tom. "Suddenly I Knew How to Film the Play." *New York Times*, July 24, 1977, section D, 9, 20. How Lumet finally decided to take on the film adaptation of *Equus*, a work that to him seemed perfectly suited for the stage alone.

Casty, Alan. "*The Pawnbroker* and the New Direction In Film Realism." *Film Heritage* 1 (Spring 1966): 3–14. Lumet on the cutting edge of an American film movement in sync with the methods and mentalities of European auteurs.

Chanko, Kenneth M. "Sidney Lumet: An Interview." *Films in Review* 35 (October 1984): 451–56. Much of what Lumet says here was already on the record in some form; the interview is most informative regarding Lumet's views on the director's relationship to his material.

Combs, Richard. "Sidney Lumet." In *Cinema, A Critical Directory: The Major Film-Makers*. Vol. 2, edited by Richard Roud, 650–52. London: Secker and Warburg, 1980. Professional entry in a European reference work.

Coursodon, Jean-Pierre. *American Directors*, vol. 2. New York: McGraw-Hill, 1983. Professional entry.

Cowie, Peter. "Five Directors of the Year." In *International Film Guide*. Vol. 5, edited by Peter Cowie, 20–25. London: Tantivy, 1968. Lumet hailed as one of the most promising of a new generation of American directors.

———. *50 Major Film-Makers*. London: Tantivy, 1975, 150–54. Professional entry.

Crist, Judith. "Two Big 'Little' Films." In *The Private Eye, the Cowboy, and the Very Naked Girl*, 123–25. New York: Paperback Library, 1970. Crist reviews *The Pawnbroker*.

Cunningham, Frank R. "The Insistence of Memory: The Opening Sequences of Lumet's Pawnbroker." *Literature/Film Quarterly*, 1 (1989): 39–43. Good analysis of editing in *The Pawnbroker*, some of which was later incorporated in Cunningham's book-length study.

Cunningham, Frank R. *Sidney Lumet: Film and Literary Vision*. Lexington: University of Kentucky Press, 1991. Cunningham argues persuasively that Lumet's work is concerned thematically with personal responsibility, and that Lumet brings print and stage properties to the screen with an artistry that demands our attention.

Cunningham, Frank R. "Sidney Lumet's Humanism: The Return to the Father in *12 Angry Men*." *Literature/Film Quarterly* 2 (1986): 112–21. Cunningham explores Lumet's first film thematically, bringing to the film the same care and intelligence Cunningham might have brought to an exegesis of a novel or play.

"Director Participation." *Life* 34 (June 8 1953): 103. Introduction of a bright young man working in a bright young medium.

Dundy, Elaine. "Why Actors Do Better for Sidney Lumet." *New York,* November 22, 1976, 82. Lumet as an "actors' director," his willingness to improvise during rehearsal.

"Economy Class Journey." *Time* 79 (June 1 1962): 50. Lumet brings Eugene O'Neill's *Long Day's Journey Into Night* to the screen.

Farber, Manny. "Hard-Sell Cinema" in *Negative Space: Manny Farber on the Movies,* 113–24. New York: Praeger, 1971. In this 1957 article, Farber dismisses—in one stroke—the "ersatz" artistry of Lumet and a number of young artists, many of whom went on to become the grand old men of American arts and letters, among them the painter Larry Rivers and writer Saul Bellow.

Farber, Stephen. "Daniel." *Film Quarterly* 39 (Spring 1984): 32–37. Lumet's attraction to the concerns of Doctorow's novel, and how he worked to actualize those concerns cinematically.

———. "Lumet in '69." *Sight and Sound* 38 (Autumn 1969): 190–95. Farber discusses Lumet's style and his willingness to experiment artistically in what is fundamentally a commercial medium.

Fenin, G. "The Face of 63—United States." *Films and Filming* 11 (March 63): 55. Professional entry.

Fisher, Bob. "Magical Matte Paintings for *The Wiz.*" *American Cinematographer* 11 (November 1978): 1078–79, 1108–9. An often fascinating, behind-the-scenes look at how the film's mattes were created and employed.

Flatly, Guy. "Lumet—The Kid Actor Who Became a Director." *New York Times,* January 20, 1974, section, 11, 13. Written while Lumet was enjoying the back-to-back success of *Murder on the Orient Express* and *Serpico;* Lumet's roots on the stage, his rise to success, his growing interest in corruption in America and the way in which money corrupts the American Dream.

"Following the Yellow Brick Road from *The Wonderful World of Oz* to *The Wiz.*" *American Cinematographer* 11 (November 1978): 1090–91. Primarily, Lumet's departure from the MGM, Judy Garland classic.

Foster, Frederick. "Filming *The Fugitive Kind.*" *American Cinematographer* 41 (June 1960): 354–55, 379–80, 382. Of particular interest when read with Kathleen Murphy's "Dead Heat on a Merry-Go-Round," cited below.

Gitlin, Todd. "The Blunder Years." *American Film* 10 (September 88): 48–52. What begins as a review of *Running on Empty* turns into a thoughtful and thought-provoking account of Lumet's concerns as an America filmmaker dealing with his country's confusions and doubts.

"Good Men and True and All Angry." *Life* 42 (April 22 1957): 137. Lumet's emergence as a film director.

Gow, Gordon. "What's Real? What's True?" *Films and Filming* 8 (May 1975): 10–16. Lumet discusses his films through *Dog Day Afternoon;* Gow is particularly interested in how Lumet fictionalizes nonfiction material.

Gronstedt, Olle, Bo Johan Hultman, and Torsten Manns. "Samtal om Pant-lanaren." *Chaplin* 64 (May 1966): 176–177. Focus on *The Pawnbroker*.

H. H. "Sidney Lumet." *Skoop* 5 (June–July 1977): 12–13, 22. Brief professional entry.

Hirschfeld, Gerald. "Low Key Lighting for *Fail Safe*." *American Cinematographer* 44 (August 1963): 462–63, 482–84. Important and informative article for anyone interested in Lumet's cinematics, especially his interest in Expressionistic techniques.

Hogan, Randolph. "Sidney Lumet's Love Affair with New York." *New York Times*, December 31, 1981, section D, 7. Lumet as one of the New York School of film makers.

Kael, Pauline. "The Making of *The Group*." In *Kiss Kiss Bang Bang*, 65–100. New York: Atlantic Monthly Press, 1968. Kael was present during much of the production, and found little if anything about Lumet and his talents she thought worthy of her time and attention.

———. "A View from the Bridge . . ." In *I Lost it at the Movies*, 172–75. Boston: Little, Brown and Company, 1965. Dismissive review of Lumet and the film.

Kaufman, Boris. "Filming *12 Angry Men* on a Single Set." *American Cinematographer* 37 (December 1956): 724–25. The best place to begin for anyone interested in Lumet's use of a camera and interest in composition.

Kauffman, Stanley. "A View From The Bridge." In *A World on Film: Criticism and Comment*, 102–6. New York: Dell, 1966. For anyone interested in Lumet's problems with his critics, a particularly telling dismissal.

Kerner, Bruce. "An Interview with Kenneth Hyman." *Cinema* 2 (Summer 1968): 5–9. On the making of *The Hill*, by its producer.

Kerr, Peter. "Campus Radicals Count the Cost of Commitment." *New York Times*, September 4, 1988, *Arts and Leisure*, 17, 20. A particularly intelligent newspaper article on *Running on Empty*.

Kilday, Gregg. "All The Prince's Men." *Los Angeles Herald-Examiner*, August 23, 1981, section E, 1, 10. On the making of *Prince of the City*, familiar career material as background.

Labarca, Daniel. "Sidney Lumet y Su Obra." *Cine al dia* 7 (March 1969): 28–29. Cursory treatment of Lumet's films through *A Deadly Affair*.

Lally, Kevin. "Versatility Gives Lumet Staying Power." *Film Journal* 89 (January 1986): 8, 26. Lumet as an interpreter of others' work, able and willing to serve it.

Lawrenson, Helen. "The Mixed Marriage of Gail Lumet." *Cosmopolitan* (February 1967): 66–68. On Lumet's interracial marriage to Lena Horne's daughter, Gail.

Loynd, Ray. "Lumet's Sterling Season." *Los Angeles Herald-Examiner*, January 23, 1977, section H, 1–2. After years of uneven work, Lumet is presented as a director who has come into his own; ominously, written as Lumet was finishing the editing of *Equus* and doing pre-production for *The Wiz*.

Lombardi, John. "Lumet: The City Is His Sound Stage." *New York Times Magazine,* June 6, 1982. Lumet as a New York director, currently at work on *The Verdict.*

Luciano, Dale. *"Long Day's Journey Into Night:* An Interview with Sidney Lumet." *Film Quarterly* 25 (Fall 1971): 20–29. Lumet is at his best and most informative about the making of this film; perhaps the single most frequently quoted document on Lumet as a director.

"Lumet, Sidney." *Filmlexicon degli autori e delle opere: Aggiormente e Integrazi, 1958–1971.* Vol 3. Edited by Aldo Bernardini, 1151, Rome: Edizioni di Bianco e Nero, 1973. Further evidence of recognition of Lumet in Europe, but, curiously, only his first three films are mentioned.

Lumet, Sidney. "How to Get The Best Out of People." *Coronet* (November 1969): 127–30. A discussion of how Lumet directs his actors, but also revealing about the man himself.

———. "Keep Them On The Hook." *Films and Filming* 11 (October 1964): 17–20. Lumet discusses risks and problems faced in the making of *The Pawnbroker.*

———. "Le Point de vue du metteur en scène." *Cahiers du Cinéma* 94 (April 1959): 32–34. Lumet speaks intelligently and in detail about how he directed television shows ("Danger"); the original English version from which the article was translated into French is not available.

———. "Notes on TV." *Cue* July 19, 1952, 6. The problems faced by a young television director, and the potential of the new medium to do more than entertain.

———. On a Film 'Journey.'" *New York Times,* October 7, 1962, sec 2, p. 7. The making of "Long Day's Journey;" Lumet distinguishes between the considerations of a stage and film director.

———. "Sidney Lumet." *Cahiers du Cinéma,* 150–51 (December 1963–January 1964): 56–57. Comparison of the American and European film industries.

———. "Why I Like It Here: A Statement by Sidney Lumet." *Making Films in New York,* 1 (March 1969): 17. Lumet distances himself from Hollywood, literally and metaphorically.

———. "Sidney Lumet on the Director," in *Movie People: At Work in the Business of Film.* Edited by Fred Baker. 35–50. New York: Douglas, 1972. A two-part article, done over the course of several years, in which Lumet discusses the trials and tribulations of moviemaking.

Margolick, David. "Again, Sidney Lumet Ponders Justice," *New York Times,* December 31, 1989, section H, 9. A recognition of thematic similarities between Lumet's work of the mid-1970s up through *Prince of the City,* and the less satisfying work to follow; useful in particular for anyone trying to find a thematic path leading toward *Running on Empty,* and *Q & A.*

McDonald, Dwight. "Good Movies, Bad Movies and *The Pawnbroker.*" In *On Movies.* 159–63. New York: Berkeley, 1971. McDonald cites failings in *The Pawnbroker,* which he suggests are Lumet's failings as a person, as well as a director.

————. "Kazanistan, Ingeland and Williams, Tenn." In *On Movies.* 164–74. New York: Berkeley, 1971. Similar arguments as in the above citation, this time in regard to *The Fugitive Kind.*

Merrill, Susan. "Sidney Lumet: *The Offence:* An Interview with Susan Merrill." *Films in Review* 9 (November 1973): 523–28, 556. The title is misleading; fundamentally a consideration of Lumet's directorial concerns and abilities up to this film.

"Midtersiderne: 107 Hollywood Instrucktorer. Et Leksikon af Per Calum og Moren Piil." *Kosmorama* 87 (1968): xiii. Professional entry in a European compendium of American film directors.

Miles, Cynthia. "Lumet in East Euro: Director's Responsibility Mulled." *Variety,* November 16, 1981, 7. Returning from a tour of Eastern block countries, Lumet discusses the freedoms and responsibilities of American directors.

Minoff, P. "Danger Is His Business." *Cue* July 21, 1951, 13. A young television director with a successful show on his hands.

Moskowitz, Gene. "The Tight Close-Up." *Sight and Sound* 29 (Winter 1959–60): 126–30. A discussion of Lumet and other young television directors who are going on to do films; most interesting for its discussion of the rigors and limitations of early television direction.

Murphy, Kathleen. "Dead Heat on a Merry-Go-Round." *Film Comment* 6 (November–December 1990): 59–62. Parallels between Lumet's *The Fugitive Kind* and David Lynch's *Wild at Heart,* made some 30 years later.

O'Toole, Lawrence. "Fast But Not Cheap." *Marquee,* August–September 1983, 17–19. On the making of *Daniel.*

————. "Sidney Lumet." *Moviegoer,* October 1983, 9–11. Standard profile, combined with more on the making of *Daniel* (see above).

"Personality of the Month: Sidney Lumet." *Films and Filming* 11 (August 1960): 5. On the eve of *The Fugitive Kind,* Lumet is recognized as a serious young director.

"Photographing *The Wiz.*" *American Cinematographer* 11 (November 1978): 1070–73, 1098–99, 1106–1107, 1129–37. An exquisite interview with cinematographer Oswald Morris; though technical, the gist of the interview will be comprehensible to anyone who has ever taken a snapshot.

Petrie, Graham. "The Films of Sidney Lumet: Adaptation as Art." *Film Quarterly* 21 (Winter 1967–68): 9–18. Lumet's adaptations of stage and print material to the screen through *A Deadly Affair;* Petrie's article was among the first to explore Lumet's directorial talents, defying the commonly held assumption that Lumet was only as good as his material.

Rafferty, Terrence. "The Current Cinema." *New Yorker,* September 19, 1988, 86–89. A dismissal of *Running on Empty,* replete with many of the common criticisms of Lumet's directorial skills.

Robyns, Gwen. *The Mystery of Agatha Christie.* 170–76. New York: Doubleday, 1978. In this section, and elsewhere, Robyns recounts the making of *Murder on the Orient Express.*

Roizman, Owen. "*Network* and How It Was Photographed." *American Cinematographer* 58 (April 1977): 384 ff. Rewarding account of production problems and solutions by one of the best cinematographers in the business.

Rosenblum, Ralph, and Robert Karen. *When the Shooting Stops . . . the Cutting Begins: A Film Editor's Story.* New York: Penguin, 1980. Admirable account of the role of the editor; see Rosenblum's account of three Lumet productions, *Long Day's Journey into Night, Fail Safe,* and *The Pawnbroker.*

Ross, Lillian. "Profiles: Kurosawa Frames." *New Yorker,* December 21, 1981, 51–78. Though devoted to a visit to New York by the famed Japanese director, Kurosawa's admiration for Lumet is worth noting.

Sarris, Andrew. *The American Cinema: Directors and Directions, 1929–1968.* 197–98. New York: Dutton, 1968. Formal, professional entry.

————. "Likeable But Elusive." *Film Culture* 28 (Spring 1963): 35. Sarris voices an ambivalence about Lumet's work that he maintained as Lumet's work progressed.

Schine, Cathleen. "Sidney Lumet Shoots Again." *Vogue* March 1982, 232. More a celebrity profile given to promote *Deathtrap* than a consideration of Lumet's films, it is of interest because the author's ambivalence toward Lumet's work is so obvious, and so common; what respect Schine can find for Lumet is, virtually by her own admission, a grudging respect.

Sharples, Win, Jr. "The Filming of *Serpico.*" *Filmmakers Newsletter* 7 (February 1974): 30–34. Lumet as a New York "realist," facing production problems while shooting on location.

Sheinman, Mort. "Sidney Lumet: Letting It Happen." *Women's Wear Daily,* October 2, 1975, 12. A glimpse at Lumet's directorial method; written while Lumet was at work on *Network,* it is most interesting for his description of shooting earlier films on location, particularly *The Pawnbroker* and *Dog Day Afternoon.*

Shewey, Don. "Sidney Lumet: The Reluctant Auteur." *American Film* (December 1982): 31–36. Shewey does his best to find an appropriate place for Lumet among contemporary American directors.

"Sidney Lumet." *Cinema* 58 (May 1958): 11. One of the first European recognitions of Lumet as a director.

"Sidney Lumet." *Current Biography* 28 (September 1967), 258–60. Lumet's life and career up to the making of *Bye, Bye Braverman;* more than 3,000 words long, among the most thoughtful, scholarly treatments Lumet had been given to date.

Smith, Gavin. "Sidney Lumet: Lion on the Left." *Film Comment* 24 (August 1988): 32–38. Sidney Lumet as a socially-conscious film maker at his most committed when working on films with a message.

Smith, Gavin. "'That's the Way it Happens.'" *Film Comment* 28 (September–October 1992): 50–56. Lumet discusses his cinematic style and his approach to movie making in this interview, with particular attention to his latest films, *Q & A* and *A Stranger among Us*.

Steele, Robert. "Another Trip to the Pawnshop." *Film Heritage* 1 (Spring 1966): 15–22. Both in form and content, Lumet's work stands apart from typical Hollywood films and from the work of other young film makers of his generation.

Swedien, Bruce F. "The Accusonic Recording Process Makes Its Debut." *American Cinematographer* 11 (November 1978): 1082–83, 1096. While of little general interest, this account of introducing a state-of-the-art sound process in the making of *The Wiz* is interesting for what it says about the scope of the production.

Turpin, Gerry. "LIGHTFLEX: A Whole New World of Color on the Screen." *American Cinematographer* 11 (November 1978):1086 ff. For someone particularly interested in Lumet's use of light values and color perhaps, but more technical than most will want.

Underwood, Lynn. "Agatha's Orient Express." In *Agatha Christie*. 39–42. New York: Harper Paperbacks, 1990. Supplies good background information on the making of *Murder on the Orient Express*.

Walton, Tony. "Of Munchkins, Winkies and the Emerald City." *American Cinematographer* 11 (November 1978): 1076, 1116–17, 1122. Lumet's desire to balance the real and the fantastic in *The Wiz*, and the part Walton played in this.

Weiler, A. H. "A Funeral Grows in Brookyln." *New York Times*, April 23, 1967, section 2, 15, 20. Lumet and the making of *Bye, Bye Braverman* on location in the neighborhood where Lumet grew up.

"What Directors Are Saying." *Action* November–December 1969, 28.

"What Directors Are Saying." *Action* May–June 1970, 30.

"Why Am I Happy?" *Newsweek* 24 (12 June 1961): 94. Lumet brings Arthur Miller's *A View from the Bridge* to the screen.

Wolf, William. "Director With A Conscience." *New York*, August 10, 1981, 54–55. On the making of *Prince of the City*, Lumet's screen adaptation of the book, Lumet's ambivalence about the protagonist.

Yakir, Dan. "Wiz Kid." *Film Comment* 14 (November–December 1978): 49–54. Discussion of *The Wiz*, along with good questions posed to Lumet and his generous responses; for anyone primarily interested in *The Wiz*, the first piece you should read.

Young, Freddie. "A Method of Pre-Exposing Color Negative for Subtle Effect." *American Cinematographer* 47 (August 1966): 537. Cinematographer Freddie Young discusses *A Deadly Affair*; the first discussion of Lumet's use of color.

FILMOGRAPHY

Films Directed by Sidney Lumet

Twelve Angry Men (1957)

Producers: Henry Fonda and Reginald Rose
Director: Sidney Lumet
Story and Screenplay: Reginald Rose, from his original teleplay
Director of Photography: Boris Kaufman
Art Direction: Robert Markell
Music: Kenyon Hopkins
Sound: James Gleason
Editor: Carl Lerner
Associate Producer: George Justin
Cast: Henry Fonda (Juror No. 8, Davis), Lee J. Cobb (Juror No. 3), Ed
    Begley (Juror No. 10), E. G. Marshall (Juror No. 4), Jack Warden
    (Juror No. 7), Martin Balsam (Juror No. 1), John Fielder (Juror No.
    2), Jack Klugman (Juror No. 5), Edward Binns (Juror No. 6), Joseph
    Sweeney (Juror No. 9, Arnold), George Voskovec (Juror No. 11),
    Robert Webber (Juror No. 12), Rudy Bond (Judge), James A. Kelly
    (Guard), Bill Nelson (Court Clerk), John Savoca (Defendant).
Distribution: United Artists
Running Time: 95 minutes
Release: April, 1957

Stage Struck (1958)

Producer: Stuart Millar
Director: Sidney Lumet
Screenplay: Ruth and Augustus Goetz, based on the play *Morning Glory* by
    Zoe Akins
Directors of Photography: Franz F. Planer and Maurice Hartzband
Art Direction: Kim Edgar Swandos
Music: Alex North
Sound: James A. Gleason, Terry Kellum
Costume Designer: Moss Mabry
Editor: Stuart Gilmore
Production Supervisor: George Justin
Production Assistant: Stephen Bono

Assistant Director: Charles H. Maguire
Second Assistant Director: William C. Garrity
In Charge of Production: William Dozier
Make-up: Bob Jiras
Hairdresser: Willis Hanchett
Cast: Henry Fonda (Lewis Easton), Susan Strasberg (Eva Lovelace), Joan
    Greenwood (Rita Vernon), Herbert Marshall (Robert Hedges),
    Christopher Plummer (Joe Sheridan), Daniel Ocko (Constantine), Pat
    Harrington (Benny), Frank Campanella (Victor), John Fielder (Adrian),
    Patricia Englund (Gwen Hall), Jack Weston (Frank), Sally Gracie
    (Elizabeth), Nina Hansen (Regina), Harold Grau (Stage Doorman)
Distribution: RKO-Radio (Buena Vista)
Running Time: 95 minutes
Color: Technicolor
Release: March, 1958

That Kind of Woman (1959)
Producers: Carlo Ponti, Marcello Girosi
Director: Sidney Lumet
Screenplay: Walter Bernstein, from a story by Robert Lowry
Photography: Boris Kaufman
Art Direction: Hal Pereira, Roland Anderson
Music: Daniel Amfitheatrof
Sound: James Gleason, Charles Grenzback
Editor: Howard Smith
Associate Producer: Ray Wander
Cast: Sophia Loren (Kay), Tab Hunter (Red), George Sanders (The Man),
    Jack Warden (Kelly), Barbara Nichols (Jane), Keenan Wynn (Harry)
Distribution: Paramount
Running Time: 92 minutes
Release: September, 1959

The Fugitive Kind (1960)
Producers: Martin Jurow and Richard A. Shepherd
Director: Sidney Lumet
Screenplay: Tennessee Williams and Meade Roberts, based on Williams's
    play *Orpheus Descending*
Photography: Boris Kaufman
Art Direction: Richard Sylbert
Set Decoration: Gene Challahan
Music Composed and Conducted by: Kenyon Hopkins
Sound: James Gleason and Philip Gleason
Costumes: Frank Thompson

Editor: Carl Lerner
Assistant Director: Charles H. Maguire
Associate Producer: George Justin
Cast: Marlon Brando (Val Xavier), Anna Magnani (Lady Torrance), Joanne
    Woodward (Carol Cutrere), Maureen Stapleton (Vee Talbot), Victor
    Jory (Jabe Torrance), R. G. Armstrong (Sheriff Talbot), Emory
    Richardson (Uncle Pleasant, the Conjure Man), Spivy (Ruby
    Lightfoot), Sally Gracie (Dolly Hamma), Lucille Benson (Beulah
    Binnings), John Baragrey (David Cutrere), Ben Yaffee (Dog Hamma),
    Joe Brown, Jr. (Pee Wee Binnings), Virgilia Chew (Nurse Porter),
    Frank Borgman (Gas Station Attendant), Janice Mars (Attendant's
    Wife), Debbie Lynch (Lonely Girl).
Distribution: United Artists
Running Time: 135 minutes
Release: May, 1960

A View from the Bridge (1961)
Producer: Paul Graetz
Director: Sidney Lumet
Screenplay: Norman Rosten, based on Arthur Miller's play
Director of Photography: Michel Kelber
Art Direction: Jacques Saulnier
Music: Maurice Leroux
Sound: Jo deBretagne
Editor: Francoise Javet
Assistant Director: Dossia Mage
Production Manager: Julien Riviere
Cast: Raf Vallone (Eddie Carbone), Jean Sorel (Rodolpho), Maureen
    Stapleton (Beatrice Carbone), Carol Lawrence (Catherine), Raymond
    Pellegrin (Marco), Morris Carnovsky (Mr. Alfieri), Harvey Lembeck
    (Mike), Mickey Knox (Louis), Vincent Gardenia (Lipari), Frank
    Campanella (Longshoreman).
Distribution: Paramount
Running Time: 114 minutes
Release: 1961
European title: *Vu Du Pont*

Long Day's Journey into Night (1962)
Producer: Ely Landau
Director: Sidney Lumet
Screenplay: Eugene O'Neill's play
Photography: Boris Kaufman
Art Direction: Richard Sylbert

Music Composed and Played by: André Previn
Costumes: Motley
Production Supervisor: George Justin
Editor: Ralph Rosenblum
Cast: Katharine Hepburn (Mary Tyrone), Ralph Richardson (James Tyrone
    Sr.), Jason Robards, Jr. (Jamie Tyrone), Dean Stockwell (Edmund
    Tyrone), Jeanne Barr (Kathleen the Maid).
Distribution: Twentieth Century-Fox
Running Time: 136 minutes
Release: 1962

Fail Safe (1964)

Producer: Max W. Youngstein
Director: Sidney Lumet
Screenplay: Walter Bernstein, based on the novel by Eugene Burdick and
    Harvey Wheeler
Director of Photography: Gerald Hirschfeld
Art Direction: Albert Brenner
Set Decoration: J. C. Delaney
Sound: Jack Fitzstephens, William Swift
Costumes: Anna Hill Johnstone
Editor: Ralph Rosenblum
Sound Editor: Jack Fitzstephens
Sound Mixer: William Swift
Assistant Director: Harry Falk, Jr.
Associate Producer: Charles H. Maquire
Special and Animated Effects: Storyboard, Inc.
Camera Operator: Al Taffett
Chief Electrician: Howard Fortune
Chief Grip: Edward Knott
Continuity: Marguerite James
Make-up: Harry Buchman
Titles: F. Hillsberg, Inc.
Cast: Henry Fonda (the President), Dan O'Herlihy (General Black), Walter
    Matthau (Groeteschele), Frank Overton (General Bogan), Edward
    Binns (Colonel Grady), Fritz Weaver (Colonel Cascio), Larry Hagman
    (Buck), William Hansen (Secretary Swenson), Rullel Hardie (General
    Stark), Russel Collins (Knapp), Sorrel Booke (Congressman Raskob),
    Nancy Berg (Isla Wolfe), John Connell (Thomas), Frank Simpson
    (Sullivan), Hildy Parks (Betty Black), Janet Ward (Mrs. Grady), Dom
    DeLouise (Sgt. Collins), Dana Elcar (Foster), Stuart Germain (Mr.
    Cascio), Louise Larabee (Mrs. Cascio), Frieda Altman (Jennie), Bob
    Gerringer (Fly).

Distribution: BLC/Columbia
Running Time: 112 minutes
Release: October, 1964

The Pawnbroker (1965)

Producers: Roger H. Lewis and Philip Langner
Director: Sidney Lumet
Screenplay: David Friedkin and Morton Fine, based on the novel by Edward
    Lewis Wallant
Photography: Boris Kaufman
Art Direction: Richard Sylbert
Set Decoration: Jack Flaherty
Music: Quincy Jones
Sound: Dennis Maitland
Costumes: Anna Hill Johnstone
Editor: Ralph Rosenblum
Associate Producer: Joseph Manduke
Executive Producer: Worthington Miner
Production Manager: Ulu Grosbard
Assistant Director: Dan Eriksen
Make-up: Bill Herman
Production Head: Alfred Markim
Cast: Rod Steiger (Sol Nazerman), Geraldine Fitzgerald (Marilyn
    Birchfield), Brock Peters (Rodriquez), Jaime Sanchez (Jesus Ortiz),
    Thelma Oliver (Mabel), Marketa Kimbrell (Tessie), Baruch Lumet
    (Mendel), Juano Hernandez (Mr. Smith, the Philosopher), Linda Geiser
    (Ruth), Nancy R. Pollock (Bertha), Raymond St. Jacques (Tangee),
    John McCurry (Buck), Charles Dierkop (Robinson), Eusebia Cosme
    (Mrs. Ortiz), Warren Finnerty (Savarese), Jack Ader (Morton),
    Marianne Kanter (Joan), E. M. Margolese (Papa).
Distribution: Planet-Landau/Allied Artists
Running Time: 115 minutes
Release: April, 1965

The Hill (1965)

Producer: Kenneth Hyman
Director: Sidney Lumet
Screenplay: Ray Rigby, based on a play by Rigby and R. S. Allen
Photography: Oswald Morris
Art Direction: Herbert Smith
Music: None
Sound Editor: Peter Musgrave
Sound Recordist: David Bowen

Recording Supervisor: A. W. Watkins
Dubbing Mixer: Fred Turtle
Film Editor: Thelma Connell
Associate Producer: Ray Anzarut
Assistant Directors: Frank Ernst and Pedro Vidal
Make-up: George Partleton
Wardrobe Supervisor: Elsa Fennell
Technical Advisor: George Montford
Camera Operator: Brian West
Continuity: Lee Turner
Cast: Sean Connery (Joe Roberts), Harry Andrews (Regimental Sergeant
    Major Wilson), Ian Bannen (Harris), Alfred Lynch (George Stevens),
    Ossie Davis (Jacko King), Roy Kinnear (Monty Bartlett), Jack Watson
    (Jock McGrath), Ian Hendry (Williams), Sir Michael Redgrave
    (Medical Officer), Norman Bird (Commandant), Neil McCarthy
    (Burton), Howard Goorney (Walters), Tony Caunter (Martin).
Distribution: MGM
Running Time: 123 minutes
Release: October, 1967

The Group (1966)
Producer: Sidney Buchman
Director: Sidney Lumet
Screenplay: Sidney Buchman, based on the novel by Mary McCarthy
Photography: Boris Kaufman
Scenic Artist: Stanley Cappiello
Production Designer: Gene Callahan
Set Decoration: Jack Wright, Jr.
Music Supervisor: Charles Gross
Music Conducted by: Robert deCormier
Sound: Jack Fitzstephens and Dennis Maitland
Costumes: Anna Hill Johnstone
Editor: Ralph Rosenblum
Production Manager: Mel Howard
Production Supervisor: Henry Spitz
Director: Dan Eriksen, Tony Belletier
Make-up: Irving Buchman
Hairstyles: Frederick Jones
Cast: Candice Bergen (Elinor Eastlake, "Lakey"), Joan Hackett (Dorothy
    Renfrew), Elizabeth Hartman (Priss Harshorn), Shirley Knight (Polly
    Andrews), Joanna Pettet (Kay Strong), Mary-Robin Redd (Pokey
    Prothero), Jessica Walter (Libby MacAusland), Kathleen Widdoes
    (Helena Davison), James Broderick (Dr. James Ridgeley), James

Congdon (Sloan Crockett), Larry Hagman (Harald Peterson), Hal
Holbrook (Gus Leroy), Richard Mulligan (Dick Brown), Robert
Emhardt (Mr. Andrews), Carrie Nye (Norine), Philippa Bevans (Mrs.
Hartshorn), Leta Bonynge (Mrs. Prothero), Marion Brash (Radio
Man's Wife), Sara Burton (Mrs. Davison), Flora Campbell (Mrs.
MacAusland), Bruno DiCosmi (Nils), Leora Dana (Mrs. Renfrew), Bill
Fletcher (Bill), George Gaynes (Brook Latham), Martha Greenhouse
(Mrs. Bergler), Russell Hardie (Mr. Davison), Doreen Lang (Nurse
Swenson), Chet London (Radio Man), John O'Liary (Putnam Blake),
Baruch Lumet (Mr. Schneider), Hildy Parks (Nurse Catherine), Lidia
Prochnicka (The Baroness), Polly Rowles (Mrs. Andrews), Douglas
Rutherford (Mr. Prothero), Truman Smith (Mr. Bergler), Loretta White
(Mrs. Eastlake), Richard Graham (Rev. Garland), Arthur Anderson
(Pokey's Husband), Clay Johns (Phil), Ed Holmes (Mr. MacAusland).
Distribution: United Artists
Running Time: 150 minutes
Color: DeLuxe
Release: March, 1966

The Deadly Affair (1967)
Producer: Sidney Lumet
Director: Sidney Lumet
Screenplay: Paul Dehn, based on the novel *Call for the Dead* by John
    Le Carre
Photography: Freddie Young
Art Direction: John Howell
Set Decorations: Pamela Cornell
Music: Quincy Jones
Sound: Les Hammond
Costumes: Cynthia Tingay
Editor: Thelma Connell
Associate Producer: Denis O'Dell
Production Manager: Victor Peck
Assistant Director: Ted Sturgis
Make-up: Jill Carpenter
Hairstyles: Betty Glasgow
Cast: James Mason (Charles Dobbs), Simone Signoret (Elsa Fennan),
    Maximilian Schell (Dieter Frey), Harriet Anderson (Ann Dobbs), Harry
    Andrews (Inspector Mendel), Kenneth Haigh (Bill Appleby), Lynn
    Redgrave (Virgin), Roy Kinnear (Adam Scarr), Max Adrian (Adviser),
    Robert Flemyng (Samuel Fennan), Colin Redgrave (Director), Les
    White (Harek), June Murphy, Frank Williams, Rosemary Load (The
    Three Witches in *Macbeth*), Kenneth Ives (Stagehand), John Dimech

(Waiter), Julian Sherrier (Head Waiter), Petra Markham (Daughter at Theatre), Denis Shaw (Landlord), Maria Charles (Blonde), Amanda Walker (Brunette), Sheraton Blout (Eunice Scarr), Janet Hargreaves (Ticket Clerk), Michael Brennan (Barman), Richard Steele and Gartan Klauber (Businessmen), Margaret Lacey (Mrs. Bird), Judy Keirn (Stewardess), and The Royal Shakespeare Company in *Edward II* by Christopher Marlowe, directed by Peter Hall: David Warner (King Edward), Michael Bryant (Gaveston), Stanley Leber (Lancaster), Paul Hardwick (Young Mortimer), Charles Kay (Lightborn), Timothy West (Matrevis), Jonathan Hales (Gurney), William Dysart, Murray Brown, Paul Starr, Peter Harrison, David Quilter, Terence Sewards and Roger Jones (Nobles).

Distribution: BLC/Columbia
Running Time: 107 minutes
Color: Technicolor
Release: February, 1967

Bye, Bye Braverman (1968)

Producer: Sidney Lumet
Director: Sidney Lumet
Screenplay: Herbert Sargent, based on the novel *To An Early Grave* by Wallace Markfield
Photography: Boris Kaufman
Art Direction: Ben Kasazkow
Set Decorations: John Godfrey
Music: Peter Matz
Sound: Dick Vorisek
Costumes: Anna Hill Johnstone
Associate Producer: Charles Maguire
Production Supervisor: Kenneth Utt
Assistant Directors: Burtt Harris and Alan Hopkins
Production Assistant: Fred C. Caruso
Cast: George Segal (Morroe Rieff), Jack Warden (Barnet Weiner), Jessica Walter (Inez Braverman), Phyllis Newman (Myra Mandelbaum), Godfrey Cambridge (Taxi Cab Driver), Joseph Wiseman (Felix Ottensteen), Sorrell Booke (Holly Levine), Zohra Lampert (Etta Rieff), Anthony Holland (Max Ottensteen), Susan Wyler (Pilar), Lieb Lensky (Custodian), Alan King (The Rabbi).
Distribution: Warner Brothers—Seven Arts
Running Time: 94 minutes
Color: Technicolor
Release: April, 1968

The Sea Gull (1968)

Producer: Sidney Lumet
Director: Sidney Lumet
Screenplay: Translation by Moūr Budberg of the play by Anton Chekhov
Photography: Gerry Fisher, B. S. C.
Camera Operator: Anders Bodin, F. S. F.
Scenic Artist: Eric Bjork
Set Decorations: Rune Hjelm and Rolf Larsson
Sound Recordist: Leslie Hammond
Costumes: Tony Walton
Editor: Alan Heim
Production Design: Tony Walton
Associate Producer: F. Sherwin Green
Production Manager: Ronald Sundberg
Assistant Director: Waldemar Bergendahl
Make-up: Tina Johansson and Kjell Gustavsson
Wardrobe: Eve Faloon, Maj Erikson
Hairstyles: Tina Johansson and Kjell Gustavsson
Continuity: Inga-lisa Bitz
Design Assistants: Lennart Clements, Philip Rosenberg
Publicist: Carl Combs
Cast: James Mason (Trigorin), Vanessa Redgrave (Nina), Simone Signoret
    (Arkadina), David Warner (Konstantin), Harry Andrews (Sorin),
    Denholm Elliott (Dorn), Eileen Herlie (Polina), Alfred Lynch
    (Medvedenko), Ronald Radd (Shamraev), Kathleen Widdoes (Masha),
    Frej Lindquest (Yakov), Karen Miller (Housemaid).
Distribution: Seven Arts
Running Time: 141 minutes
Color: Technicolor
Release: December, 1968

The Appointment

Producer: Martin Poll
Director: Sidney Lumet
Screenplay: James Salter, from an original story by Antonio Leonviola
Photography: Carlo Di Palma
Art Direction: Piero Gherardi
Set Dresser: Arrigo Breschi
Music: John Barry
Additional Music and Orchestration: Don Walker
Sound: David Hildyard
Wardrobe: Alda Marussig

Film Editor: Thelma Connell
Production Supervisor: Orazio Tassara
Make-up: Otello Fava
Hair Stylist: Renata Magnanti
Props: Lamberto Verdeneli
Cast: Omar Sharif (Federico Fendi), Anouk Aimee (Carla), Lotte Lenya
    (Emman Valandier), Paola Barbara (Mother), Didi Perego (Navy),
    Luigi Proiette (Fabre), Fausto Tozzi (Renzo), Inna Alexeieff (Old
    Woman on Train), Ennio Balbo (Ugo Perino), Linda De Felice
    (Fisherman's Wife), Sandro Dori (Cutter), Cyrus Elias (Apprentice
    Lawyer), Gabriella Grimaldi (Anna), Isabella Guidotti (Perino's
    Secretary), Angelo Infanti (Antonio), M. Grazia Marescalchi (Mrs.
    Delfini), Serena Michelotti (Lucia), Nerina Montagnani (Head
    Seamstress), Germana Palolieri (Maid), Monica Pardo (Olghina).
Distribution: Metro
Running Time: 100 minutes
Color: Metrocolor
Release: 1969

King: A Filmed Record . . . Montgomery to Memphis
Producer: Ely Landau
Directors of connecting sequences: Sidney Lumet and Josph L. Mankiewicz
Associate Producer: Richard Kaplan
Editing Staff Headed by: Lora Hays and John Carter
Distribution: Maron
Running Time: 153 minutes
Release: September, 1969

Last of the Mobile Hot-shots (1970)
Producer: Sidney Lumet
Director: Sidney Lumet
Screenplay: Gore Vidal, based on *The Seven Descents of Myrtle* by Tennessee
    Williams as produced on stage by David Merrick
Photography: James Wong Howe
Set Direction: Leif B. Pedersei
Production Design: Gene Callahan
Music: Quincy Jones
Sound: Nat Boxer
Recording Mixer: Richard Vorisek
Costume Design: P. Zipprodt
Editor: Alan Heim
Assistant Directors: Burtt Harris, Bob Brand
Associate Producer: Jim DiGangi

Hair Stylist: F. Jones
Publicist: Jim Merrick
Cast: James Coburn (Jeb), Lynn Redgrave (Myrtle), Robert Hooks (Chicken), Perry Hayes (George), Reggie King (Rube).
Distribution: Warner Brothers
Running Time: 108 minutes
Color: Technicolor
Release: January, 1970
British Title: *Blood Kin*

The Anderson Tapes (1971)
Producer: Robert M. Weitman
Director: Sidney Lumet
Screenplay: Frank R. Pierson, based on the novel by Lawrence Sanders
Photography: Arthur J. Ornitz
Art Direction: Philip Rosenberg
Set Decoration: Alan Hicks
Music Composed and Conducted by: Quincy Jones
Sound: Dennis Maitland, Jack Fitzstephens and Al Gramaglia
Costumes: Gene Coffin
Editor: Joanne Burke
Production Design: Benjamin J. Kasazkrow
Assistant Director: Alan Hopkins
Associate Producer: George Justin
Make-up: Saul Meth
Hairstyles: Ian Forrest and Betty Destefano
Casting: Marion Dougherty
Cast: Sean Connery (John Anderson), Dyan Cannon (Ingrid Everleigh), Martin Balsam (Tommy Haskins), Ralph Meeker (Captain Delaney), Alan King (Pat Angelo), Christopher Walken (The Kid), Val Avery (Socks Parelli), Dick Williams (Spencer), Garrett Morris (Everson), Stan Gottlieb (Pop), Paul Benjamin (Jimmy), Anthony Holland (Psychologist), Conrad Bain (Dr. Rubicoff), Richard B. Schull (Werner), Margaret Hamilton (Miss Kaler), Judith Lowry (Mrs. Hathaway), Max Showalter (Bingham), Janet Ward (Mrs. Bingham), Scott Jacoby (Jerry Bingham), Norman Rose (Longene), Med Miles (Mrs. Longene), Ralph Stanley (D'Medico), John Call (O'Leary), John Bradon (Vanessi), Paula Trueman (Nurse), Michael Miller (First Agent), Michael Prince (Johnson), Frank Macetta (Papa Angelo), Jack Doroshow (Eric), Michael Clary (Eric's Friend), Hildy Brook (Receptionist), Robert Dagny (Doctor), Bradford English (TV Watcher), Reid Cruckshanks (Judge), Tom Signorelli (Sync Man), Carmine Caridi (Detective A), Michael Fairman (Sgt. Claire), Philip

Larson (Policeman), Charles Frank (Medic), George Patelis (Detective B), William Da Prato (Detective C), Sam Coppola (Private Detective).
Distribution: Columbia-Warner Brothers
Running Time: 98 minutes
Color: Technicolor
Release: June, 1971

Child's Play (1972)

Producer: David Merrick
Director: Sidney Lumet
Screenplay: Leon Prochnik, based on the play by Robert Marasco produced on the Broadway stage by David Merrick
Photography: Gerald Hirschfield
Production Design: Philip Rosenberg
Music Composed and Conducted by: Michael Small
Sound: William Edmondson
Costumes: Ruth Morley
Make-up: Saul Meth
Editors: Edward Warschilka and Joanne Burke, A. C.
Wardrobe Supervisor: George Newman
Associate Producer: Hank Moonjean
Associate Director: Hank Moonjean
Unit Production Manager: Jim DiGangi
Script Supervisor: Nick Sgarro
Casting Director: Geri Windsor
Cast: James Mason (Jerome Malley), Robert Preston (Joseph Dobbs), Beau Bridges (Paul Reis), Ronald Weyand (Father Mozian), Charles White (Father Griffin), David Rounds (Father Penny), Kate Harrington (Mrs. Carter), Jamie Alexander (Sheppard), Brian Chapin (O'Donnell), Bryant Fraser (Jennings), Mark Hall Haefeli (Wilson), Ton Leopold (Shea), Julius Lo Iacono (McArdle), Christopher Man (Travis), Paul O'Keefe (Banks), Robert D. Randall (Medley), Robbie Reed (Class President), Paul Alessio, Anthony Barletta, Kevin Coupe, Christopher Hoag and Stephen McLaughlin (Students).
Distribution: Paramount
Running Time: 100 minutes
Color: Movielab
Release: December, 1972

The Offence (1973)

Producer: Dennis O'Dell
Director: Sidney Lumet
Screenplay: John Hopkins, based on his play *This Story of Yours*

Photography: Gerry Fisher
Art Direction: John Clark
Music: Harrison Birtwhistle
Sound: Simon Kaye
Costumes: Vangie Harrison
Editor: John Victor Smith
Production Manager: Victor Park
Location Manager: Barry Melrose
Assistant Director: Ted Sturgis
Cast: Sean Connery (Detective Sergeant Johnson), Trevor Howard
     (Cartwright), Vivien Merchant (Maureen Johnson), Ian Bannen
     (Baxter), Derek Newark (Jessard), John Hallam (Panton), Peter Bowles
     (Cameron), Ronald Radd (Lawson), Anthony Sager (Hill), Howard
     Goorney (Lambeth), Richard Moore (Garrett), Maxine Gordon (Janie).
Distribution: United Artists
Running Time: 113 minutes
Color: Deluxe
Release: May, 1973

Serpico (1974)

Producer: Martin Bregman
Director: Sidney Lumet
Screenplay: Waldo Salt and Norman Wexler, based on the book by Peter
     Maas
Photography: Arthur J. Ornitz
Art Direction: Douglas Higgins
Set Decoration: Thomas H. Wright
Music Composed by: Mikis Theodorakis
Music Arranged and Conducted by: Bob James
Sound Editors: John J. Fitzstephens, Edward Beyer, Robert Reitano and
     Richard P. Cirincione
Costume Design: Anna Hill Johnstone
Film Editor: Dede Allen
Associate Producer: Roger M. Rothstein
Production Design: Charles Bailey
Assistant Directors: Burtt Harris and Alan Hopkins
Make-up: Redge Tackley
Extra Casting: Talent Service Associates
Co-Editor: Richard Marks
Assistant Editor: Ronald Roose
Unit Manager: Martin Danzig
Script Supervisor: B. J. Bachman
Camera Operator: Louis Barlia
Property Master: Joe Caracciolo

Set Dresser: Les Bloom
Scenic Artist: Jack Hughes
Assistant Cameraman: James Hovey
Re-recordist: Richard Vorisek
Sound Mixer: James J. Sabat
Boom Operator: Robert Rogow
Gaffer: Willy Meyerhoff
Key Grip: Charles Kolb
Production Secretary: Shari Leibowitz
Transportation Gaffer: Raymond Hartwick
Locations: Cinemobile Systems, Inc.
Publicity: Solters/Sabinson/Roskin
Cast: Al Pacino (Serpico), John Randolph (Sidney Green), Jack Kehoe (Tom
    Keough), Biff McGuire (Inspector McClain), Barbara Edayoung
    (Lourie), Cornelia Sharpe (Leslie), Tony Roberts (Bob Blair), John
    Medici (Pasquale), Allan Rich (D. A. Tauber), Norman Ornellas
    (Rubello), Ed Grover (Lombardo), Al Henderson (Peluce), Hank Garre
    (Marlone), Damien Leake (Joey), Joe Bova (Potts), Gene Gross
    (Captain Tolkin), John Stewart (Waterman), Woodie King (Larry),
    James Tolkin (Steiger), Ed Crowley (Barto), Bernard Barrow (Palmer),
    Sal Carollo (Mr. Serpico), Mildred Clinton (Mrs. Serpico), Nathan
    George (Smith), Gus Fleming (Dr. Metz), Richard Foronjy (Corsaro),
    Alan North (Brown), Lewis J. Stadlen (Berman), John McQuade
    (Kellogg), Ted Beniades (Sarno), John Lehne (Gilbert), M. Emmet
    Walsh (Gallagher), George Ede (Daley), Charles White (Delaney).
Distribution: Paramount
Running Time: 130 minutes
Color: Technicolor
Equipment: Panavision
Release: February, 1974

Lovin' Molly (1974)

Producer: Stephen Friedman
Director: Sidney Lumet
Screenplay: Stephen Friedman, based on the novel *Leaving Cheyenne* by
    Larry McMurtry
Photography: Edward Brown
Art Direction: Robert Drunheller, Paul Hefferan
Music: Fred Hellerman
Music Direction: Samuel Matlovsky
Sound Recordist: Jack Fitzstephens, John Sabat
Sound Re-recordist: Sound Shop Inc.
Costumes: Gene Coffin

Editor: Joanne Burke
Associate Producer: David Golden
Production Manager: John Robert Lloyd
Assistant Director: Charles Okun
Make-up: Robert Laden
Production Design: Gene Coffin
Titles: F. Hillsberg Inc.
Cast: Anthony Perkins (Gid), Beau Bridges (Johnny), Blythe Danner
    (Molly), Edward Binns (Mr. Fry), Susan Saranson (Sarah), Conrad
    Fowkes (Eddie White), Claude Traverse (Mr. Tayler), John Henry
    Faulk (Mr. Grinson).
Distribution: Gala
Running Time: 98 minutes
Color: Movielab
Release: March, 1974

Murder on the Orient Express (1974)
Producer: John Brabourne and Richard Goodwin
Director: Sidney Lumet
Screenplay: Paul Dehn, from the novel by Agatha Christie
Photography: Geoffrey Unsworth, B. S. C.
Art Direction: Jack Stephens
Production Design and Costumes: Tony Walton
Music Composed by: Richard Rodney Bennett
Orchestra of the Royal House, Covent Garden Conducted by: Marcus Dods
Sound: Peter Handford, Bill Rowe
Sound Editor: Jonathan Bates
Wardrobe: Brenda Dabbs
Editor: Anne V. Coates
Production Associate: Richard Du Vivier
Production Manager: Jack Causey
French Production Manager: Louis Fleury
First Assistant Director: Ted Sturgis
Make-up: Charles Parker, Stuart Freeborn, John O'Gorman
Hairdressing Supervisor: Ramon Gow
Camera Operator: Peter MacDonald
Unit Manager: Jim Brennan
Location Manager: Norton Knatchbull
Continuity: Angela Allen
Production Secretary: Elisabeth Woodthorpe
Process Photography: Charles Staffell, B. S. C.
Cast: Albert Finney (Hercule Poirot), Lauren Bacall (Mrs. Hubbard), Martin
    Balsam (Bianchi), Ingrid Bergman (Greta Ohlsson), Jacqueline Bisset

(Countess Andrenyi), Jean-Pierre Cassel (Pierre Paul Michel), Sean Connery (Colonel Arbuthnot), John Gielgud (Beddoes), Wendy Hiller (Princess Dragomiroff), Anthony Perkins (Hector McQueen), Vanessa Redgrave (Mary Debenham), Richel Roberts (Hildegarde Schmidt), Richard Widmark (Ratchett), Michael York (Count Andrenyi), Colin Blakely (Hardman), George Coulouris (Doctor Constantine), Der Quilley (Foscarelli), Vernon Dobtcheff (Concierge), Jeremy Lloyd (A. D. C.), John Moffatt (Chief Attendant).

Distribution: Paramount
Running Time: 128 minutes
Color: Technicolor
Cameras and Lenses: Panavision
Release: December, 1974

Dog Day Afternoon (1975)

Producers: Martin Bregman and Martin Elfand
Director: Sidney Lumet
Screenplay: Frank Pierson, based on magazine articles by P. F. Kluge and Thomas Moore
Photography: Victor J. Kemper
Art Direction: Doug Higgins
Set Decoration: Robert Drumheller
Sound Editors: Jack Fitzstephens, Richard Cirincione, Sanford Rackow and Stephen A. Rotter
Sound Mixer: James Sabat
Re-recording Supervisor: Richard Vorasek
Costume Design: Anna Hill Johnstone
Wardrobe Supervisors: Cliff Capone, Peggy Farrell
Make-up: Reginald Tackley
Editor: Dede Allen
Associate Producer: Robert Greenhut
Assistant Director: Burtt Harris
Second Assistant Director: Alan Hopkins
Script Supervisor: B. J. Bjorkman
Unit Publicity: Solters and Roskin
Assistant Editor: Angelo Corrao
Production Coordinator: Lois Kramer
Scenic Artist: Stanley Cappiello
Production Designer: Charles Bailey
Casting: Don Phillips and Michael Chinich
Cast: Al Pacino (Sonny Wortzik), John Cazale (Sal), Penny Allen (Sylvia, the head teller), Sully Boyar (Mulvaney), Beulah Garrick (Margaret), Carol Kane (Jenny), Sandra Kazan (Deborah), Marcia Jean Kurtz

(Miriam), Amy Levitt (Maria), John Marriott (Howard), Estelle Omens (Edna), Gary Springer (Stevie), James Broderick (Sheldon), Charles Durning (Moretti), Carmine Foresta (Carmine), Lang Henriksen (Murphy), Floyd Levine (Phone Cop), Thomas Murphy (Policeman with Angie), Dominic Chianese (Sonny's Father), Marcia Haufrecht (Vi's Friend), Judith Malina (Vi, Sonny's Mother), Susan Peretz (Angie), Chris Sarandon (Leon), William Bogert (TV Studio Anchorman), Ron Cummins (TV Reporter), Jay Gerber (Sam), Philip Charles Mackenzie (Doctor), Chu Chu Malave (Maria's Boyfriend), Lionel Pina (Pizza Boy), Dick Williams (Limo Driver).

Distribution: Columbia–Warner Brothers
Running Time: 130 minutes
Color: Technicolor
Release: October, 1975

Network (1976)

Producer: Howard Gottfried
Director: Sidney Lumet
Original story and screenplay: Paddy Chayefsky
Photography: Owen Roizman
Production Design: Philip Rosenberg
Set Decoration: Edward Stewart
Original music composed and conducted by: Elliot Lawrence
Sound Editors: Jack Fitzstephens, Sanford Rackow, and Marc M. Laub
Re-Recordist: Dick Vorisek
Sound Mixer: James Sabat
Costume Design: Theoni V. Aldredge
Editor: Alan Heim
Associate Producer: Fred Caruso
First Assistant Director: Jay Allan Hopkins
Second Assistant Director: Ralph Singleton
Make-up: John Alese
Hair Stylist: Phil Leto
Casting: Juliet Taylor/MDA
Camera Operator: Fred Schuler
Assistant Cameraman: Tom Priestley, Jr.
Second Assistant Cameraman: Gary Muller
Assistant Editor: Michael Jacobi
Still Photographer: Michael Ginsburg
Key Grip: Kenneth Goss
Gaffer: Norman Leigh
Costumers: George Newman, Marilyn Putnam
Script Supervisor: Kay Chapin

Property Master: Conrad Brink
Location Coordinator: John Starke
Office Coordinator: Connie Schoenberg
Production Auditor: Selma Brown
Extra Casting: Todd-Champion, Ltd.
UBS video logo: Steve Rutt, EUE Video Services
Scenic Artist: Eugene Powell
Television Consultant: Lynn Klugman
Cast: Faye Dunaway (Diana Christensen), William Holden (Max
    Schumacher), Peter Finch (Howard Beale), Robert Duvall (Frank
    Hackett), Wesley Addy (Nelson Chaney), Ned Beatty (Arthur Jensen),
    Arthur Burghardt (Great Ahmed Khan), Bill Burrows (TV Director),
    John Carpenter (George Bosch), Jordan Charney (Harry Hunter),
    Kathy Cronkite (Mary Ann Gifford), Ed Crowley (Joe Donnelly),
    Jerome Dempsey (Walter C. Amundsen), Conchata Ferrell (Barbara
    Schlesinger), Gene Gross (Milton K. Steinman), Stanley Grover (Jack
    Snowden), Cindy Grover (Caroline Schumacher), Darry Hickman (Bill
    Herron), Mitchell Jason (Arthur Zanwill), Paul Jenkins (TV Stage
    Manager), Ken Kercheval (Merrill Grant), Kenneth Kimmins (Associate
    Producer), Lynn Klugman (TV Production Assistant), Carolyn
    Krigbaum (Max's Secretary), Zane Lasky (Audio Man), Michale Lipton
    (Tommy Pellegrino), Michael Lombard (Willie Stein), Pirie MacDonald
    (Herb Thackeray), Russ Petranto (TV Associate Director), Bernard
    Pollock (Lou), Roy Poole (Sam Haywood), William Prince (Edward
    George Ruddy), Sasha Von Scherler (Helen Miggs), Lane Smith
    (Robert McDonough), Theodore Sorel (Giannini), Beatrice Straight
    (Louise Schumacher), Fred Stuthman (Mosaic Figure), Cameron
    Thomas (TV Technical Director), Marlene Warfield (Laurene Hobbs),
    Lydia Wilen (Hunter's Secretary), Lee Richardson (Narrator).
Distribution: United Artists
Running Time: 121 minutes
Color: Metrocolor
Release: December, 1976

Equus (1977)

Producers: Lester Persky and Elliot Kastner
Director: Sidney Lumet
Screenplay: Peter Shaffer, adapted from his play *Equus*
Photography: Oswald Morris
Art Direction: Simon Holland
Production Design: Tony Walton
Music: Richard Rodney Bennett
Sound Mixer: Jimmy Sabat

Costume Design: Tony Walton
Editor: John Victor-Smith
Associate Producer: Denis Holt (U. K.)
Production Supervisor: Colin Host
First Assistant Director: David Tringham
Make-up: Ron Berkley and Ken Brooke
Hairdresser: James Keeler
Technical Adviser (horses): Yakima Canutt
Continuity: Blanche McDermaid
Production Accountant: Arthur Carroll
Wardrobe Supervision: Branda Dabbs
Still Photography: Beverly Rockett
Property Master: Dave Jordan
Set Dresser: Gerry Holmes
Special Effects: Kitt West
Electrical Supervisor: John Tythe
Construction Manager: Jack Carter
Production Assistant: Iris Rose
Casting: Rose Tobias Shaw and Clare Walker
Cast: Richard Burton (Dr. Martin Dysart), Peter Firth (Alan Strang), Colin
    Blakely (Frank Strang), Joan Plowright (Dora Strang), Harry Andrews
    (Harry Dalton), Eileen Atkins (Magistrate Hester Saloman), Jenny
    Agutter (Jill Mason), John Wyman (the Horseman), Kate Reid
    (Margaret Dysart)
Distribution: United Artists
Running Time: 137 minutes
Color: Technicolor
Release: November, 1977

The Wiz (1978)
Producer: Rob Cohen
Director: Sidney Lumet
Executive Producer: Ken Harper
Associate Producer: Burtt Harris
Director of Photography: Oswald Morris
Film Editor: Dede Allen
Screenplay: Joel Schumacher, from the play by William F. Brown, music
    and lyrics by Charles Smalls
Production Design/Costumes: Tony Walton
Art Director: Philip Rosenberg
Special Visual Effects: Albert Whitlock
Musical Score: Charles Smalls
Music Adapted and Supervised by: Quincy Jones

Cast: Diana Ross (Dorothy), Michael Jackson (the Scarecrow), Nipsey
   Russell (the Tinman), Ted Ross (the Lion), Mabel King (Evillene),
   Theresa Merritt (Aunt Em), Thelma Carpenter (Miss One), Lena
   Horne (Glenda The Good), Richard Prior (The Wiz), Stanley Greene
   (Uncle Harry), Clyde J. Barrett (Subway Peddler), Derrick Bell
   (Crow), Roderick-Spencer Sibert (Crow), Kashka Banjomo (Crow),
   Ronald "Smokey" Stevens (Crow), Tony Brealond (Gold Footman),
   Joe Lynn (Gold Footman), Charles Rodriguez (Green Footman),
   Clinton Jackson (Green Footman), Carlton Johnson (Head Winkie), Ted
   Williams (Munchkin #1), Mabel Robinson (Munchkin #2), Damon
   Pearce (Munchkin #3), Donna Patrice Ingram (Munchkin #4), Harry
   Madsen (Cheetah), Rolls Royce Lady (Glory Van Scott), Green Lady
   (Vicki Baltimore)
Distribution: Universal
Running Time: 133 minutes
Color: Technicolor
Release: October, 1978

Just Tell Me What You Want (1980)
Producers: Jay Presson Allen, Sidney Lumet
Director: Sidney Lumet
Executive Producer: Burtt Harris
Screenplay: Jay Presson Allen
Director of Photography: Oswald Morris
Editor: John J. Fitzstephens
Production Designer: Tony Walton
Cast: Ali MacGraw (Bones Burton), Alan King (Max Herschel), Keenan
   Wynn (Seymor Berger), Myrna Loy (Stella), Dina Merril (Connie
   Herschel), Peter Weller (Stephen Routledge), Tony Roberts (Mike
   Berger), Sara Truslow (Cathy), Judy Kae (Baby), Dr. Coleson (Joseph
   Maher), Lothar (Michael Gross)
Distribution: Warner Brothers
Running Time: 114 minutes
Color: Technicolor
Release: February, 1980

Prince of the City (1981)
Producer: Burtt Harris
Director: Sidney Lumet
Executive Producer: Jay Presson Allen
Screenplay: Jay Presson Allen, Sidney Lumet, from the book by Robert
   Daley
Director of Photography: Andrzej Bartkowiak
Editor: John J. Fitzsimmons

Production Design: Tony Walton
Cast: Treat Williams (Danny Ciello), Lindsay Crouse (Carla Ciello),
    Matthew Laurance (Ronnie), Norman Parker (Richard Capallino), Paul
    Roebling (Brooks Paige), Jerry Orbach (Gus Levy), Carmine Foresta
    (Ernie Fallaci), Tony Turco (Danny's father), E. D. Smith (Edelmann),
    Carl Allegretti (Dave Benedetto), Michael Beckett (Michael Blomberg),
    Ron Maccone (Nick Napoli), Tony Munafo (Rocky Gazzo), Tony
    DiBendedetto (Carl Allegretti), Cosmo Allegretti (Marcel Sardino),
    Lane Smith (Tug McGraw), Eddie Jones (Ned Chippy), King (Robert
    Christian), Steve Inwood (Mario Vincente), Bob Balaban (Sandrocino),
    Bobby Alto (Kantor), James Tolkan (Polito), Tony Page (Ralph
    Alvarez), Kenny Marino (Dom Bando), Richard Foronjy (Joe
    Marinaro), Don Billett (Bill Mayo), Peter Michael Goetz (Charles
    Deluth), Carmine Caridi (Gino Moscone), Jose Santa (Jose), Lionel
    Pina (Sancho) Cynthia Nixon (Jeannie)
Distribution: Orion
Running Time: 168 minutes
Release: August, 1981

Deathtrap (1982)
Producer: Burtt Harris
Director: Sidney Lumet
Executive Producer: Jay Presson Allen
Associate Producer: Alfred de Liagre, Jr.
Editor: John J. Fitzstephens
Production Design: Tony Walton
Screenplay: Jay Presson Allen, adapted from the play *Deathtrap* by Ira Levin
Director of Photography: Andrzej Bartkowiak
Cast: Michael Caine (Sidney Bruhl), Christopher Reeve (Clifford
    Anderson), Dyan Cannon (Myra Bruhl), Irene Worth (Helga van
    Dury), Henry Jones (Porter Milgrim), Joe Silver (Seymor Starger),
    Tony DiBenedetto (Burt, the bartender), Jenny Lumet (Stage
    Newsboy), Jeffrey Lyon (himself), Steward Klein (himself)
Distribution: Warner Brothers
Running Time: 118 minutes
Color: Technicolor
Release: March, 1982

The Verdict (1982)
Producers: Richard D. Zanuck, David Brown
Director: Sidney Lumet
Executive Producer: Burtt Harris
Screenplay: David Mamet, from the novel by Barry Reed
Director of Photography: Andrzej Bartkowiak

Editor: Peter Frank
Production Designer: Edward Pisoni
Cast: Paul Newman (Frank Galvin), Charlotte Rampling (Laura Fischer),
    Jack Warden (Mickey), James Mason (Ed), Milo O'Shea (Judge Hoyle),
    Lindsay Crouse (Kaitlin Price), Edward Binns (Bishop Brophy)
Distribution: Twentieth Century-Fox
Running Time: 129 minutes
Color: Technicolor
Release: December, 1982

Daniel (1983)

Producer: Burtt Harris
Director: Sidney Lumet
Executive Producers: E. L. Doctorow, Sidney Lumet
Editor: Peter C. Frank
Screenplay: E. L. Doctorow, from his novel *The Book of Daniel*
Director of Photography: Andrzej Bartkowiak
Cast: Timothy Hutton (Daniel Isaacson), Amanda Plummer (Susan
    Isaacson), Mandy Patinkin (Paul Isaacson), Lindsay Crouse (Rochelle
    Isaacson), John Rubenstein (Robert Lewin), Maria Tucci (Lisa Lewin),
    Edward Asner (Jacob Ascher), Ellen Barkin (Daniel's wife), David
    Marguiles (Susan's psychiatrist), Lee Richardson (Reporter), Carmen
    Matthews (Fanny Ascher), Joseph Leon (Selig Mindish), Tovah
    Feldshuh (Linda Mindish), Dan W. Mitchell-Smith (young Daniel),
    Jena Greco (young Susan)
Distribution: Paramount
Running Time: 129 minutes
Release: August, 1983

Garbo Talks (1984)

Producers: Burtt Harris, Elliott Kastner
Director: Sidney Lumet
Associate Producer: Jennifer M. Ogden
Editor: Andrew Mondshein
Production Designer: Philip Rosenberg
Director of Photography: Andrzej Bartkowiak
Screenplay: Larry Grusin
Cast: Anne Bancroft (Estelle Rolfe), Ron Silver (Gilbert Rolfe), Carrie
    Fisher (Lisa Rolfe), Jane Mortimer (Catherine Hicks), Walter Rolfe
    (Steven Hill), Howard DaSilva (Angelo Dekakis), Dorothy Loudon
    (Sony Apoltinar), Harvey Fierstein (Bernie Whitlock), Hermione
    Gingold (Elizabeth Rennick)
Distribution: MBM/UA
Running Time: 103 minutes

Color: Technicolor
Release: November, 1984

Power (1986)
Producers: Reene Schisgal, Mark Tarlov
Director: Sidney Lumet
Screenplay: David Himmelstein
Editor: Andrew Mondshein
Director of Photography: Andrzej Bartkowiak
Cast: Richard Gere (Pete St. John), Julie Christie (Ellen Freeman), Gene
    Hackman (Wilfred Buckley), Kate Capshaw (Sydney Betterman),
    Denzel Washington (Arnold Billings), E. G. Marshall (Senator Sam
    Hastings), Beatrice Straight (Claire Hastings), Fritz Weaver (Wallace
    Furman)
Distribution: Twentieth Century-Fox
Running Time: 111 minutes
Release: January, 1986

The Morning After (1986)
Producer: Bruce Gilbert
Director: Sidney Lumet
Associate Producer: Wolfgang Glattes
Director of Photography: Andrzej Bartkowiak
Screenplay: James Hicks
Editor: Joel Goodman
Cast: Jane Fonda (Alex Sternbergen), Jeff Bridges (Turner Kendall), Raul
    Julia (Jaoquin Morero), Diane Salinger (Isabel Harding), Richard
    Foronjy (Sergeant Greenbaum), Jeffrey Scott (Bobby), James Haake
    (Frankie)
Distribution: Lorimar/American Filmworks
Running Time: 103 minutes
Color: Deluxe
Release: December, 1986

Running on Empty (1988)
Producers: Amy Robinson, Griffin Dunne
Director: Sidney Lumet
Executive Producers: Naomi Foner, Burtt Harris
Screenplay: Naomi Foner
Director of Photography: Gerry Fischer
Editor: Andrew Mondshein
Production Design: Philip Rosenberg
Cast: Judd Hirsch (Arthur Pope), Christine Lahti (Annie Pope), River
    Phoenix (Danny Pope), Jonas Abry (Harry Pope), Laura Plimpton

(Lorna Phillips), Ed Crowley (Mr. Phillips), L. M. "Kit" Carson (Gus Wynant), Steven Hill (Annie's father), Lynne Thigpen (Underground Contact), David Marguiles (Jonah)
Distribution: Lorimar/Warner Brothers
Running Time: 117 minutes
Color: Technicolor
Release: September, 1988

Family Business (1989)

Producer: Lawrence Gorden
Director: Sidney Lumet
Executive Producers: Jennifer Ogden, Burtt Harris
Screenplay: Vincent Patrick, from his novel
Director of Photography: Andrzej Bartkowiak
Editor: Andrew Mondshein
Production Designer: Philip Rosenberg
Cast: Sean Connery (Jesse), Dustin Hoffman (Vito), Matthew Broderick (Adam), Rosana DeSoto (Elaine), Janet Carroll (Margie), Victoria Jackson (Christine), Bill McCutcheon (Doheny), Marilyn Cooper (Rose), Deborah Rush (Michelle), Salem Ludwig (Nat), Rex Everhardt (Ray), James Tolkan (Judge)
Distribution: Tri-Star
Running Time: 113 minutes
Color: Technicolor
Release: December, 1989

Q & A (1990)

Producers: Arnon Milchan, Burtt Harris
Director: Sidney Lumet
Executive Producer: Patrick Wachsberger
Screenplay: Sidney Lumet, from the novel by Edwin Torres
Editor: Richard Cirincione
Production Design: Philip Rosenberg
Director of Photography: Andrzej Bartkowiak
Cast: Timothy Hutton (Al Reilly), Nick Nolte (Mike Brennan), Patrick O'Neal (Kevin Quinn), Paul Caulderon (Roger Montalvo), Harry Madsen (Tony Vasquez), Lee Richardson (Blumenfeld), Luis Guzman (Luis Valentine), Charles Dutton (Sam "Chappie" Chapman), Dominick Chianese (Larry Pesch), Jenny Lumet (Nancy Bosch), Armand Assante (Bobby Texador), International Chrysis (José Malpico), Martin E. Brens (Armand Segal), Gustavo Brens (Alfonso Segal), Leonard Cimino (Nick Petrano), Maurice Schell ("The Virgin")
Distribution: Tri-Star
Running time: 132 minutes

Color: Technicolor
Release: May, 1990

A Stranger among Us (1992)
Producers: Steve Golin, Sigurjon Sighvatsson, Howard Rosenman
Director: Sidney Lumet
Executive Producers: Sandy Gallin, Carol Baum
Screenplay: Robert J. Averich
Director of Photography: Andrzej Bartkowiak
Production Designer: Philip Rosenberg
Film Editor: Andrew Mondshein
Cast: Melanie Griffith (Emily Eden), Eric Thal (Ariel), John Pankow
    (Levine), Tracy Pollan (Mara), Lee Richardson (Rebbe), Mia Sara
    (Leah), Jamey Sheridan (Nick), Jake Weber (Yaakov), David Marguiles
    (Lt. Oliver), James Gandolfini (Tony Baldessari), Chris Collins (Chris
    Baldessari), David Rosenbaum (Mr. Klausman), Ruth Vool (Mrs.
    Klausman), Burtt Harris (Emily's father), Ira Rubin (French Rebbe),
    Shayna (Rena Sofer)
Distribution: Buena Vista Films
Running time: 96 minutes
Color: Technicolor
Release: July, 1992

INDEX

207

THE AUTHOR

Jay Boyer teaches courses in literature and film at Arizona State University.

Twayne's Filmmakers Series

These recently published Twayne titles are available by mail. To order directly, return the coupon below to: Twayne Publishers, Att: LP, 866 Third Avenue, New York, N.Y. 10022, or call toll-free 1-800-323-7445 (9:00 A.M. to 9:00 P.M. EST).

Line	Quantity	ISBN	Author/Title	Price
1	_____	080579297X	Pogel/	$22.95 (hc)
2	_____	0805793097	WOODY ALLEN	$13.95 (pb)
3	_____	0805793127	Cohen/	$28.95 (hc)
4	_____	0805793313	INGMAR BERGMAN: THE ART OF CONFESSION	$16.95 (pb)
5	_____	0805793178	Kaleta/	$22.95 (hc)
6	_____	0805793232	DAVID LYNCH	$13.95 (pb)
7	_____	080579316X	Reimer & Reimer/	$23.95 (hc)
8	_____	0805793224	NAZI RETRO FILM: HOW GERMAN NARRATIVE CINEMA REMEMBERS THE PAST	$13.95 (pb)
9	_____	0805793151	Keyser/	$26.95 (hc)
10	_____	0805793216	MARTIN SCORSESE	$13.95 (pb)
11	_____	0805793119	Mott & Saunders/ STEVEN SPIELBERG	$10.95 (pb)

Sub-total _____

Please add postage and handling costs—$2.00 for the first book and 75¢ for each additional book _____

Sales tax—if applicable _____

TOTAL _____

	Lines	Units
Control No. [ ] Ord. Type [SPCA]		

__ Enclosed is my check/money order payble to Macmillan Publishing Company.
__ Bill my ☐AMEX ☐MasterCard ☐Visa ☐Discover   Exp. date _____

Card # _____ Signature _____
Charge orders valid only with signature

Ship to: _____

_____

_____ Zip Code

For charge orders only:

Bill to: _____

_____

_____ Zip Code

For information regarding bulk purchases, please write to Managing Editor at the above address. Publisher's prices are subject to change without notice. Allow 4–6 weeks for delivery.   Promo # 78724 FC2611

Twayne's Oral History Series

These recently published Twayne titles are available by mail. To order directly, return the coupon below to: Twayne Publishers, Att: LP, 866 Third Avenue, New York, N.Y. 10022, or call toll-free 1-800-323-7445 (9:00 A.M. to 9:00 P.M. EST).

Line	Quantity	ISBN	Author/Title	Price
1	_____	0805791108	Dunar & McBride/	$27.95 (hc)
2	_____	0805791337	BUILDING HOOVER DAM: AN	$15.95 (pb)
			ORAL HISTORY OF THE GREAT DEPRESSION	
3	_____	0805791078	Owsley/	$26.95 (hc)
4	_____	0805791159	HISPANIC AMERICANS: HISTORY	$14.95 (pb)
			OF THE AMERICAN DREAM	
5	_____	0805791035	Jones-Eddy/	$26.95 (hc)
6	_____	0805791140	HOMESTEADING WOMEN: AN	$13.95 (pb)
			ORAL HISTORY OF COLORADO 1890-1950	
7	_____	0805791124	Stannard/	$26.95 (hc)
8	_____	0805791175	INFANTRY: AN ORAL HISTORY OF	$14.95 (pb)
			A WORLD WAR II AMERICAN INFANTRY	
			BATTALION	
9	_____	0805791000	Lewin/	$20.95 (hc)
10	_____	0805791264	WITNESSES TO THE HOLOCAUST:	$12.95 (pb)
			AN ORAL HISTORY	

Sub-total _____

Please add postage and handling costs—$2.00 for the first book and
75¢ for each additional book _____

Sales tax—if applicable _____

TOTAL _____

Lines   Units

Control No. [_____]   Ord. Type [SPCA]   [____]

__ Enclosed is my check/money order payble to Macmillan Publishing Company.

__ Bill my ☐AMEX ☐MasterCard ☐Visa ☐Discover   Exp. date _____

Card # _____ Signature _____
Charge orders valid only with signature

Ship to: _____

_____

_____ Zip Code

For charge orders only:

Bill to: _____

_____

_____ Zip Code

For information regarding bulk purchases, please write to Managing Editor at the above address. Publisher's prices are subject to change without notice. Allow 4–6 weeks for delivery.
Promo # 78726 FC2613

Critical Essays Series on American Literature

These recently published Twayne titles are available by mail. To order directly, return the coupon below to: Twayne Publishers, Att: LP, 866 Third Avenue, New York, N.Y. 10022, or call toll-free 1-800-323-7445 (9:00 A.M. to 9:00 P.M. EST).

Line	Quantity	ISBN	Author/Title	Price
1	____	0816173206	Scharnhorst, ed./ THE ADVENTURES OF TOM SAWYER	$42.00
2	____	0816173168	Davis, ed./ ROBERT BLY	$42.00
3	____	081617315X	Karpinsky, ed./ CHARLOTTE PERKINS GILMAN	$42.00
4	____	0816173176	Burkholder, ed./ HERMAN MELVILLE'S *BENITO CERENO*	$42.00
5	____	0816173184	Parker & Higgins, eds./ HERMAN MELVILLE'S *MOBY DICK*	$45.00
6	____	0816173109	Thesing, ed./ EDNA ST. VINCENT MILLAY	$42.00
7	____	0816173192	Gottesman, ed./ HENRY MILLER	$42.00
8	____	081618884X	McKay, ed./ TONI MORRISON	$42.00
9	____	0816173222	McAlexander, ed./ PETER TAYLOR	$42.00
10	____	0816173087	Petry, ed./ ANNE TYLER	$42.00
11	____	0816173095	Torsney, ed./ CONSTANCE FENIMORE WOOLSON	$42.00

Sub-total _____

Please add postage and handling costs—$2.00 for the first book and 75¢ for each additional book _____

Sales tax—if applicable _____

TOTAL _____

Control No. [ ]   Ord. Type [SPCA]   Lines [ ] Units [ ]

__ Enclosed is my check/money order payble to Macmillan Publishing Company.
__ Bill my ☐AMEX ☐MasterCard ☐Visa ☐Discover   Exp. date ____

Card # _____   Signature _____
Charge orders valid only with signature

Ship to: _____

_____

_____ __ Zip Code

For charge orders only:

Bill to: _____

_____

_____ __ Zip Code

For information regarding bulk purchases, please write to Managing Editor at the above address. Publisher's prices are subject to change without notice. Allow 4–6 weeks for delivery.   Promo # 78720 FC2617